LAUNCHING WHILE FEMALE

SMASHING THE SYSTEM THAT HOLDS
WOMEN ENTREPRENEURS BACK

SUSANNE ALTHOFF

BEACON PRESS
BOSTON

BEACON PRESS
Boston, Massachusetts
www.beacon.org

Beacon Press books
are published under the auspices of
the Unitarian Universalist Association of Congregations.

23 22 21 20   8 7 6 5 4 3 2 1

This book is printed on acid-free paper that meets the uncoated paper
ANSI/NISO specifications for permanence as revised in 1992.

Text design and composition by Kim Arney

Library of Congress Cataloging-in-Publication Data

Names: Althoff, Susanne, author.
Title: Launching while female : smashing the system that holds women
     entrepreneurs back / Susanne Althoff.
Description: Boston : Beacon Press, [2020] | Includes bibliographical references.
Identifiers: LCCN 2020011350 (print) | LCCN 2020011351 (ebook) |
     ISBN 9780807042977 (hardcover ; alk. paper) | ISBN 9780807043035 (ebook)
Subjects: LCSH: Women chief executive officers. | Businesswomen. | Minority
     businesswomen. | Sexism. | New business enterprises—Finance. | Women-owned
     business enterprises. | Sexual minority business enterprises. | Entrepreneurship.
Classification: LCC HD6054.3 .A48 2020 (print) | LCC HD6054.3 (ebook) |
     DDC 658.4/21082—dc23
LC record available at https://lccn.loc.gov/2020011350
LC ebook record available at https://lccn.loc.gov/2020011351

CONTENTS

AUTHOR'S NOTE

FOR THIS BOOK I interviewed a hundred women entrepreneurs, as well as nonbinary entrepreneurs, between July 2017 and January 2020, with follow-ups in early 2020. Start-ups are fast moving, so details on the companies and founders here may have changed in the meantime.

Most of the available research and data on entrepreneurship examine only women and men. For this reason, this book primarily focuses on people who identify as women (cisgender and transgender), but it's important to note that the hurdles faced by women tend to be shared by gender-expansive people, too.

Finally, while gender is the focus, my aim in these pages is to show how other identities—such as race, class, and sexual orientation—also play a significant role in someone's entrepreneurial experience.

INTRODUCTION

CHRISTINA HARBRIDGE thinks women entrepreneurs are a lot like women political candidates. She should know; she works with both. They often discount their own qualifications, especially when they're just starting out. People tend to define them in terms of their family relations—"she's a mom"—rather than their professional life. And they have to be better than men, probably way better, just to have a chance to compete.

Harbridge's San Francisco–based company, Allegory, coaches entrepreneurs, executives, and others to be better leaders and communicators. She also volunteers for Emerge, a nationwide organization that recruits Democratic women to run for political office and trains them how to win.

She remembers one particular woman vying for a statewide position of Democratic Party chair. "She got super-passionate about something, and she was told to calm down," Harbridge tells me. "And the guy she was running against pounded his fist on the table in anger, and no one said anything."

There was plenty of evidence of a double standard on the campaign trail leading up to the 2020 presidential election. Questions about US senator Elizabeth Warren's "likability," or lack thereof, repeatedly popped up.[1] CNN political analyst David Gergen, bristling at the way she seemed to have a plan for everything, complained that Warren has a "hectoring quality."[2] US senator Amy Klobuchar noted that a woman with a political résumé as skimpy as that of Pete Buttigieg, her fellow candidate and the former mayor of South Bend, Indiana, would not have been taken seriously. "We have to work harder, and that's a fact," she said during one of the debates.[3]

Women entrepreneurs going after funding get similar treatment. Different setting, different stakes, but the assumptions are the same. "These funders use language with women that they would never say to a guy," says Harbridge. "I've sat in the rooms and heard it. 'It doesn't sound like you're ready,' and this is like a thirty-five-year-old woman who's done all this stuff. Then they look at a twenty-year-old guy with an idea in the garage and say, 'Oh, my God, you're so ahead of your time!' It's really fascinating."

Early in her career, Harbridge showed how a woman's insight can fundamentally change the way a business operates. In the late 1980s, while a college student in Northern California, she needed to get a full-time job that would help pay her father's medical expenses (his Parkinson's disease was worsening) and still allow her to take classes at night. She answered an ad for a collector, not even knowing what it was. She thought maybe it had to do with antiques.

She got hired as a file clerk at what turned out to be a debt collection agency. On her first day, the people she encountered in the break room were some of the nicest she'd ever met. But she was shocked when she walked out onto the floor for the first time. "My hands shook listening to people on the phone being just so cruel to people," she tells me. "I thought, 'Why are they doing it this way? There should be a collections unit that collects debts by being nice.'"

Once she had the idea, she couldn't let go of it. In her early twenties, she launched a firm with the idea of making it the world's first "nice" debt collection agency. The industry ran on the belief that you should intimidate people. Harbridge intuitively understood that this was wrong, and it would make people resent the companies that were owed money. "I believed the purpose of a collection call wasn't to collect money," she says. "It was to establish enough relationship so the person explained their situation so we could help them. Often the person didn't owe the money, didn't understand they owed it, or couldn't afford it. Once it was clear what was going on, we could help them— find jobs, dispute it, make a payment plan, file for bankruptcy.

"Other agency owners made fun of me, called me 'Little Red Riding Hood about to get eaten by a wolf,'" Harbridge says. "This whole 'nice' thing, I got a lot of ridicule, but I was super-stubborn."

Even Harbridge assumed her approach would result in a lower rate of repayments, but she had a background in computer programming and thought that what her company lacked in collections, she could make up in efficiency. Imagine everybody's surprise, then, when her business ended up raking in collections at triple the industry rate. "The industry average is 9.9 percent. We did 32.2," she says. It turned out people liked it when the collection agency was nice to them.

"People often criticize the genius right out of the woman," says Harbridge, who sold her debt collection business in 2006 and soon after launched her second company. "I have sat in rooms and watched a woman [who's pitching her business] nail it, just do something so profound, and then somebody will raise their hand and correct her. Women get a lot of negative messaging: 'Wow, you don't have any experience in that.' 'It doesn't sound like you have a competitive advantage.' 'I think you're too late to the game.' 'Wow, it's kind of a dog-eat-dog industry—are you tough enough?'"

You might say, okay, just shrug it off and move on. Or offer a rebuttal. But a woman has to be careful about how she responds.

Harbridge says, "One of the challenges is, if the female founder or CEO challenges that investor, makes him feel small or corrected, their discomfort and fragility may cause them not to fund her. She's got to be strategic around keeping them open. This sucks, and it makes me vomit a little in my mouth when I have to coach women this way. The same is true with a candidate running for office. If the voter gets fragile and shuts down, a qualified, incredible female candidate will be less likely to win the race. This is especially true for women of color."

Harbridge often gets asked why she's only training women in politics. "I don't think women are better than men," she tells me. Instead, she's motivated by the numbers. Women make up 51 percent of our population, but, for example, only 24 percent of the seats in the US Congress were filled by women as of early 2020.[4] "If it was men, I'd be training men. The perspective is off in our country because we don't have enough women in positions of leadership."

Women are likewise missing from the entrepreneurial space. They own fewer companies than men, and those businesses have access to significantly less start-up capital, make significantly less revenue, and employ far fewer people. An entrepreneurial gender gap exists, and it leaves us with fewer jobs, a weaker economy, and less innovation. Building a start-up world that's open and inclusive would benefit us all.

I've been studying and interviewing women entrepreneurs for years, and I've seen versions of Harbridge's story play out in a hundred different ways. I came to the topic not as an entrepreneur but as a journalist. I worked for a dozen years as an editor at the *Boston Globe*'s Sunday magazine, the last six of those as the magazine's editor-in-chief. The newspaper industry has become entrepreneurial by default because its original business model has collapsed. To replace revenue no longer coming from advertisers and subscribers, we experimented at the *Globe* with apps, events, e-books, and other money-making schemes.

In 2007, I represented the newsroom on a team of seven women from all over the company who came together to develop an idea for a magazine for young women who weren't already reading the *Globe*. We studied the market, made financial projections, put together prototypes, and convened focus groups. After six months, we launched a free monthly publication called *Lola*. It was about the size of a paperback, designed to be carried in your bag as you hurried around the city. Readers immediately loved it. I found the process exhilarating, but it taught me yet another entrepreneurial lesson. When the financial crisis hit in 2008, the advertising that supported *Lola* started to drop, and the publication shut down after a two-year run. I learned that you can't just have a product that people like. You need to have good timing, too.

I left the *Globe* in 2015 to take a teaching position at Emerson College in Boston, with a focus on the business of publishing. I brought my entrepreneurial mindset with me, because what's true of the newspaper industry is true of the publishing industry all over. Everywhere I looked, publishers were in a struggle to figure out how to make money in a society that now assumed information should be free. But as I taught entrepreneurship to my students, most of whom are women, one thing became painfully clear: almost every entrepreneur they'd ever heard of was a man. Does that matter? I've seen that it does. It subtly erodes the confidence of the young women I teach. They love learning about the next big start-up but have a vague notion that the arena isn't for them.

Maya Rafie, an ambitious woman with a love of photography and a French accent (her family is Lebanese, but she was born and raised in France), was one of the first student entrepreneurs I met at Emerson. In 2015, at the age of nineteen, she launched a platform called Bistara where college students could find freelance gigs doing creative work. Rafie secured just under $30,000 in seed money and eventually drew in more than four thousand users at over fifty universities nationwide. Yet she told me she still wasn't being taken seriously.

In 2017, Rafie made it to the second round of MassChallenge, one of the world's top accelerator programs for up-and-coming entrepreneurs, and pitched in front of a panel of five men and one woman. She could tell, especially in the minds of the male judges, that her gender and her age were both strikes against her. "It was clear that they loved the idea, but they weren't a fan of me," she says.

Also while in college, Rafie attended a marketing conference that featured a noted business author as a speaker. "I was a big fan," she says. "I was very excited. He finished up his speech talking about how we should empower young entrepreneurs. At lunch break, I saw him at a food truck. I went up to him, probably a little nervous, but I said, 'Thank you so much for your words. I myself am starting a company.' He actually looked at me and said, 'Is your mom here?' I caught myself and said, 'That was kind of rude.' He was like, 'I'm so sorry. It's just that you look young and I'm so tired.'" Rafie just walked away. "It was a shocking experience," she says.

After two years, Bistara needed more capital and paid employees, neither of which Rafie could secure. She reluctantly shut it down at the end of 2017. In the years since, Rafie has been working full-time in marketing jobs and doing side projects with friends, hoping one might blossom into her next start-up. "It's not the end of my entrepreneurial endeavors," she tells me.

As I set out to write this book, I knew I wanted to clearly understand what made some women-owned companies flourish, when others withered or died. I wanted to learn about the hurdles women entrepreneurs face, the ways they've been held back, and the persistence they've shown to succeed anyway. And I wanted to find out what we stand to gain if these hurdles are smashed for good. More jobs and a stronger economy, certainly, but what else? What happens when people with different experiences and needs and points of view innovate? To answer these questions, I've interviewed a hundred women entrepreneurs, as well as nonbinary entrepreneurs, working all over the country in fields such as tech, food, health care, and finance. They told me stories that are raw, honest, uplifting, and disturbing.

In these pages, you'll meet people like Hannah Wei. In the fall of 2017 in Boston, I observed her workshop on how to build credibility as a first-time founder. It was part of an all-day conference for aspiring women student entrepreneurs called Four94. At the time, Wei was herself a student, getting dual degrees at Wellesley College and MIT. She described her struggles trying to get a social media app named CliqBit off the ground. She and a woman classmate had managed to raise $2.5 million in funding and employed a dozen people. But still they had to deal with the questions from investors: "Are you pregnant now?" "What happens when you are?" "Won't you lose your motivation when you have a family and kids?" Once, Wei recalled, a male judge at an accelerator told her: "Love the idea. Love the company. Love the app. The only thing wrong with your company is it doesn't have enough men in it."

The Four94 conference was put on by five young women studying at Harvard who'd witnessed the obstacles women entrepreneurs face and wanted to change things. The conference name references the fact that only 4.94 percent of all venture capital deals in the United States in 2016 went to women-led companies. Risham Dhillon started the conference idea. During her sophomore year at Harvard, Dhillon, a computer science major, and her female roommate began tinkering with their own project: a sensor and app that would alert parents to a baby accidentally left behind in a hot car. They called it Chirp. "We just wanted to see what we could build and where we could go," she tells me. In their junior year, Dhillon and the roommate took a

Harvard class called Startup R&D to continue work on Chirp. Dhillon was struck by the fact that only one-sixth of the students in the class were women. Dhillon and some friends, including Janet Chen, a computer science major, felt that one big problem was a lack of community among women entrepreneurs. They envisioned a conference, followed by other events, that would give young women the inspiration and step-by-step guidance they'd need to start a business.

"I can name very few women who are leading companies," says Chen. I think even if it's not a conscious thing, where you feel burdened by those statistics, it's still very unconsciously powerful. I think it goes a really long way to be able to see a leader who looks like you."

With just a few months of planning and very little publicity, the Four94 conference attracted a hundred women students from as far away as Texas. The women entrepreneurs and executives giving the talks and workshops encouraged attendees to think about new businesses that could solve common problems, to be scrappy and self-motivated, to accept that sometimes they'll feel crushed and dismissed and probably harassed, but to keep going anyway.

That advice was echoed by many of the people I interviewed for this book. After several years of research, I came to see that there's a lot women entrepreneurs can do to improve their odds of success—everything from networking effectively to injecting bold aspirations into the financial projections they pitch to investors. But these women can't overcome a patriarchal system on their own. We all have a part to play.

The following chapters offer an unvarnished look at the challenges women entrepreneurs face and show that, in many cases, these obstacles have stood in women's way for generations. But change is possible, and as you'll see, there are real, practical ways we can open the entrepreneurial system to everyone.

CHAPTER 1

ENTREPRENEURSHIP'S MERITOCRACY MYTH

How we all lose out

FORBES MAGAZINE MAKES A LOT OF LISTS. There are over 130 of them, including the World's Most Powerful People, the Billionaires List, America's Best Employers, America's Top Colleges, and Best Places to Retire.[1] In September 2019, the magazine released another, America's Most Innovative Leaders, crowning "the most creative and successful business minds of today."[2] Tied for the number-one spot were entrepreneurs Jeff Bezos of Amazon and Elon Musk of Tesla and SpaceX. More entrepreneurs followed, including Mark Zuckerberg of Facebook (number three), Marc Benioff of Salesforce (number four), Reed Hastings of Netflix (number five), and Larry Page and Sergey Brin of Alphabet and Google (number ten).

In all, 102 founders and CEOs were featured. Of those, 101 were men. Only one was a woman, Barbara Rentler, the CEO of Ross Stores (number seventy-five).

Readers quickly attacked *Forbes* on social media, calling the lack of women "inexcusable" and "truly astonishing."[3] Aileen Lee, the prominent tech investor who coined the term "unicorn" to describe start-ups valued at $1 billion, described the list as "an example of how privilege can be blinding" and "the consequences of institutional bias."[4] In the following days, the magazine's editor, Randall Lane, offered an apology—"We blew it," he tweeted—and promised to set up a task force to inject fairness into future lists.[5] Soon after, more than fifty women CEOs, most of them founders of the companies they run, signed an open letter criticizing the list and explaining the damage:

> Though important, this isn't about equity and inclusion: This is about economic imperative. Growth in the global marketplace happens only by big business and start-ups opening the doors to women. We cannot compete on half our brain power. That's like hopping long distances, up mountains even, on one leg. . . . A list like this also has major ripple impacts. It governs who gets tapped for boards, which candidates get to interview, who speaks at conference podiums, and who gets funding for their next gig, which all then further reinforce the status quo of business realm as boy's club.[6]

At the highest levels of entrepreneurial success, you'll find men everywhere. From 2009 to early 2016, women led less than 4 percent of the US companies debuting on a major stock exchange, according to S&P Global Market Intelligence.[7] Then there are the members of the Global Unicorn Club, a list of private companies valued at over $1 billion, compiled by research firm CB Insights.[8] In early 2020, 216 US companies were part of the club, but only five were founded solely by women, and only nineteen had a woman cofounder.

Women in this country are opening businesses at a remarkable rate—they went from owning 5 percent of all firms in 1972 to 42 percent in 2019—but dig deeper and the situation seems a lot less cheery.[9] Women-owned businesses were responsible for just 8 percent of all employment and 4 percent of total revenues in 2019. Hitting $1 million or more in annual revenue is an important early marker of success for a company, yet in 2018 a mere 2 percent of women-owned firms had this distinction.[10]

But why? Maybe there's a good reason. Maybe women are just interested in running smaller, more flexible companies, and the industries they choose aren't conducive to high revenues or fast growth. Or maybe their ideas aren't as good. The evidence I've gathered points to another cause: women are operating within an entrepreneurial system rife with bias and discrimination, a system built by and for men.

The one hundred women entrepreneurs I interviewed over the last four years have witnessed the consequences. They've overcome funding shortages. They've struggled to find mentors and role models. They've been belittled, disregarded, and harassed. Their male counterparts receive almost double the start-up capital as women, and it's been shown that a lack of early money can stunt a company's growth.[11] In 2019, start-ups founded only by women pulled in just 2.7 percent of the total venture capital investment in the United States.[12] Women of color receive an even tinier slice.

As Mara Zepeda was hunting for capital to grow Switchboard, her Portland, Oregon–based tech start-up that helps colleges and other groups build strong networks, she came to see that the current approach to funding boxes out a ton of promising businesses, especially those aiming to combine profit and social good, often founded by women and people of color. Her frustration led her and other women entrepreneurs in 2017 to form a group called Zebras Unite that pushes for an ethical, inclusive approach to entrepreneurship. "We are right now held prisoner in the status quo of old, outdated models, and those models extend to corporate structure, capital systems, financing, business models," Zepeda tells me. "We desperately need new models, new experiments, courageous capital to reimagine a future that isn't extractive, but is focused on repair and broad economic development."

Entrepreneurs have changed the world in ways big and small, from how we use data and diagnose diseases, to how we brew coffee and find someone to date. An entrepreneur is anyone who creates a new business and assumes financial risk to do so. But the entrepreneurs glorified by our culture and sought after by investors are the ones who infuse their business with innovation and offer the potential for significant, often rapid growth.[13] This innovation can come in several forms, such as a new product or service, or an old product or service made or delivered in a new way. Researchers have shown that young companies are key producers of jobs, rivaling job creation by older firms.[14] Entrepreneurial ventures can generate wealth for people and communities and improve the ways we live and work.[15]

We live in a time when traditional industries are vanishing and robots are nudging out human workers. In January 2020, the World Bank declared global economic prospects "fragile"—and this was weeks before the COVID-19 pandemic wreaked further havoc.[16] It's a crucial time for entrepreneurship, yet the rate of all Americans starting new businesses declined over the last four decades.[17] Savvy mayors and governors are looking for ways to reverse this.[18] Even Wytheville, home to eight thousand residents in southwest Virginia's coal country, has committed to spurring entrepreneurship, testing out free business classes and a competition that awarded up to $20,000 apiece to the best business ideas.[19]

The Kauffman Foundation, a philanthropy in Kansas City, Missouri, has been investigating how to goose entrepreneurial activity across the country for decades and has repeatedly sounded alarms about women getting nudged aside. "The nation has fewer jobs— and less strength in emerging industries—than it could if women's entrepreneurship were on par with men's," one Kauffman report notes.[20] "Women capable of starting growth companies may well be our greatest under-utilized economic resource." The researchers who created the Global Women Entrepreneur Leaders Scorecard second this: they report that if women started high-growth companies at the same rate as men, we'd add 15 million jobs to the US economy in only two years.[21] Researchers looking at MIT data estimated that if the school's female faculty launched biotech start-ups at the same rate as its male faculty, we'd all have the benefits of about forty companies that don't exist today, companies that would be creating jobs and searching for cures.[22]

The problem isn't unique to the United States. Men have higher rates of entrepreneurship than women in every country but Mexico, Indonesia, Vietnam, and the Philippines.[23] The Boston Consulting Group showed that if women worldwide launched new businesses at the same rate as men, global GDP could increase by as much as 6 percent, improving the global economy by $2.5 trillion to $5 trillion.[24]

And women are good at running companies. According to research by the Boston Consulting Group and MassChallenge, women-led start-ups make seventy-eight cents for every dollar of investment they receive, compared to thirty-one cents for companies led by men.[25] Venture capital firm First Round Capital concludes that the companies it invested in over a ten-year period that had at least one woman founder performed 63 percent better than firms with all-male founders.[26] An analysis by PitchBook and All Raise showed that start-ups with at least one woman founder on the team take a median of 6.4 years to reach an exit (meaning the company is sold or goes public), compared to a median of 7.4 years for all start-ups.[27] These statistics join a growing body of research that finds that women CEOs typically run companies with better returns and happier employees.[28]

We like to believe that America is a meritocracy. That those with the best brains and best ideas and a willingness to work hard will ultimately succeed. But the evidence reveals otherwise. A 2019 study by Georgetown University's Center on Education and the Workforce showed that it's better to start life as a rich kid than a smart one.[29] Affluent kindergartners with low test scores have a seven in ten chance of attaining a high socioeconomic status when they grow up, the researchers found. Meanwhile, poor kindergartners with high test scores have just a three in ten chance. "The American Dream," the researchers write, "promises that individual talent will be rewarded, regardless of where one comes from or who one's parents are. Based on this ideal of equal opportunity, it's tempting to believe that education and career outcomes reflect a natural sorting according to merit. But this presumption risks suggesting that those who do not thrive in school or the workforce lack talent—when, in fact, they more often lack sufficient systemic support on the journey to reach their full potential."

Systemic support is lacking for women entrepreneurs, too. They've seen that their gender matters, as do their race, sexual orientation, and other factors.

Not many entrepreneurs have experienced the role of gender in quite the same way as Allison Clift-Jennings has. She cofounded the Reno, Nevada–based blockchain company Filament in 2012, just four years after the technology debuted, making her a veteran in this exploding, much-hyped industry. Blockchain technology offers a way to share data that's secure, tamper resistant, and decentralized, something that's tantalizing to fields such as finance, manufacturing, and health care. Filament is focusing on transportation—in particular, equipping vehicles to collect and communicate information or payments. For example, with Filament's product, a car could keep and share its own trusted record of usage and maintenance, which would be valuable if the owner needed to access the warranty or sell the car. Filament has also been working with Clift-Jennings's alma mater, the University of Nevada at Reno, to test how self-driving cars can "talk" to sensors along the road.

Clift-Jennings knows start-ups. Filament is the seventh start-up that she's either founded or helped to grow. As CEO, she's seen Filament raise more than $22 million in funding.

On New Year's Eve of 2016, as the company was closing a round of investments, Clift-Jennings decided it was time to make an announcement to her investors. On her blog, she explained that she is transgender and in the process of transitioning.[30] She would no longer use "Eric" and instead go by "Allison." She noted that all of her employees already knew about and supported her transition (as did her spouse, children, and parents) and that nothing would change with Filament. "I feel more centered, at peace, focused, and motivated than I ever have in my entire life," she wrote. "I'm hopeful that by being public about my own journey and being proud of every part of myself—while I help build Filament—I can help inspire others who may not know why they feel the way they feel, or don't have the inspiration to make the leap to their true self."

Clift-Jennings understood that some investors might walk away from her company. And she recognized these repercussions would be felt not just by her but by her colleagues as well. "I was cognizant that every person who goes through a process like mine has to align the fact that every single person that they have a relationship with could disown them after this. That's a heavy concept. And I knew that if I was going to experience negative blowback from this, it could drastically affect the future of the company."

As it turned out, her investors were overwhelmingly positive. "I consider myself very lucky," she says, "and I carry a ton of privilege still, and I recognize that, and that probably contributed to it to some degree. I recognize it doesn't work out great for everybody, but I couldn't have asked for more wonderful investors."

Since her transition, Clift-Jennings has come to realize how her years of being viewed as a white, heterosexual, cisgender man brought unearned advantages. "Most males experience this in day-to-day life: It's the assumption that you know what you're talking about and have the experience," she says. "It's the assumption that you are not a sex object, but you're a walking, cognizant human being. It's the assumption that you have a career and you're self-made and you're a rugged individualist. We call it 'mankind,' for God's sake. All these sorts of things tend to be implied towards men. The truth is that, for much of my life being perceived as male, and in the early days assuming I was male, I did not even understand that not everybody gets that benefit. When I started to experience being perceived as female, some of these things were not automatically given to me. It was shocking. . . . That was something that was very revealing to me and sobering, and it took me a while to really come to terms with it. What did I just get on easy mode that others don't get?"

One episode from about a decade ago, before she transitioned, now makes her cringe. She was on stage as part of a panel discussion on the start-up ecosystem and made the claim that entrepreneurship is a meritocracy, with everyone having the same shot at launching a company. "In my [old] worldview, that was absolutely true," she says. "But it absolutely is not true across the board. In the start-up community, Black queer women do not start at the same starting line as perceived cisgender heterosexual white males. Not even close."

She adds, "I wish I could box up that experience or that ability to see from both gender presentations—how people treat people— and portray that in a way that everyone could actually feel and see. That would probably open up so many eyes across the board, men and women."

Farah Allen has also observed that some entrepreneurs have access to an "easy mode"—and she knows she isn't one of them. Her Atlanta-based start-up, The Labz, offers a blockchain platform where music creators can collaborate on songs and then securely document their copyright and keep track of other legal details. I met Allen in Atlanta in 2018, when she was pitching The Labz at an event hosted by digitalundivided's BIG incubator, which supports Black and Latinx women entrepreneurs with mentoring, networking, and instruction. In her five-minute pitch on stage, Allen built a convincing case that she's discovered an urgent need in the music industry and created a solution with lots of potential.

Before she launched The Labz in 2017, Allen had spent more than a decade working in the Atlanta area as an IT management consultant for companies such as Delta Airlines and Voya Financial. "I was trying to figure out how to become a chief technology officer," she tells me. "My lack of ability to get into the next level of management really made me want to be an entrepreneur."

Allen's experience is common among women entrepreneurs, especially women of color. Hitting a glass ceiling in the corporate world, frustration with the gender and racial wage gap, or simply unemployment inspires them to strike out on their own.[31] In the United States, women of color entrepreneurs are opening businesses at a much faster pace than all women entrepreneurs.[32] The number of companies owned by Black women jumped 50 percent from 2014 to 2019, while it increased 41 percent for women who are Native Hawaiian or Pacific Islander, 40 percent for Latinx women, 37 percent for Asian American women, and 26 percent for Native American and Alaska Native women. Yet there's a troubling component: companies owned by women of color tend to pull in less money. In 2019, the average revenue for a business owned by a woman of color was $65,800, while it was $218,800 for a white woman. "The disparity has an enormous effect on the U.S. economy," declare the researchers of the 2019 State of Women-Owned Businesses report. "Four million new jobs and $981 billion in revenue would be added if average revenue of minority women-owned firms matched that of white women-owned businesses."

Allen tells me that investors often start with the assumption that she doesn't know what she's doing. "When I've talked to investors, I've witnessed their different perceptions of me," she says. "It's like they're perceiving that I don't know technology. They think that I have to name some of the companies I worked for. I don't get the benefit of the doubt. I have to be more prepared than my counterparts. We're in a world where a white guy, probably a twenty-one-year-old guy, would have a great idea. Maybe he'll have a tech background. But he hasn't built anything, probably doesn't have a whole team. He would get funded over me, especially if he has a network or went to a certain school. I've seen that. On the other hand, I will keep getting, 'Well, you don't have a CFO,' or 'Well, you don't have traction.' 'You don't have this, you don't have that.'" Allen tells me that even when she addresses each issue an investor flags—she's built out a big team with deep experience, she's increased the number of paying customers—it doesn't seem to be enough. "I still have those obstacles."

Allen says she's not looking for any kind of special privileges. She just wants to be seen for what she is: "I don't really want to be treated as a Black woman who has a technology company. I want to be treated like anyone who has a really good idea and has a really good business."

Erasing entrepreneurship's gender gap would lead to more businesses. But not just more. Also different: companies that approach problems in ways that others haven't thought of, ones that recognize needs others have ignored. When only half the population is considered eligible to create new products and services, we risk significant missteps. We get an app from Apple that promises to monitor your total health but leaves out menstruation.[33] We get artificial hearts and smartphones and safety gear all sized for men's bodies.[34] We get wearable heart-rate trackers and automated soap dispensers that don't work properly on darker skin tones.[35]

Rajia Abdelaziz created a product that led one *PopSugar* reporter to declare, "How this didn't exist until now completely baffles me."[36] Abdelaziz got the idea when she was an engineering and computer science undergrad at the University of Massachusetts at Lowell. She felt unsafe walking around campus after dark, but when she looked into what kind of devices were available to alert people if you were in trouble, all she could find were big, bulky panic buttons. "I told a friend of mine, 'Well, my grandma is eighty years old, and you know what she says about those panic buttons? She'd rather fall and not be able to get up than be seen wearing one of those things.'" Abdelaziz thought, what if we disguised the hardware by putting it inside a piece of jewelry? Nobody would know it was there.

In 2016, while still in school, Abdelaziz and fellow engineering student Ray Hamilton started a company to produce her idea. They now sell their invisaWear jewelry charms for $129 and up. If the wearer is ever in an emergency, pressing the back of the charm two times will alert 911 and up to five personal contacts. As Abdelaziz suspected, college-age women have clamored for it, but they've also received orders from people who work late at night and real estate agents who show houses to clients they barely know. A customer used the charm after she was severely injured in a car accident.

But one group still sometimes has a hard time grasping the need for the product: investors. She's heard things like: "This is the United States. This isn't India. People don't get kidnapped right off the street." A judge in a *Shark Tank*–style competition told Abdelaziz that his wife never complains about feeling unsafe, so he doesn't believe there's a need. "A lot of the investors are older males," she says, "and they don't really understand that women worry about their safety every single day."

In 2018, the e-cigarette company Juul, cofounded by former Stanford classmates Adam Bowen and James Monsees, hauled in $12.8 billion in corporate investment.[37] As *Fortune* magazine pointed out, that's $10 billion *more* than all the venture capital investment made that year in all women-founded start-ups combined.[38]

It's not only the amount of money men get, it's the start-ups that get it.

Prominent Boston-based angel investor Barbara Clarke can rattle off a list of questionable start-ups led by male entrepreneurs that won heaps of venture capital funding. That makes her fume, especially considering that worthwhile women-led businesses go unfunded. She points to Doug Evans's Juicero, which attracted about $120 million in VC dollars.[39] Juicero was a $700 Wi-Fi–connected juicing machine that used single-serving packets of chopped fresh fruits and vegetables that sold for up to $10 each, were only available by subscription, and required the user to scan a QR code before the juicing began. In 2017, a year after the machine debuted and not long after *Bloomberg* produced a video showing the packets could simply be squeezed with your hands to create juice, the company collapsed. Clarke notes: "With $120 million, you could have funded every Black woman entrepreneur coming out of every accelerator. It's just such a terrible use of capital."

Then there's Untuckit, a clothing company cofounded by Chris Riccobono and Aaron Sanandres that sells $100 men's casual dress shirts made to be worn untucked. It's received $30 million in VC dollars and is looking for more—despite critics who say the shirts are overpriced and lacking in true innovation.[40] An *Esquire* headline in 2018 declared: "Don't Waste Money on An 'Untucked' Shirt. Just Un-Tuck Your Damn Shirt."[41]

"We are not talking about a capital scarcity issue," Clarke tells me. "This is absolutely not the case. There's plenty of capital, and where this money is going is absurd." In a world of Juiceros and Untuckits, she says, "The rigor which I have seen firsthand that Black and Latina women have to go through to get their funding is ludicrous."

The business world is flush with examples of two sets of standards, one for men (especially white men) and another for everyone else. Multiple studies have shown that when you replace a man's name on a résumé with a woman's name, the applicant is viewed less favorably and is offered a lower starting salary.[42] Researchers Ashleigh Shelby Rosette and Robert W. Livingston have found that Black women executives are judged more critically when their companies stumble, most likely because both their gender and race differ from what's considered a typical leader.[43] "Black women leaders suffered *double jeopardy*, and were evaluated more negatively than Black men and White women, but only under conditions of organizational failure," Rosette and Livingston write. "Under conditions of organizational success, the three groups were evaluated comparably to each other, but each group was evaluated less favorably than White men."

Then consider Elon Musk. The billionaire entrepreneur behind Tesla, SpaceX, and PayPal has long been deemed an eccentric, but in 2018 he took it up several notches. In May of that year, during a combative earnings call for Tesla, his publicly traded electric-car company that has struggled to turn a profit, he ripped into analysts, saying they were offering "boring, bonehead questions."[44] One analyst called the episode "downright bizarre." A stock sell-off followed. In July, he made an unfounded accusation that one of the rescuers in a Thai cave accident was a pedophile, drawing international scorn.[45] In early August, he boasted on Twitter that he was going to take Tesla private and already had the funds to do so, triggering a fraud charge by the Securities and Exchange Commission, a $40 million fine, and an agreement that he step down as chairman of Tesla's board.[46] In mid-August, he choked up during an interview that appeared on the front page of the *New York Times*, confessing that he's under extreme stress, not sleeping, and neglecting his personal life.[47] "This past year has been the most difficult and painful year of my career," he told the *Times*. "It was excruciating."

"What If a Female CEO Acted Like Elon Musk?" was the question *The Atlantic* posed in a headline.[48] "Both men and women take a risk when they reveal stressors or struggles, but their candor doesn't usually garner the same reaction," staffer Marina Koren writes. "For women, the risks of being open are far greater, and they can manifest in tangible ways." Amy Nelson, a former corporate litigator who's the founder and CEO of The Riveter, an online community for working women based in Seattle, chimed in with a *Forbes* essay of her own.[49] "I don't believe I could cry in an interview or any public setting," she writes. "In a world where women have few opportunities to lead and where I find myself in the fortunate position to do so, my perception is that I must show up every day as strong (but not too strong), calm (but with enough assertiveness), and kind (but demanding of excellence). Female founders must constantly consider how they are perceived in both business and life, which creates a tension that doesn't allow us to be fully vulnerable or transparent."

When Musk stumbled, nobody said, *Well, that's what happens when a man runs a company!* After all, he's one male entrepreneur among thousands—why should he represent all of them? Yet the same can't be said for women entrepreneurs. Elizabeth Holmes, founder and former

CEO of the now-defunct blood-testing start-up Theranos, once valued at $9 billion, was rightfully exposed as a fraud and is facing the legal consequences.[50] But with that example in hand, women entrepreneurs in biotech are being compared to Holmes simply because they share her gender.

It happened to Alice Zhang, cofounder and CEO of Verge Genomics, a Bay Area start-up that uses human genomics and artificial intelligence to identify new treatments for ALS, Parkinson's, and other neurodegenerative diseases. Her company isn't doing anything remotely similar to the blood-test technology that Theranos was trying to develop, yet after Zhang had raised a round of funding, she started to hear her name linked to Holmes's on social media and in conversations. "I'm being compared to a company that's committed fraud. My male colleagues in other biotech companies have never received such a comparison," Zhang tells me. "It's always challenging when that's someone's initial impression of you." She's seen multiple prominent male VCs tweet these comments, which is both hurtful and maddening. They're obviously doing it simply because, like Holmes, she's a woman—and yet no one is calling them on it.

"Any time you have a negative story central to an underrepresented group, it's going to have a disproportionate impact on that group," Elizabeth Jennings, founder of the Austin, Texas–based commercialization and research firm Venture Atlas Labs, told *Forbes* in 2019.[51] "It would be hard to imagine that any reinforcement of negative ideas about women in leadership positions could have a positive outcome."

Having more women entrepreneurs won't come at the expense of men and won't diminish the number of companies that men launch. More women-led high-growth firms mean a stronger economy and potentially new industries, all of which aid men-owned businesses, too.[52] As S&P Global executive Courtney Geduldig told NBC News in 2019, "I think one of the biggest misconceptions about gender equality is that it only benefits women, but the data shows that this is not true."[53]

Women entrepreneurs often operate their businesses outside of the norms, in ways that aid all of us. Many of the women I interviewed tell me they're eager to collaborate with competitors. They insist on hiring diverse teams. They set up their companies to respect work-life balance, with flexible schedules and paid parental leave. They prioritize their communities, offering jobs with living wages, mentoring local kids, and making donations. The findings of a 2018 survey echo this last point: women business owners reported a stronger urge than men to use their companies to make a positive economic and charitable impact on their communities.[54]

"I'm sure that you probably every day drive by people that you see need jobs," says Jennifer Labit, whose company, the Fenton, Missouri–based Cotton Babies, makes cloth diapers sold around the world, including at Walmart, and allows many of its employees to bring their infants to work. "You can tell that they're hungry, or you can tell that maybe they've had some kind of an economic event that has affected their housing situation, or they're underemployed, or maybe they're new in this country. Everybody has a story of some kind. As business owners, we get to create opportunities or we get to eliminate opportunities. I have made the decision that as a business owner, it's my job to create opportunities."

CHAPTER 2

CENTURIES OF SECOND-CLASS STATUS

Early women entrepreneurs

ON APRIL 26, 1988, the first of six days of congressional hearings on women entrepreneurs, it was Lillian Lincoln Lambert's turn to testify.[1] Leaning toward the microphone, elbows on the table, she introduced herself to the six US representatives, all men except one, seated before her. She told them she was the president and founder of Centennial One, a janitorial services company in a Maryland suburb of Washington, DC. She explained that she started the company in late 1975 with $4,000 of her own savings, and a dozen years later was making more than $8 million in annual sales and employing more than eight hundred people. She detailed the janitorial contracts she had secured with government agencies, despite roadblocks put up by the US Small Business Administration; while its program for minority business owners was supposed to support her, she often felt thwarted by it. Then, Lambert dug into her final point:

> It was when I first hired my first salesman, a young aggressive white male, I was confronted with the realities of sex and race discrimination in the marketplace. Previously, clients had been rather subtle in dealing directly with me, but it was through this young man that it became obvious that people were frequently dubious about doing business with a female, particularly a black female. I have been

blessed over the last 12 years, and, with hard work, I have built a fine track record. I am now taken seriously, but it has not always been that way. Credibility continues to be an issue with women in business.

Lambert told the committee that she has "good credentials." She was being modest, having earned an MBA from Harvard Business School in 1969, the first Black woman to do so.[2] (Women have only been allowed in Harvard's full MBA program since 1963.)[3] Credentials, she testified, only get women so far: "Clients, suppliers, and financial bankers are slow to believe in a business plan if it is submitted by a woman. She still has to prove herself, and she is put to a much more difficult test than her male counterpart."

When I reach Lambert by phone in Sarasota, Florida, where she's now retired and spending half of every year, she tells me she was pleased to be a part of those historic hearings in 1988, but confesses, "I probably didn't have a lot of confidence that it was going to do a lot."

The goals of the hearings were ambitious: to call attention to the fact that, since the 1970s, the number of women entrepreneurs was multiplying and having a big economic impact, and to erase the discrimination and inequality that were preventing them from making an even larger impact.[4] John LaFalce, then a Democratic US representative from New York and chairman of the House Committee on Small Business, held the hearings at the urging of a politically savvy group of women entrepreneurs who had banded together in 1975 and called themselves the National Association of Women Business Owners (NAWBO). "We always promoted women's entrepreneurship as a way of growing the economy, not as a social program," says Virginia Littlejohn, onetime president of the group and now president and cofounder of Quantum Leaps, a Washington, DC–area nonprofit that promotes women's entrepreneurship globally. By 1988, NAWBO felt the time was right to push for major legislation that would help women business owners; "it's very, very important to use opportunities like a presidential election year to move the agenda," Littlejohn tells me. Hearings would be the first step toward this legislation.

She explains: "John LaFalce said that they were fairly thinly staffed on women's entrepreneurial expertise. Would NAWBO be able to assist fairly substantially with the hearings? And we said, 'Oh, yes, we would.'"

In early 1988, Littlejohn and four other women held what she calls a "strategic slumber party" in a cabin in the Virginia woods. Those with children left them at home. "We basically stayed up all night and knocked out what we were going to be doing," she explains. First, they wanted to show the ways that women entrepreneurs were deprived of funding (at the time, for example, women couldn't get a business loan from a bank in many states without a husband or other male relative cosigning). Second, they planned to argue that the government was significantly undercounting women-owned businesses and their revenue (Littlejohn says the prevailing but highly inaccurate view was that the typical woman entrepreneur was running a home-based business making crafts like candles or macramé and pulling in only about $10,000 a year). Finally, they wanted women entrepreneurs to have a say in public policy, receive help securing federal contracts, and get access to more education and training.

The women of NAWBO hoped the hearings would be well attended by the male-dominated House Committee on Small Business, so they enlisted Polly Bergen, a veteran actor whose roles included the movie *Cape Fear* and the TV miniseries *The Winds of War*, to be the first witness. Bergen would talk about her cosmetics and fashion companies.[5] "We needed to have a movie star who would be the right age, that the members of the House Small Business Committee would be interested in and want to have their photograph taken with her," Littlejohn tells me. "She ensured that all the men would want to come in and be there for the hearing, whereas normally they wouldn't have been so interested." The NAWBO leaders helped select more witnesses to address each of the pressing issues and coached them on what to say, making sure to build the case that women entrepreneurs, especially women of color, were not being taken seriously and facing discrimination and prejudice. "Basically, we barely did any work for our companies during this period," Littlejohn says. "We just were flat out on getting the hearings organized."

The NAWBO members had one other interesting strategy: they targeted male politicians who had daughters—but not sons. "In the

1980s, the ones we found who were madly passionate and supportive about women's entrepreneurship were men who had only daughters," says Littlejohn. "That became a very conscious strategy for us, to recruit men as champions who had only daughters."

Joining Bergen and Lambert were witnesses such as Christine Bierman, president and founder of a safety products distributor, Colt Safety, in St. Louis.[6] Bierman testified that she struggled to find a bank that would give her a business loan, and once she located one, her husband had to cosign. "I have been turned down for a loan by every bank in St. Louis," she explained. "It always got down to the question of personal assets and can you bring your husband back to sign? This, to me, is blatant discrimination." Mary Farrar told the committee that despite having millions of dollars in billings for her Kansas City construction company, Systems Erectors, she couldn't get lenders to take her seriously.[7] "Every time I walk into the bank, it is like I was starting all over again. I generally get the pat on the back." The one time she did a business deal with her brother, the first bank they approached loaned them money right away. She noted, "That one experience pointed out to me that it helped to have a man for a partner." While starting and growing PureCycle, a water recycling company, and three other businesses in Boulder, Colorado, Margaret Hansson said, "I faced all of the same problems that most of the women here have faced in terms of banking, with insulting comments about going home and taking care of my family. Why do I not do something that is really going to make some money like get a secretary's job and so forth."[8]

Barbara Gentry, director of the Women Business Owners Service in the Michigan Department of Commerce, testified that public hearings with 435 women business owners in Michigan in 1986 found banking discrimination to be widespread.[9] "Lenders perceive women-owned businesses as high-risk investments due to misperceptions about women's ability, experience, and commitment to operate successfully. Women are, therefore, charged excessive amounts of interest and collateral, up to five times the amount of the loan, and co-signatures are required for husbands, fathers, or sons when women have attained personal credit in comparable amounts."

Government contracts featured prominently in the hearings, especially since the federal government was then and still is considered the world's biggest buyer of goods and services.[10] In 1979, women-owned businesses received a mere 0.2 percent of federal prime contracting dollars, and at the time of the hearings in 1988, that number had inched up to about 1 percent.[11] (Today, the federal government's goal is to award at least 5 percent of procurement dollars to women-owned businesses—yes, equality is a slow march.)[12] Phyllis Hill Slater, president and owner of engineering and architectural support firm Hill Slater in Lynbrook, New York, testified that while she had secured some of those government contracts, firms founded by people of color, like hers, are still treated as less "capable"—"even though our architects and engineers went to the same schools, took the same licensing tests."[13] She noted that those awarding government contracts would always choose a white woman business owner over a Black woman business owner: "This is a fact, and this is how people think, and we cannot change how people think right now. It is not going to happen in our lifetime." To address this, Hill Slater urged that the procurement assistance to women and people of color be handled separately. "If there is going to be $10 million worth of contracts given out, then a certain percentage should be going to women business owners, and a certain percentage should be going to minority business owners. Separate, not thrown into the same pot."

Charlotte Taylor testified that, in 1977 and 1978, she had led a task force set up by President Jimmy Carter to investigate "why there were so few women business owners."[14] She said they found barriers for women entrepreneurs, especially related to accessing capital and training, and both Carter and President Ronald Reagan had pledged to follow the task force's recommended fixes. Yet, a decade later, little progress had been made. "I am sure you will find," she told the committee, "that if work has happened at the Federal level, it has been surface at best, and window dressing without major action."

The hearings—with twenty-six witnesses—had the kind of impact that Littlejohn and other NAWBO leaders hoped for. The House committee's report offered conclusions such as, "Discrimination is both overt and subtle in form and makes it more difficult for women to acquire capital, managerial experience and skill, and market opportunities," and "The Committee hearings provided documentation that the response of the Federal government to the special problems of women entrepreneurs has been weak and ineffectual."[15]

Two months later, on July 14, 1988, Representative LaFalce introduced the legislation H.R. 5050—the numbers "5050" were deliberately chosen to reflect equality—and on October 25, 1988, President Reagan signed the bill into law.[16] The Women's Business Ownership Act of 1988, as it was called, accomplished almost all of the goals set out in NAWBO's "strategic slumber party." It barred the requirement for male cosigners on business loans and opened access to credit in other ways. It launched the National Women's Business Council, which makes policy recommendations to the president, Congress, and Small Business Administration. It led to the creation of Small Business Administration–affiliated Women's Business Centers around the country that provide training and other assistance. And it required that the federal government accurately count women-owned businesses. There was one notable omission: the final bill didn't include assistance to secure federal contracts. After some in Congress objected, Littlejohn says, "With great heartbreak, we decided to drop that from the legislation."

It was a pivotal moment in the history of women's entrepreneurship, showing how far women had come and how much work remained. "After centuries of second class status," declared the House committee report, "women are emerging as entrepreneurs in record numbers. But inequities in the marketplace tend to retard the achievement of business success for women entrepreneurs. . . . The legislation attempts to promote equality of business opportunities for fully one-half of our nation's population."[17]

From the days of our agricultural and household economy to industrialization and beyond, women have carved out their own businesses. Gender norms, as well as class, race, and ethnicity, usually dictated their choice of business.[18] Notions of male supremacy and white supremacy were ever looming (as they continue to be), and women's competence and suitability for business were doubted. Even as late as 1946, a public opinion poll found that only 35 percent of Americans considered women as intelligent as men, while a 1945 poll showed that 60 percent of Americans believed married women whose husbands made enough to support them should not be allowed to hold a job.[19] Then there's twentieth-century economist Joseph Schumpeter, considered the father of entrepreneurship, who deemed men the ideal innovators.[20]

In her book *Enterprising Women: 250 Years of American Business*, historian Virginia G. Drachman explains that early women entrepreneurs tended to create companies making and selling products for women, children, and the home—things like dress patterns, cosmetics, and herbal remedies.[21] Until the late 1900s, women operating in traditionally male industries, like iron production and aviation, were often picking up a company passed on to them by deceased husbands. Family relations played a significant role for women entrepreneurs— whether it was male relatives assisting their entry into business, their marital status dictating their rights, or the birth and care of children complicating their work lives. They often struggled to find sufficient capital and credit to grow their businesses and were denied educational opportunities. The typical early woman entrepreneur was white. According to Drachman, African American women, as well as Jewish immigrant women, were rare as entrepreneurs until the early 1900s; while both groups saw growth afterward, Jim Crow laws slowed the rise for African American women. Latinx women and Asian American women didn't enter the entrepreneurial space in noteworthy numbers until the second half of the 1900s.

An example of the patriarchy that early women entrepreneurs faced can be seen in the common law doctrine called coverture, in place from the Colonial period to the mid-nineteenth century.[22] It played a key role in dictating the things free women could and couldn't do. Coverture applied only to married women—which were the vast majority of women at that time[23]—and stipulated that they had no legal identity of their own. "The husband and wife became one—and that one was the husband. As a symbol of this subsuming of identity, women took the last names of their husbands," writes historian Catherine Allgor for the National Women's History Museum.[24] "Because they did not legally exist, married women could not make contracts or be sued, so they could not own or work in businesses. Married women owned nothing, not even the clothes on their backs." Allgor notes that coverture, despite being on the books, was not always followed. "Though a woman could not make a contract, plenty of women did business and trade, either on their own, in a legal exception called 'feme sole,' or for absent husbands. Wives often ran businesses alongside their mates, with the local community acting as monitors and enforcers." Single free women, fewer in number, were not bound by coverture and had property rights.

Ending coverture was on the minds of Lucretia Mott, Elizabeth Cady Stanton, and the other women and men who gathered for the Seneca Falls Convention in upstate New York in 1848. While their call for a woman's right to vote is perhaps best remembered, their Declaration of Sentiments also demanded that married women have the ability to own property and keep wages earned.[25] In listing the "injuries" man has made to woman, they wrote: "He has made her, if married, in the eye of the law, civilly dead." The declaration underscored other ways that women's standing needed to improve: "He has monopolized nearly all the profitable employments, and from those she is permitted to follow, she receives but a scanty remuneration. He closes against her all the avenues to wealth and distinction, which he considers most honorable to himself."

In the mid-1800s, the power of coverture began to diminish: individual states started passing laws giving married women control of property and their earnings, as well as the ability to enter into contracts.[26] The motivation for these laws was sometimes the protection of families from creditors, not fairness to women. No matter, these shifts opened up entrepreneurial possibilities for women. For example, economist Zorina Khan found that the number of women applying for patents in the nineteenth century "jumped significantly in states with legal reforms and was lowest in states without such laws."[27]

Coverture, Allgor writes, "has been eroded bit by bit. But it has never been fully abolished. The ghost of coverture has always haunted women's lives and continues to do so. Coverture is why women weren't regularly allowed on juries until the 1960s, and marital rape wasn't a crime until the 1980s."[28] Allgor suggests a constitutional amendment might be the best way to erase the impact of coverture for good.

Early women entrepreneurs were operating in an emerging capitalist system inextricably linked to slavery. Some of these businesswomen enslaved people, giving them a labor force built on exploitation and brutality. But even those not directly involved with slavery felt its economic impact. In the 2016 book *Slavery's Capitalism: A New History of American Economic Development*, sixteen scholars knock down the myth that "slavery was merely a regional institution" and detail the ways this system of human bondage permeated everything—from Northern tool and boot makers profiting from sales to Southern enslavers running plantations, to the wealth generated by cotton grown by enslaved people aiding the development of the nation's banking system, to management and accounting practices created during slavery and used by generations of businesspeople.[29] Studies like this also connect the dots between slavery and who has wealth today and who doesn't. And, of course, having generational wealth is an advantage for present-day entrepreneurs bootstrapping their start-ups.

Eliza Pinckney has been called the nation's "first important agriculturist" and "credited with changing the economy of the Colonial South"—but she also enslaved people and helped to perpetuate the institution of slavery.[30] In 1739, when Pinckney was sixteen, her father left his South Carolina plantations behind for military service in Antigua with the British Army.[31] His wife was ill, so he put Pinckney in charge of plantation business.[32] On her own initiative, she directed the cultivation of a large indigo crop, with the idea of selling the valuable blue dye that could be produced from the plant to cloth manufacturers.[33] In 1744, she decided her plantations should focus on producing indigo seeds to the exclusion of all else.[34] This was risky but paid off. With Pinckney's help, indigo farming spread across the region, and by the 1770s, the annual export of indigo from South Carolina to England amounted to 1,107,660 pounds.[35]

Another woman entrepreneur who enslaved people is Mary Katherine Goddard.[36] A Baltimore-based printer and newspaper publisher, she was selected by the Continental Congress in 1777 to produce the first signed copy of the Declaration of Independence.[37] She attached her full name to this demand for liberty—the bottom of the document reads "Printed by Mary Katharine Goddard," with an alternate spelling of her middle name—whereas typically she used her initials to sign her work.[38] Goddard also served as the postmaster of Baltimore beginning in 1775, probably the first woman postmaster in Colonial America.[39]

Born in 1738 in Connecticut, Goddard started life on a comfortable, traditional path, but that changed when her father died when she was nineteen and her mother gave the primary inheritance to her younger brother, William, then seventeen.[40] For most of the rest of her life, Goddard followed her brother in his business pursuits. She never married or had children. Goddard accompanied her brother to Providence, Philadelphia, and then Baltimore, each time running the printing shops and newspapers he had opened but then left behind. While he had poor work habits and money troubles, she experienced repeated success.

In Baltimore in 1775, Goddard took over her brother's *Maryland Journal* as her own independent operation.[41] She also opened a bookshop and published an almanac, while serving as the city's postmaster. In *Enterprising Women*, Drachman writes that "these ventures established Goddard as one of the remarkably successful entrepreneurs of her day—male or female." But she adds, "One-time sibling loyalty and support gradually deteriorated into sibling conflict and competition." In 1784, Goddard's brother apparently forced her out of the *Journal*; the two had a falling out and likely never reconciled. And then, five years later, Goddard was axed as postmaster when the Postmaster General claimed that the position, with its new travel demands, was unsuitable for a woman.[42] A politically connected man was named as her replacement. Thereafter, Goddard focused solely on running her shop.

Goddard died in 1816, and in her will, she freed Belinda Starling, the only enslaved person living with her at the time, and bequeathed to Starling all of her property "to recompense the faithful performance of duties to me."[43] Goddard's brother was left out of the will.

Today, Goddard appears in many films and articles about women's business history, yet the fact that she kept Starling and other people in bondage is often omitted.[44] I've never seen a discussion of the ways slavery contributed to Goddard's business success.

When so much of the business world was closed to women, creating companies whose main customers were also women was an option that made sense. Historian Edith Sparks calls industries such as beauty and fashion "feminized economic niches."[45] In these niches, there were fortunes to be made. The successful women who followed this path include Lydia Pinkham, who in 1876 patented her herbal remedy for "female complaints," called Lydia E. Pinkham's Vegetable Compound.[46] Based in Lynn, Massachusetts, Pinkham encouraged her vast number of customers to write in with their intimate gynecological questions, which she then answered. Many Vegetable Compound users reported that regular doctors offered them no relief and no answers; with Pinkham's product, they finally felt someone was listening to them.

Lena Bryant was another entrepreneur who catered to an overlooked female market.[47] In 1900, as a newly widowed seamstress with an infant son, she pawned the diamond earrings her late husband (a jeweler) had gifted her so she could buy a sewing machine and set up a business in her apartment. Four years later, she opened a clothing shop in New York City under the name Lane Bryant ("Lena" was misspelled as "Lane" on bank paperwork, and the name stuck). Bryant went on to make two wise decisions: she introduced what's considered the first commercially available maternity dress, going against the thinking of the time that women should hide themselves during pregnancy, and then she added plus-size clothing, seeing that other designers were neglecting larger women. Both lines were a hit.

Madam C. J. Walker got rich in the early 1900s by addressing the hair-care needs of Black women and employing innovative marketing and distribution strategies. She then used her wealth and status to advocate for people of color and social change. Journalist A'Lelia Bundles, Walker's great-great-granddaughter, wrote the 2001 biography *On Her Own Ground: The Life and Times of Madam C. J. Walker*, which offers a gripping portrait of this entrepreneur's rise. Born Sarah

Breedlove in 1867 on a Louisiana plantation to parents who were once enslaved, Walker was orphaned at age seven and managed only three months of formal schooling.[48] She married at the age of fourteen; three years later had her only child, a daughter; and by twenty was widowed. She would later marry two other men, but neither union lasted long. After marrying her third husband, she took the name Madam C. J. Walker.

Hard work was a constant for Walker. Her first jobs were as farm laborer and laundress.[49] In 1889, she and her three-year-old daughter moved to St. Louis to live near her brothers, and it was there that she was exposed to their thriving barbershop business. Walker began experimenting with scalp ointments and other remedies to treat her own hair loss. "The complaint was a common one for women of the era," Bundles writes, "due usually to a combination of infrequent washing, illness, high fever, scalp disease, low-protein diets and damaging hair treatments."[50] Around 1903, eager to find a job that would pay more than washing clothes, Walker began working as a sales agent for hair-products entrepreneur Annie Pope-Turnbo, first in St. Louis and then in Denver.

Three years later, Walker felt ready to try her own hair-care business.[51] She developed a formula she called Madam Walker's Wonderful Hair Grower and traveled the country, pitching her product, giving demonstrations, and training other Black women to be her sales agents. In each new city, Walker used church connections to find audiences and, sometimes, places to spend the night (during that time, few hotels were open to her as a Black woman).[52] She frequently ran ads for her Hair Grower in Black newspapers. "She had also discovered that she was a natural teacher, a leader with a gift for drawing crowds and persuading skeptics," Bundles writes.[53] In 1909, just three years after launching her company, she made $8,782, equivalent to about $250,000 today, and in the following years, as profits climbed, she built a factory in Indianapolis, acquired real estate around the country, and grew her army of sales agents.[54] "I have made it possible," Walker once said, "for many colored women to abandon the wash-tub for more pleasant and profitable occupation."[55] There was one area in which Walker struggled: finding investors to help her grow her company.[56]

Harvard Business School professor Nancy F. Koehn, who teaches her MBA students about Walker, has said: "She had an indomitable spirit that prevailed through the difficulties of finding capital, and through the difficulties of her own very limited social position. In a market in which there weren't many realms where women could play, she found a way. . . . She lived on a fascinating threshold between the end of slavery, the beginnings of the great migration northward by African Americans, and the opening up of consumer capitalism."[57]

As Walker's profile and wealth grew, she began generously donating to programs for African Americans and engaging in political activism, such as anti-lynching protests. "Now my object in life is not simply to make money for myself or to spend it on myself in dressing or running around in an automobile," Walker told the crowd at Booker T. Washington's National Negro Business League convention in Chicago in 1912.[58] "But I love to use a part of what I make in trying to help others." Bundles notes that Walker closely followed the work of Washington and his Tuskegee Institute and "fully embraced his self-help, up-from-slavery philosophy and his faith in entrepreneurship as an underpinning of African American progress."[59]

In 1918, Walker built a thirty-four-room mansion near the Hudson River in Irvington, New York, not far from the estates of the Rockefellers and Vanderbilts.[60] She was feeling confident that her business would keep expanding and had more philanthropic projects in mind. But the following year, Walker died of kidney failure at age fifty-one. On May 26, 1919, the *New York Times* gave her obituary a prominent spot on page fifteen, not far from a story on Germany's chemical exports and an ad for a Fifth Avenue diamond seller.[61] (It's remarkable that Walker got a mention at all, since, by its own admission, the *Times*'s obits "have been dominated by white men" since 1851.)[62] "Her death recalled the unusual story of how she rose in twelve years from a washerwoman making only $1.50 a day to a position of wealth and influence among members of her race," the *Times* wrote in its obituary. "She said herself two years ago that she was not yet a millionaire, but hoped to be some time, not that she wanted the money for herself, but for the good she could do with it." At the time of her death, almost forty thousand African American women had gone through the training to be Walker's sales agents.[63]

Though Walker's company closed in the mid-1980s, her impact continues.[64] In the spring of 2020, Netflix released *Self Made*, a miniseries loosely based on Walker's life. In 2016, Richelieu Dennis and his Sundial Brands, maker of the skin- and hair-care lines SheaMoisture and Nubian Heritage, resurrected the Madam C. J. Walker brand; Unilever later acquired Sundial Brands. Then, in 2018, Dennis's nonprofit New Voices Foundation purchased Walker's mansion with plans to turn it into a center that trains and supports Black women entrepreneurs.[65] I heard Darryl Thompson, managing partner of the New Voices Fund, affiliated with the New Voices Foundation, speak at a June 2019 Babson College conference on women's entrepreneurship, held outside Boston. He said buying Walker's home is a significant step toward educating women entrepreneurs of color and helping them access capital. "The revolution," he said, "must be financed."

While women entrepreneurs found success targeting female customers, they frequently failed to win the respect of the larger business community, which considered companies with male customers and male leaders the gold standard. As an example, historian Kathy Peiss points to the series of articles titled "Women in Business" in *Fortune* magazine in 1935 that claimed that only businesses dominated by men were "vital industries."[66] The magazine dismissed the work of women entrepreneurs in fields like fashion and beauty, noting that "feminine success in the exploitation of women proves nothing but the fact that women are by nature feminine." It didn't seem to matter to the magazine that in 1930, according to Peiss, beauty was estimated to be the tenth-largest industry in the country.[67]

The women entrepreneurs who entered these so-called vital industries—such as manufacturing, transportation, and energy—were repeatedly thwarted and discouraged. In her book *Boss Lady: How Three Women Entrepreneurs Built Successful Big Businesses in the Mid-Twentieth Century*, historian Edith Sparks notes that about 40 percent of women working in this era experienced sexual harassment on the job.[68] When Olive Ann Mellor applied for her first position in aviation, working as a secretary-bookkeeper at a Kansas company called Travel Air Manufacturing in 1924, the owner told her, "You've got pretty good-looking legs, I guess you'll do."[69] The twenty-year-old Mellor, then the company's only woman employee, was hired on the condition that she follow a "hands-off policy" with her male coworkers, most of whom were married. Sparks notes that it was a common assumption at the time that single women became secretaries in the hopes of finding husbands at work.

Growing up, Mellor had shown an aptitude for finance; by age eleven, she was writing the checks and paying the bills for her family.[70] Instead of going to high school, she attended the American Secretarial and Business College. At the age of eighteen, she started work as an office manager and bookkeeper for an electrical firm; she stayed three years before moving to Travel Air.

As it turned out, Mellor did end up marrying the owner, Walter Beech, in 1930. The Beeches built a partnership both personal and professional that led the two to cofound Beech Aircraft in Wichita, Kansas, in 1932.[71] Walter, a former army pilot, took the title of president and was in charge of design and production, while Olive Ann, secretary-treasurer and then director, handled finance and administration. Without Walter and his reputation, connections, and money, Sparks writes, it's unlikely that Olive Ann could have broken into aviation and manufacturing in that era; for one, as a woman, she probably wouldn't have been able to raise the start-up capital needed.

Beech Aircraft specialized in commercial and then military planes.[72] To promote their Staggerwing biplane, Olive Ann devised a shrewd marketing ploy: In the 1930s, major airplane races were just beginning to allow women pilots to compete alongside men.[73] Olive Ann decided they should enter the 1936 Bendix Trophy race with a woman pilot, who, if successful, would prove how easy it was to fly the Staggerwing. (Using another company's plane, Amelia Earhart had placed fifth in the Bendix the year before.)[74] Louise Thaden and her navigator, Blanche Noyes, maneuvered the Staggerwing from New

York to Los Angeles in under fifteen hours, becoming the first women to win the Bendix Trophy.[75] Sparks notes that the company's decision to elevate women pilots, while pushing the message that they required easy-to-handle planes, "both subverted and reinforced common gender norms."[76]

In 1940, Walter was hit with encephalitis, or inflammation of the brain, and was hospitalized for almost a year.[77] The timing was bad, as the family now included two daughters, a three-year-old and an infant, and Beech Aircraft was prepping for wartime production. Olive Ann took over as the sole leader, fending off a takeover attempt by fourteen male executives of the company. Sparks writes, "Her dismissal of all fourteen executives involved in the coup displayed assertiveness and authority and consolidated her family's control of the company as well as her own leadership." During World War II, Beech Aircraft employed fourteen thousand workers, and Olive Ann secured millions of dollars in loans.

Walter died of a heart attack in 1950 at the age of fifty-nine.[78] Olive Ann served as president until 1968 and board chair until 1980, when the company was acquired by Raytheon. She died in 1993, just before turning ninety. Olive Ann managed to thrive in the testosterone-fueled aviation industry—she was often called the "First Lady of Aviation" and was once crowned "Man of the Month" by the National Aviation Club—but her abilities and place were challenged again and again. Consider the headline used for a 1959 *Saturday Evening Post* article about Beech: "Danger: Boss Lady at Work."[79] Sparks writes, "In contrast to the legions of female clerical workers who supported the business world . . . the women who led businesses in the middle of the twentieth century were transgressors whose very presence seemed a threat to those anxious to preserve men's power."

Like Olive Ann Beech, Bette Nesmith Graham started out as a secretary, built a thriving company in a male-dominated industry, and fought back a male attempt to wrest control of the company.[80] In 1954, as a divorced mother of one working at a Texas bank, Graham struggled with her typing skills. Erasers weren't concealing her mistakes. Inspired by her interest in art, she retreated to her Dallas kitchen, mixed up white paint in a blender, and poured it into nail polish bottles. Back at work, Graham discovered that her invention had the potential to cover up typos. She worked on improving the formula and then started marketing and selling her product around Texas. Her teenage son, Michael Nesmith, and his friends were her first employees; Michael would later become a member of the music group the Monkees. When Graham was fired by the bank in 1958, she turned to her invention full-time, filed for a patent, and picked the name the Liquid Paper Company. She soon had a bestseller on her hands, as well as competitors. She used some of her earnings to set up two foundations, one that financially supported women in business, another for women in the arts. A second marriage soured, and the husband tried to take control of the company, but Graham prevailed. In 1979, she sold Liquid Paper to Gillette for $47.5 million. She died the following year at age fifty-six, after a stroke. "Most men are ignorant—they don't really understand," Graham told a 1977 interviewer. "And so women have to just keep on with their determination and be relentless. We have to not relent."

On December 1, 1968, the *New York Times* stopped sorting job postings into the categories "Help Wanted—Female" and "Help Wanted—Male."[81] If you scanned the section the Sunday before, you found eighteen pages of openings for women, dominated by ads for secretaries, keypunch operators, nurses, and bookkeepers.[82] Many listings asked for "attractive" applicants, even those requiring a college degree. A sample:

- "Executive Secretary. Be part of the executive suite. Complete with financial VP for a boss! He's looking for a gal that blends well with the plush atmosphere of the executive floor. Good basic skills in addition to initiative and a strong sense of responsibility desirable."
- "Receptionists. $96. With ability to type 30 w.p.m. 9 to 4:30. One of America's foremost concerns is seeking girls who have the ability to converse with sales-minded men."

- "Airline. Be a TWA Flight Hostess. Step up to this rewarding career! . . . Primary qualifications. Minimum age 19½. High school graduate. Excellent health. Unblemished complexion. Height 5'2"–5'9" with proportionate weight by TWA standard. Glasses permitted. Single."

The men's help-wanted section, meanwhile, was almost double in size and stuffed with postings for engineers, programmers, accountants, salesmen, and foremen, such as:

- "Engineers. $12-$16K. Experience in M.E./Chem E./I.E. Diversified non-defense company seeks men to handle increasing responsibility."
- "Programmer Analyst. To $18,000. Airlines. Top Int'l carrier utilizing 360/65 (real-time applications) needs man familiar with COBOL and some PL/I definite asset."
- "Production Supervisors. Are you a born leader? That's what it takes to land one of the several supervisory positions available in our Bronx & Queens processing plants. Nights to start, but these spots will lead to other areas of plant management for the guy who has the ability to get people to do things."[83]

Passed in 1964, Title VII of the Civil Rights Act outlawed employment discrimination on the basis of race, color, religion, national origin, or sex.[84] While it put a quick stop to help-wanted ads stipulating that only certain races should apply, the labeling of jobs for him and her continued.[85] The US Equal Employment Opportunity Commission and newspapers such as the *New York Times* didn't see a problem with the practice.[86] In 1966 and 1967, the newly formed National Organization for Women (NOW) urged the agency to reconsider and staged protests outside its offices, as well as the *Times*, hoisting signs that said, "Women can think as well as type."[87] A *Times* executive was reported as telling NOW members that if the help-wanted ads were no longer separated by gender, "there might be fewer jobs for women because men would be applying for them. After all, men can be just as militant as women."[88] Eventually, NOW achieved its goal: in 1968, the Equal Employment Opportunity Commission reversed its opinion and the *Times* effectively stopped gender-segregating its ads; by 1973, most other US newspapers had done so as well.[89]

The Civil Rights Act joined other legal reforms—such as the Equal Pay Act of 1963, Equal Credit Opportunity Act of 1974, and Pregnancy Discrimination Act of 1978—that changed the employment and financial outlook for women.[90] These reforms stripped away prohibitions on when and where women could work, boosted their wages (though still not matching men's), and provided financial tools such as a personal credit card in their own name. When combined with an increasing number of women in the labor force and more educational opportunities, the result was a marked rise in women's entrepreneurship.[91] Before the 1970s, the federal government counted women as owning less than 5 percent of the nation's businesses.[92] By 1985, the number had climbed to 28 percent.

The increase in women in the labor force was remarkable. Consider that in 1900, less than 20 percent of all women engaged in paid labor outside the home.[93] In 1950, about a third of women were in the labor force, and by 1999, the number had peaked at 60 percent.[94] Since then, it has declined slightly, coming in at 57 percent in 2018. In her book *Understanding the Gender Gap: An Economic History of American Women*, economist Claudia Goldin explains that women's employment shot up after World War II for several reasons—ranging from the new option of part-time work to the abandonment of so-called marriage bars.[95] Large firms and school districts began adopting marriage bars in the late 1800s to prohibit the hiring of married women for office work and teaching jobs; single women were fired once they wed.[96] Companies justified this policy by saying that married women were unreliable and inefficient and belonged in the home; the policy also prevented many women from achieving seniority and therefore better pay. By the 1950s, most marriage bars were dropped, and married women, especially white ones, streamed into the labor force. Marriage bars typically didn't cover manufacturing and domestic service jobs, frequently held by foreign-born or Black workers. It's important to note that Black women have always participated more in the labor force than white women, as Goldin explains, "even when both have the same family income, education, and number of children, among other factors."[97] Also, between 1930 and 1960, many women of color were able to leave domestic service jobs and move into other options; during this time, for example, the number of African American women in clerical and sales jobs grew eightfold, and the share of Chinese American women in clerical jobs tripled.[98]

Despite these changes, women still struggled to find jobs in many fields and get promoted to upper management. The patriarchy was maintaining its grip on the business world. In a 1965 *Harvard Business Review* survey titled "Are Women Executives People?" only 35 percent of male executives said their attitude toward women in management was favorable and just 27 percent said they'd feel okay working for a woman.[99] Entrepreneur Virginia Littlejohn, one of the forces behind the Women's Business Ownership Act of 1988, wrote in 1983 that many women began pursuing entrepreneurship in the 1970s precisely because they couldn't land the jobs they wanted: "[M]any women feel their career expectations cannot be met in the world of large corporations, where their experience does not match the traditional (male) career path. Instead, they elect to compete on their own."[100] In the 1980s, the term "glass ceiling" began to circulate to describe the forces keeping women from advancement, and articles at the time often noted that women responded by starting their own companies. In the 1984 book *The Working Woman Report: Succeeding in Business in the 80s*, editor Gay Bryant and her *Working Woman* magazine team write: "Women have special reasons for becoming entrepreneurs. One is frustration. After years of experience in corporations, a woman may find that she hits a glass ceiling, that despite long service and considerable managerial talent, she is not getting near a top position. She's ambitious, has the self-confidence and business acumen to make it, and is tired of waiting indefinitely for someone to give her the chance to do so."[101]

Better educational opportunities were aiding women's embrace of entrepreneurship. In 1860, women were allowed into only three private colleges in the United States, but in the following decades, the

options expanded greatly.[102] By 1960, 38 percent of all college graduates were women, and the figure climbed to 50 percent in 1981. Still,
some elite schools, such as Yale, Princeton, and Dartmouth, didn't accept women as undergraduate students until the 1960s and 1970s.[103]
When Harvard Business School first admitted women to its full MBA
program in 1963, they got a chilly reception from some professors,
weren't allowed to live on campus, and took classes in at least one
building without a women's bathroom.[104] Lynne Sherwood was in the
first MBA class with women—a group of 8 women and 660 men—
and once told an interviewer that professors liked to call on women
students when class discussions centered on home products such as
laundry detergent. "Maybe without intending to do so, they were
making it evident that we were different," she said. "I didn't want to
be singled out. I just wanted to be another person in the classroom,
getting an education."

One of those early women at Harvard Business School was Lillian
Lincoln Lambert, the Centennial One founder whose testimony before Congress helped lead to the Women's Business Ownership Act
of 1988. Lambert was born in 1940 in rural Virginia and grew up in
a house without a bathroom and, for several years, without electric-
ity.[105] She was bright and driven enough to get accepted into Howard
University, where one of her teachers was H. Naylor Fitzhugh, one of
the first African American men to attend Harvard Business School.[106]
Fitzhugh saw something in Lambert and planted the idea in her mind
that she was Harvard material.

Lambert entered Harvard Business School in the fall of 1967,
where out of eight hundred students in her first-year MBA class, she
was one of eighteen women.[107] Of the eighteen women, she was the
only African American. Black women were also absent from the teaching and administrative staff. People didn't know how to respond to
her, she says, so they ignored her. Her professors would rush by her in
the hallways with their eyes down.

There were other problems. Groups of students met on campus at
night to discuss the case studies, but since women weren't allowed to
live on campus, they had to choose between skipping the study groups
or taking the half-mile walk across the Charles River in the dark.[108]

There was no shuttle bus. Few of the women braved the walk, which put them at a huge disadvantage in keeping up with the coursework.

It wasn't until after Lambert graduated, in 1969, that she learned that she was the first-ever Black woman to earn a Harvard MBA.[109]

After Harvard she bounced around various jobs for a few years but couldn't find anything that stuck.[110] She got a position at an investment brokerage where the president of the company told her that his white clients would welcome her as their broker because they'd be able to relate to her as their servant. "It was depressing to know that even with a Harvard MBA, I was having a hard time finding my niche," she wrote in her 2010 autobiography, *The Road to Someplace Better: From the Segregated South to Harvard Business School and Beyond.* Years later she found the same was true for other women in her graduating class—Harvard gave you critical-thinking and leadership skills but not necessarily the ability to change a male-dominated business world.

In 1973 one of Lambert's contacts asked her if she'd be willing to help get her father's Washington, DC–based janitorial company back on track.[111] "He was having problems with his bank," Lambert tells me. "He had horrible IRS problems. He owed the IRS over $100,000 in withholding taxes, which is the worst kind of tax you can owe. They'll shut your company down. I was able to negotiate a way for him to pay off his taxes and work out an arrangement with the bank, with financing." It was a messy situation, but Lambert enjoyed the challenge, and after several weeks, the owner offered her a full-time job.

Within a few years she began to see that the janitorial services business was a good one and wondered if it might be time to start her own company. "There were very few women in that industry, except as workers," she says. "I didn't know any women who owned companies in that industry. I finally met one out of Pennsylvania."

Despite the lack of role models, she pushed ahead and in 1975 founded Centennial One.[112] She started with $4,000 of her own money and was able to get a $12,000 line of credit at a bank where she had already built up a good credit rating, even though she didn't yet have any customers. The banker asked both Lambert and her husband to sign the loan. Lambert didn't think twice about it; it was just something that had to be done.

In 1978, when she was negotiating a government contract with the Naval Research Center, one of the negotiators casually asked her if she had any kids.[113] When she said yes, she had two daughters, ages four and six, the man told her that her kids were too young for her to be out in the workforce. She assured the man calmly that her children were well cared for, not only by her but by her husband. She won the contract.

She tells me she had to assess each individual situation and decide whether being a Black woman would be a positive or a negative. "I didn't try to fight battles that seemed impossible to win," she says. "At that time, I'm trying to run my business. I used whatever strategy I needed to make sure the company ran successfully. If I needed to send somebody else out to do the job instead of me going, then I did that." As an example, Lambert recognized that most of the people awarding contracts were white men. "So I hired a white guy to do the marketing, because I thought he could relate to these people better than I could or even a Black man could," she says. "I used the tools I had to serve me and the company in the best way possible."

By the time Lambert sold Centennial One in 2001, she had twelve hundred employees, was operating in six states, and was generating $20 million in annual sales.

The politicians championing the Women's Business Ownership Act of 1988 often repeated a bold prediction: that this legislation would allow women to own half of the nation's businesses by the year 2000.[114] "It is impossible to overestimate the social and economic importance of this new economic reality," Representative John LaFalce wrote in 1988. "No other Nation has opened itself to the tremendous entrepreneurial potential of its women as has the United States. Women-owned businesses may well provide the cutting edge—and the American advantage—in the worldwide economic competitiveness fast upon us."

So did the prediction come true? In 2002, the year closest to 2000 for which data are available, only 28 percent of all US firms were owned solely by women.[115]

In 2008, then US senator John Kerry used the occasion of the twentieth anniversary of the Women's Business Ownership Act to host a congressional roundtable to see what kind of progress had been made. Kerry, who at the time was chairman of the Senate Committee on Small Business and Entrepreneurship, shared good news—that the number of women-owned businesses had increased by 824 percent from 1977 to 2002—but there was bad news, too.[116] "Women-owned firms have lower revenues and fewer employees than their male-owned counterparts," Kerry said. "And in Federal procurement, women-owned firms receive less than 3.5 percent of all Federal contracts, and that is deeply troubling. . . . It is disturbing to see that the issues that were hindering women entrepreneurs from achieving their full potential 20 years ago are still barriers today."

Those in attendance—women business owners and the leaders of programs that work with these entrepreneurs—pointed out the roadblocks they encounter. Several focused on money: their difficulties securing loans, lines of credit, and venture capital, and banks continuing to ask for husbands to cosign loans. They reported a lack of women role models and mentors and insufficient professional networks, and said they sometimes get around this by hiring men who can provide an entry into male-dominated networks. Getting contracts with government agencies continued to be a problem. They reported being viewed as less capable than their male peers, especially in science, and mistaken for the secretary. They underscored that these hurdles were multiplied for women of color.

Near the end of the meeting, one entrepreneur made a brief statement, offering a flashback to the 1988 hearings: "I am Christine Bierman with Colt Safety out of St. Louis, Missouri, and Las Vegas, Nevada. I just want to go on record saying I testified—I came to Washington and testified for H.R. 5050 20 years ago and I am very disappointed that we need to continue to have this conversation today. We, I feel, haven't gone very far."

CHAPTER 3

THE BOYS' CLUB

Today's complicated hunt for funding

BORN IN MISSISSIPPI, raised in Texas, Arlan Hamilton liked to hustle from the very start.[1] In elementary school, she bought candy in bulk and resold it to classmates at a profit. In a scheme she likens to the stock market, Hamilton asked kids to give her one sticker each, which she held onto and enjoyed, and then at the end of the school year, she'd raffle off the sticker collection to one of the participants. A string of odd jobs followed in junior high and high school, such as serving pizza, ushering at concerts, and painting house numbers on curbs. The money was very much needed, as Hamilton and her mother and brother were struggling financially. She was always looking for opportunities others were ignoring.

The trait is very much on display some thirty years later, as Hamilton carves out an unconventional and important spot in the start-up investing community. As she concisely explains in a 2018 tweet: "My name is Arlan. I'm a 37-year old Black woman from Texas, based in LA. Four years ago, I was on food stamps. Today, I have built a venture capital fund from the ground up, and have invested in 100 start-up companies led by women, people of color, and LGBTQ founders."[2] Since then she has put over $10 million into more than 130 companies, still only those led by entrepreneurs she calls underrepresented and underestimated.

I first met Hamilton in October 2018 in downtown St. Louis at a private dinner for about two dozen members of the city's entrepreneurial and investment community. The following day I saw her give the keynote at a conference called "Vision" for St. Louis entrepreneurs who are women, people of color, and immigrants. At both events she was received like the start-up celebrity she is, with admirers lining up to take a photo with her and share a fist bump (a germophobe, Hamilton prefers not to shake hands). And at both events she was accompanied by her mother, Earline Butler Sims, explaining that she brings her to these events because her mom made her aspire for more.

It was her mom who, in 1994, helped a then thirteen-year-old Hamilton achieve what she describes as a "life-changing" experience. It happened at a Janet Jackson concert in Dallas, her first concert ever. Because her mother could only afford one ticket, Hamilton attended alone while her mom waited outside. "Aside from screaming my butt off at Janet and losing my mind," says Hamilton, who is gay, "I saw a room that had different races and different ages and orientations and this and that. They were all singing the same lyrics. All doing this for a Black woman. I said, 'Oh my goodness. Whatever this feeling is, I want to feel this again.'

"That night really told me I could dream bigger than I had already been dreaming. There's a lot out there. When you have that, where you can dream bigger, and then you have someone like my mom who says, 'Let me take you where you want to go, show me the map of where you're dreaming or where in the universe you want to go,' that's a wonderful combination."

Instead of college, Hamilton spent her twenties running her own entertainment magazine and working as a music-tour manager and production coordinator. The tour work began when she cold-emailed a Norwegian pop-punk band called goldenboy, asking if she could set up concerts for them across the United States, something she actually didn't know how to do. "I taught myself how to book them a full summer tour," she explains. She went on to do work for Toni Braxton, Jason Derulo, Janine, and others, and says the experience taught her the power of asking for what you want and pushing past frequent rejections.

Around 2012, she began noticing that celebrities like Ellen De-Generes and Ashton Kutcher were investing in start-ups.[3] "It was just so intriguing to me that someone like Ellen, who had it all, in my opinion, who was famous, rich, would also go spend some time in some place called Silicon Valley and put $50,000 on a team of two founders, working odds. 'What was that? What was that?' I studied it and understood it, and then I was like, 'Oh my goodness, this is amazing.'" She embarked on what she calls "an intensive home study" to learn all she could about venture capital.

"I was always an oddball. In school, I was always a little bit off center and outside the box," Hamilton explains. "Once I learned about [entrepreneurship], I said, 'These are my people. These founders, oh, that's what I am.' It was really like I came out for the second time in my life."

It didn't take long for Hamilton to realize how grim the funding picture is for people like her. Venture capital, the fuel that propels this country's high-growth start-up scene, particularly for tech companies, got its start when the first VC firm opened in Boston in 1946.[4] That firm was headed up by influential Harvard Business School professor Georges Doriot, who groomed legions of venture capitalists in his classrooms. (In the book *VC: An American History*, Harvard Business School professor Tom Nicholas writes that Doriot could be "down-right bigoted" with "a strong gender bias," noting that he "seeded a narrowmindedness on gender issues that the industry still grapples with today."[5] Nicholas documents the industry's long-running lack of racial diversity, too.) In the following decades, the VC industry flourished in Silicon Valley. The idea was that firms would pool money from pension funds, insurance companies, and other sources and then find and write checks to promising entrepreneurs, taking some equity from their companies and hoping for a big payout years later when the companies are sold or go public. Since the beginning, the firms have largely been run by white men, and women entrepreneurs and others have been iced out. From 2008 to 2019, companies founded solely by women have never pulled in more than 2.8 percent of each year's total venture capital invested in start-ups in the United States.[6] The numbers are especially bleak for women of color. For example, according to digitalundivided's 2018 ProjectDiane research, the majority of companies launched by Black women fail to raise a single dollar.[7] A 2016 study by the nonprofit StartOut concludes that gender poses more of a funding obstacle for entrepreneurs than LGBT status, noting that female LBT entrepreneurs raise less money than male GBT founders.[8]

For a long time, the thinking's been that women and people of color haven't received VC funding simply because they're not launching quality start-ups in significant numbers. They don't have the interest in or aptitude for this sort of thing.

Hamilton considered this thinking crazy. She pledged to build a venture capital fund that would cater to underrepresented entrepreneurs. She knew in her bones that investing in their companies is not an act of charity—it could generate big returns for the entrepreneurs and the investors. What Hamilton was attempting was pretty audacious. She wasn't a man (88 percent of the decision makers at US venture firms are male).[9] She wasn't white or Asian (one survey found 70 percent of VC investors in this country are white and 26 percent identify as Asian).[10] She didn't have an Ivy League degree (the same survey found 40 percent went to either Harvard or Stanford).[11] She didn't have other qualities common in venture capitalists: personal wealth, connections to monied people who could invest in her fund, or a track record of building and selling her own company.

In the spring of 2015, with the help of a scholarship and crowdfunded money, Hamilton bought a one-way plane ticket so she could attend a two-week crash course on how to be a VC investor, hosted by the accelerator and venture firm 500 Startups on Stanford's campus. Hamilton says she stood out from her classmates: "By far I was the poorest person there. Everybody there had some sort of money. They had family money, or they were partners at a fund, or they worked at a corporation, and a couple of them were just very successful executives." She ate the breakfasts and lunches provided by the training course and skipped dinner because she didn't have the cash to cover it.

Hamilton stayed in Silicon Valley for the next few months, spending the night wherever she could, often on the floor of the airport. She continued her research of the VC world, meeting with anyone who would give her time and advice. As she told people about her dream to fund promising start-ups led by women, people of color, and people who are LGBTQ, she repeatedly heard the standard line, that those groups weren't launching quality companies in significant numbers.

In June 2015, Hamilton wrote a blog post about what she was seeing in Silicon Valley, titled "Dear White Venture Capitalists: If you're reading this, it's (almost!) too late."[12] In it, she criticized the investor community for viewing Black entrepreneurs as in need of pity or handouts, and she argued that these founders could bring significant financial returns. "This isn't me begging you to help us all out because we're all down and out and we have flies around our faces," she says. Filled with scolding and humor, the blog post went viral.

By the fall of 2015, Hamilton convinced Bay Area angel investor Susan Kimberlin to make the first investment, $25,000, in her VC fund. A few other investors followed. Hamilton amassed enough so that her firm, which she named Backstage Capital and set up in Los Angeles, could begin writing checks to entrepreneurs. She required that the companies in her portfolio have at least one founder who is a woman, person of color, or LGBTQ. The checks, ranging from $25,000 to $100,000, went to start-ups creating such things as facial-recognition software, renewable energy, and dolls with natural hair.[13]

Hamilton promised that she would invest in a hundred companies by 2020, but she reached that goal in 2018, giving out more than $4 million.[14] "We are a drop in the bucket," Hamilton acknowledged on PBS, "and really set out to be an example, really be a case study for what other funds and firms could do. Usually venture funds will have at the very least $25 million under management for one fund."[15]

Despite being a drop in the bucket, Hamilton got attention for her work. A lot of attention. She made the October 2018 cover of *Fast Company*—with the magazine declaring her "the only black, queer woman to have ever built a venture capital firm from scratch"—and landed on *Vanity Fair*'s 2018 New Establishment list, one spot behind Alexandria Ocasio-Cortez. That year she also set up Backstage Accelerator for early-stage underrepresented entrepreneurs in four cities—Los Angeles, Detroit, Philadelphia, and London—with each participant getting $100,000 of investment.[16] Nearly two thousand applications for the accelerator flooded in six weeks—for only twenty-four spots.[17]

But there have been stumbles. In 2018 she announced to great fanfare a $36 million fund that would invest exclusively in Black women founders—referring to it as the "it's about damn time" fund.[18] Entrepreneurs would each get $1 million checks. But, after key investors backed out, *Axios* reported in 2019 that the fund was kaput.[19] Hamilton insists it's only delayed, not scrapped, saying it's taking longer than expected to raise the money, and complaining that other fund managers aren't as scrutinized as she is.[20]

Hamilton frequently speaks at entrepreneur and tech conferences around the world, getting attention with her droll humor and self-deprecating stories about her life. Her own book of advice, *It's About Damn Time: How to Turn Being Underestimated into Your Greatest Advantage*, came out in May 2020. She's also using her growing stature to call out discrimination and bias. While on her speaking tours, Hamilton often flies first class and stays in fancy hotels—and vents to her vast social media followers about the number of times she's mistaken for the hired help and asked to show credentials before entering rooms.[21] In 2016 she voiced her frustration about investor and PayPal cofounder Peter Thiel because of his financial support of then candidate Donald Trump.[22] She turned down a much-needed $500,000 investment in Backstage because it would have come from a group with business ties to Thiel.

Hamilton's work is having a real impact, but for women founders to get their fair share of venture capital dollars, not the measly amount they currently pull in, we need dozens more Arlan Hamiltons. Until that time, women entrepreneurs are left to navigate a funding landscape that can often feel like a boys' club—unwelcoming, sometimes creepy, sometimes hostile. It's a place where even the language is off-putting, such as when businesspeople use phrases like "key man" to identify a company's indispensable executive in investor paperwork and "getting a look up your skirt" to describe sharing company secrets with potential investors.

Seattle entrepreneur Mina Yoo, who invented a gadget that functions as a third hand and is named Heroclip, recalls the feedback she received after pitching one group of investors: she wasn't charming enough. Then a woman investor told Yoo, a former business professor and a mother of two, that she should dress more conservatively next time because a male investor had commented that Yoo was "hot."

Neha Narkhede tells me that, in the early days of raising money for her Mountain View, California–based data-management company Confluent, investors directed all of their questions to her two cofounders, who are men. "I wouldn't get people even looking at me," she says. Narkhede suspects her company would have faced more obstacles had it been solely founded by women. Instead, Confluent has pulled in over $205 million in funding, counts companies like Audi, Capital One, and Ticketmaster as customers, and has been valued at $2.5 billion. "Women in tech," she says, "are largely ignored until they're super successful."

Karen Frame, whose third tech start-up, Makeena, connects shoppers with natural brands and is based in Boulder, Colorado, says that in the eyes of investors, she has three strikes against her: She's a woman. She's a former lawyer. ("You would think an investor would be super-excited about that," she explains, "but people don't like lawyers for the most part.") And she's over fifty-five. ("The good thing is I still look like I'm in my forties.") And Frame, Makeena's CEO, has seen how investors assess women entrepreneurs in ways that have nothing to do with their product or market. Years ago, when she wanted to meet with a potential investor, he had to pull up her LinkedIn page first—to see what she looked like. When she said she was happily married, he asked if she had any pretty friends.

Melonee Wise, CEO of San Jose, California–based Fetch Robotics, which makes robots that work in warehouses, recalls that when she was seeking money for an earlier company she cofounded, investors asked if she planned on having kids in the next couple of years. The male entrepreneurs she's friends with have told her they've never received that question. Other times, the probing was done less directly, with questions like "So, you're married. What are your plans for you and your husband?"

Rachel Lee is the founder of Heartwork Videos, a St. Louis company that takes raw surgery footage and turns it into educational videos, with contracts at Columbia University and elsewhere. She's struggled to get investors excited about her company. Most tell her they don't see it exploding in size. "What I really felt like was that people were lazy in not seeing my potential," she tells me. "They would see that I was by myself. They would assume that there was nothing beyond me." Lee has seen race figure into investment decisions. She tells me about a friend, an entrepreneur and woman of color, who's been advised that she should add a white man as a cofounder: "She said she had to be very calm about it, but she said, 'Can you tell me what our other deficiencies are that would make you say that?' He was like, 'Oh, you don't have any deficiencies. I know your company, you are great at what you do, but if you really want to get money then you need, basically, a white face to head the company.'"

Michelle Dalzon had heard the dismal statistics concerning women's lack of funding and says they caused her to delay the expansion of her business, the Black-Owned Market, an online shopping site and series of pop-ups in New York City and Boston selling items by Black vendors. "It made me think that it was impossible for me to raise money, especially for this concept," says Dalzon, who eventually found an investor. Nonetheless, she says, "Raising money is still daunting."

Robin Chase, the cofounder of Zipcar, says it was only after she stepped away from her role as CEO of the car-sharing company that she began to notice the ways investors treat company leaders differently. "When I was raising money for Zipcar, I believed—and I want to use that word carefully—I believed I was not being discriminated against. When I passed leadership over to a white male and I was at the introductory cocktail party introducing some investors, I was so dramatically struck by the speed at which those investors embraced him," Chase tells me. "What I saw and what I believe is that for a good percentage of those people, they aren't thinking, 'I'm prejudiced against women.' But they have a really special and fast bond with the white or Indian male who went to their business schools, did their sports, did their same consulting firms. . . . I just thought, 'Wow, this is incredible that in two breaths they are able to make him feel comfortable in a relationship that's taken me a while to build.'"

Many of the women I interviewed noted that investors directed their worst behavior to them when they were just starting their companies, when they were rich in ideas but lacking in power and money. According to a 2018 survey of women founders by *Inc.* and *Fast Company* magazines, 62 percent of respondents who sought funding experienced bias during the fundraising process.[23] More than half the women surveyed encountered harassment or discrimination while running their companies. The number-one source of this behavior? Investors and bankers.

Venture capital is just one way to finance a new business, suited only for companies with the potential for rapid, significant growth. There are other funding options to choose from—and gender plays a role in each.

Dipping into personal savings makes sense during the very early days of a company. One survey, published in 2014 by the Kauffman Foundation, found that nearly 80 percent of women launching tech start-ups tap their own savings as a main funding source.[24] But women are at a disadvantage here: they make 82 cents for every dollar a man earns. Broken down by race or ethnicity, it comes out to 90 cents for Asian American women, 79 cents for white women, 62 cents for Black women, 61 cents for Native Hawaiian or other Pacific Islander women, 57 cents for Native American or Alaska Native women, and 54 cents for Hispanic women.[25] This pay gap means an average woman loses out on about $10,000 each year—over several years, you're talking about a decent amount of seed money for a new company.[26] Women, especially women of color, are also less likely than men to reach senior-level positions that come with higher pay, again limiting the amount of savings they can accumulate before they strike out on their own.[27]

Another financing option is turning to friends and family. Ideal when a company is in its earliest stages, this approach quickly lets an entrepreneur test if others believe in the concept. The 2014 Kauffman Foundation survey found that almost a third of women launching tech start-ups relied on friends and family as a main funding source.[28] This option, though, can be tricky for women: researchers have found that they tend to have social networks with fewer connections that could lead to funding, when compared to men's networks.[29]

Leaning on friends and family is a time-tested option—even for those our culture idolizes as self-made business titans. A popular meme in the last few years claims that Apple, Google, Amazon, Harley-Davidson, Disney, and Mattel all had humble beginnings in one person's garage, but in reality the founders of these companies benefited from rich relatives, generous benefactors, and other outside help.[30] Researchers have shown that people with personal or family wealth are the most likely to start companies, have the best chances of securing external funding, and have better access to potential employees and customers.[31] A headline in *Quartz* had the right idea: "Entrepreneurs don't have a special gene for risk—they come from families with money."[32]

Entrepreneurs whose friends and family have suffered from the gender pay gap are out of luck. The same goes for the racial wealth gap, created by our country's history of discrimination, as well as public policies that favor white people.[33] A 2016 survey, for instance, showed that white families have a median net worth of $171,000, compared to only $17,600 for Black families and $20,700 for Hispanic families.[34] This lack of generational wealth makes pursuing a start-up a riskier choice. It means there's no financial cushion while a new business gets off the ground. It means a grandparent likely isn't ready to step in and make a missed student loan or medical payment. It means a parent probably isn't able to bail out a daughter whose start-up collapsed and who needs to move back home.

An entrepreneur can also consider bank loans. The 2014 Kauffman Foundation survey found that 6 percent of women who launched tech start-ups used loans as a main funding source.[35] Yet researchers have shown that women-owned businesses pay higher interest rates and are required to put up more collateral, and people of color experience similar penalties.[36] And a 2018 report from the National Women's Business Council noted that women-owned businesses receive only a small fraction of the funding from the Small Business Administration's two biggest loan programs.[37]

Angel investors, high-net-worth people who pour their own money into companies in exchange for equity, are another option for entrepreneurs. Researchers have found that women are less likely than men to receive early-stage funding from angel investors, and women founders are responsible for only 9 percent of the proposals submitted to these investors.[38] One likely reason: the ranks of angel investors are dominated by men. In 2018, just under one-third were women.[39]

Crowdfunding is perhaps the only fundraising option in which women founders have an advantage. The most popular type, so-called reward-based crowdfunding, happens on websites such as Kickstarter and Indiegogo. Any entrepreneur can pitch a project to ordinary people, who can then make pledges as low as $1 and in return receive a product, service, or other reward (but not equity in the company). Some crowdfunding sites, such as iFundWomen and Women You Should Fund, cater specifically to women entrepreneurs. A particularly big haul happened in 2017 when Antonia Saint Dunbar used both Kickstarter and Indiegogo to introduce her idea for women's high heels and flats that "feel like sneakers on the inside," raising more than $2 million.[40]

A 2017 report by PwC found that in the United States, men are twice as likely as women to start a crowdfunding campaign, but women have a higher success rate and receive higher average pledge amounts.[41] It appears that gender bias may, in the case of crowdfunding, be a good thing for women: In 2018, a team of three researchers who studied Kickstarter data and did their own experiment found that amateur investors—the kind who participate in crowdfunding—tend to view women entrepreneurs as more trustworthy, leaving women more likely to be funded than men.[42] The researchers contrast this to the views of professional investors in the venture capital world, who, they write in the *Journal of Business Venturing*, "tend to have a funding bias against women."

Hoping to tease out why men collect more start-up funding than women, researcher Dana Kanze and her colleagues pored over seven years' worth of Q&A sessions from the funding competition TechCrunch Disrupt New York. They discovered that male and female entrepreneurs get asked different questions by investors. In a 2017 article in *Harvard Business Review*, Kanze and her team detailed their findings, explaining that men are typically quizzed about their company's potential for gains, while women are usually asked about potential losses.[43] They describe the questions aimed at men as focusing on "hopes, achievements, advancement, and ideals," while women get peppered with queries about "safety, responsibility, security, and vigilance." The gender of the investor doesn't seem to matter—the questions lobbed at women entrepreneurs remain the same. "Both men and women who evaluate start-ups," the researchers write, "appear to display the same bias in their questioning, inadvertently favoring male entrepreneurs over female ones." After doing their own follow-up experiment, Kanze and her colleagues conclude that there are real repercussions to these different lines of questioning: entrepreneurs who are asked the more positive questions raise seven times more money.

In 2017, shortly after these results were announced, I spoke to Sophia Yen, who told me she gets asked these critical questions all the time, and the aspirational ones less so. A doctor who specializes in adolescents and young adults and who teaches at Stanford, Yen is the CEO and cofounder of Pandia Health, a Sunnyvale, California–based online service that prescribes, sells, and delivers birth control. "There is subliminal bias," she told me at the time. "It'd be fine if you ask everybody the same questions, but it's not okay if you're asking people different questions. I hear it over and over again. Women are evaluated on what they've accomplished, men are evaluated on their potential. It's like, can't you see my potential? Because I do."

When I spoke to Yen two years later, she told me she thinks the research actually inspired a lot of investors to tweak the kinds of questions they ask. "That study and the efforts to promote it have opened the minds of the investors," she says, "and hopefully they're more aware." This is a promising development, but it hasn't eased the gender gap in funding. Yen notes that there are several birth-control-delivery companies operating in the United States, and hers is the only one that's founded and led by women. Her competitors have managed to raise more money showing lesser results. "We came at different times, and I know that I had more customers than they did at the exact same stage asking for the exact same amount of money. They got funded. I did not." (In the meantime, Yen has raised investor dollars.) Could it really be that investors view men as the ideal people to run a company selling birth control to women? "As a female, I understand the market," Yen says. "I know where to find the customers. And as a physician and as a female, I can think of new products that apply to this population that a person without my plumbing is not going to understand.

"I've heard from a lot of investors, 'I don't care that you're woman-founded, woman-led. It is about the bottom line, it is about the numbers, it is about the question of whether or not you can execute.' But really? You're telling me that an MIT-educated, UCSF-grad Stanford professor is not on par with a twenty-one-year-old dude who graduated Stanford. It's ageism. It's sexism. It's anti-anybody that they don't know."

Maia Heymann, cofounder of and general partner at Converge, a venture capital firm in Cambridge, Massachusetts, that focuses on business-to-business technology, says industry contacts sometimes talk about women entrepreneurs as less capable and needing "help." For experienced women entrepreneurs, Heymann has heard phrases like: "She's a first-time founder. She hasn't fundraised before. Can you help her with her pitch?" Most entrepreneurs require fundraising assistance, Heymann says, but she hasn't heard this same language used to describe male entrepreneurs who are being referred to her. "Men seem to endorse each other in a different way," Heymann tells me.

In 2009 and 2010, researchers were given a rare opportunity: to silently observe governmental venture capitalists in Sweden as they held closed-door meetings and discussed their honest opinions about entrepreneurs seeking funding. The research team, which published its findings in 2017, discovered radically different words used to describe male versus female applicants.[44] The men were labeled "young and promising," for example, while the women were "young, but inexperienced." A typical guy was a "very competent innovator and already has money to play with," while the ladies were "good-looking and careless with money." And, no surprise, the women applicants received significantly less funding. "Our research suggests that stereotyping through language underpins the image of a man as a true entrepreneur while undermining the image of a woman as the same," the researchers wrote in *Harvard Business Review* in 2017.[45] "Because the purpose of government venture capital is to use tax money to stimulate growth and value creation for society as a whole, gender bias presents the risk that the money isn't being invested in businesses that have the highest potential. This isn't only damaging for women entrepreneurs; it's potentially damaging for society as a whole."

In experiments where the exact same entrepreneurial pitch is delivered by male and female actors, researchers have found that investors favor those given by men.[46] And if the men are considered physically attractive, their pitches generate the most excitement. Attractiveness doesn't appear to play a role for women founders.

Women seeking bank loans also get evaluated differently. Writing in *Harvard Business Review* in 2018, a team of European researchers explain that bankers often give women applicants more critical assessments, especially when sizing them up on paper.[47] Women may be able to overcome this and convince lenders of their business potential if they meet in person, but, the researchers caution, as more banks make the cost-saving moves of closing local branches, women will miss out on this ability to interact face-to-face with local bankers. "Women entrepreneurs who seek to finance their ventures using bank financing are increasingly forced to find solutions elsewhere," the researchers warn. "And compared to men, women entrepreneurs are pushed into desperate and extreme types of financing."

In the provocatively titled paper "Don't Pitch Like a Girl!" published in 2017, researcher Lakshmi Balachandra and her colleagues dispute that investors have a bias against *all* women entrepreneurs.[48] Instead, they found that investors are turned off by "feminine-stereotyped behaviors"—such as warmth and expressiveness—and even men who show these behaviors will lose out. Balachandra and her team believe these behaviors make investors doubt if an entrepreneur has "business competence."

In front of investors and bankers, women entrepreneurs can perform maleness in a number of ways. Alice Zhang, the cofounder and CEO of Bay Area biotech start-up Verge Genomics, used to order wine or cocktails during business meetings at a restaurant or bar. But a friend suggested that she'd fit into these male-dominated settings if she drank whiskey, so she started doing that. "I just feel like I can be on the same wavelength as them, more guy-to-guy," Zhang says. Over time, she grew to appreciate different kinds of whiskeys. "I could drink them for pleasure now, not just for business. I love Japanese whiskeys."

In the early years of her company, Ridhi Tariyal had several tactics for attempting to fit in with male investors: In conversations she used military jargon, references to the movie *The Godfather*, and phrases like "Monday morning quarterbacking." But eventually, Tariyal had had enough. "It was a tax that I was paying," she tells me. "I am exhausted from putting on this act. I am exhausted from accentuating my maleness."

Playing up her masculine traits required a special kind of mental gymnastics because Tariyal is building a health-tech company focused on menstruation and frequently talking about her period. NextGen Jane, started in 2014 and based in Oakland, California, has developed a smart tampon that allows the collection and testing of cells from the reproductive tract that are shed during menstruation, giving users solid data on their fertility and health. Clinical trials are examining the tampon as a test for endometriosis and other reproductive conditions. Tariyal, the cofounder and CEO, was inspired to launch the company at the age of thirty-three, when she unsuccessfully tried to convince her doctor to test her fertility. At the time, Tariyal was eager to learn if she could delay childbearing, as her focus was on growing her career and paying down school debt (she has degrees from Harvard, MIT, and Georgia Tech).

When a male investor directed his questions and eye contact to Tariyal's male cofounder, not to her, a mentor suggested that she let her partner take over the pitching. Other mentors advised that she avoid descriptions that might make male investors squeamish. "Menstrual blood," they suggested, could be replaced with "novel female substrate." Tariyal recalls one male investor who asked if her smart tampon could test the level of testosterone in older men. She was floored that he'd look at a device made to capture cells from a uterus and try to engineer a use for male biology. "It was like it didn't even matter. 'Can this tampon be useful to me and anyone like me?'"

Now that her company is several years old, Tariyal realizes how important it is to find investors who are truly enthused about backing a reproductive health business, and that attempting to convert others is not worth her time. And she has ditched the "act like a man" approach, striving to be as authentic to herself as a woman of color as she can. The more she and others do this, she reasons, the less pressure for role-playing for everyone—for men being coached to be more "alpha," people of color urged to play "white," gay people pressed to act "straight." The change in approach appears to be working: in 2019, Tariyal's company raised $9 million from investors.

"To me, it boils down to that one question, does representation matter?" Tariyal says. "There's so many people that have pushed back on me, saying that if an investor is smart, they just let the data make the decision. If they saw that there's a big market for women's health, then the money would go there. And it's just not true. The suggestions that investors are free of bias and go where the money goes doesn't actually line up with reality. Women make most of the buying decisions in the household. They actually should be your target customer for basically everything. And yet when I'm sitting there, across from an investor asking me what my tampon can do for testosterone detection in older men, I can assure you you're not paying attention to the data. You're asking a sort of self-serving, biased question."

Entrepreneur Reetu Gupta recalls the video clip that went viral in 2017 showing a white male professor giving a live TV interview from his home office, interrupted by his two young children when they sneak into the room.[49] A frantic Asian woman slips in to pull the kids away. Many people at first assumed the woman was the nanny. It turned out she was the wife and mother. "I thought she was a nanny, too," Gupta tells me. "We all have implicit biases." Gupta, whose Redmond, Washington–based start-up, Cirkled In, helps colleges recruit high school students and lets those students show off their accomplishments, recognizes that when she's pitching investors, when they're sizing her up, they probably think of a maid or a secretary. "When I walk in a room, people don't see a businesswoman. People don't see a CEO. People don't see Mark Zuckerberg," says Gupta, who has master's degrees in business and engineering and twenty years of corporate experience. "They will not see CEO of a company, who can create a unicorn, who can create a billion-dollar company."

Once, Gupta pitched her company to a room filled with forty-five investors, all men, and one woman administrative assistant. "People invest in people who look like them. When they saw me in that room, I knew. I was like, 'There's no way I'm getting a check in this room,' and I didn't. Why? Because they could only see that administrative assistant—they did not have a role model or an example of a woman who had run a company, made a successful exit, and now was an investor. Nope. There was not even one investor woman in that room. Forty-five people."

Complicating the matter is that Gupta believes investors flock to start-ups in fields considered "sexy"—such as artificial intelligence, space travel, and cloud computing—fields where male founders are plentiful. She believes investors are less interested in companies where women founders proliferate: "Many education-related companies are started by women. Many fashion industry start-ups are started by women. House cleaning, baby sitting, daycare, education—all these are often started by women, because women take a majority role in any household for those things. So if I'm an investor, it may not look as sexy as cloud computing, but if you think critically, that's where the money should be. . . . We need to redefine what is sexy. Sexy is day-to-day, mundane problems and the solutions that are fixing those problems, problems that are experienced by the whole planet."

Investors like to put money into companies they understand—perhaps they have worked in the industry, have studied the market, or could imagine using the product or service themselves. So when most venture capital investors are white males, you can imagine the understanding gap that results. Women founders tell me they feel this acutely if their company targets women customers.

When serial entrepreneur Heidi E. Lehmann was pitching one of her early companies, SWSI Media, which produces videos and other content that focuses on women, she encountered a typical response from male investors: "When we were raising capital for it, a lot of the men would say, 'It sounds like a really interesting idea, and I could see where there would be a lot of potential here, but I don't really know. I'm going to go home and ask my wife.' I remember feeling so insulted," says Lehmann, now working on a wearable health diagnostics start-up called Kenzen in New York City.

Not only did Melanie Elturk have to introduce investors to a product for women, she had to tackle religion, too. Growing up in the suburbs of Detroit, Elturk struggled to find fashionable, easy-to-wear hijabs at the mall and elsewhere. In 2010, after a short career as a civil rights lawyer, she cofounded the New York City–based Haute Hijab with her husband and took the role of CEO. Their hijabs come in an astounding variety—chiffon, leopard print, embellished with crystals, and more—and are sold on their own website. Their chic Instagram account has over three hundred thousand followers. "We found that many potential investors just have no clue about hijab, about Muslim women, about Islam," Elturk tells me. "We've gotten some really bizarre questions and assumptions about women being forced to wear it by their husbands, or how they're oppressed, and it's just so disheartening." The topic Elturk's most interested in discussing can get overshadowed: "I want to talk about numbers. Just look at our numbers, and you'll see that we're on the path to an incredible growth trajectory."

"Early entrepreneurs are so dependent on the personal preferences of investors," notes angel investor Barbara Clarke. "You have the issue of people wanting to invest in people like themselves. That's issue one. Issue two would be investing in industries that they care about. Every woman of color and a lot of white women have had the experience where they're talking about a particular market, and the investor will just be like, 'I don't get it. Is that really a big market? I don't understand it,' or 'I'm not the target demographic to use that product.'"

Ishveen Anand has created a company in a field that plenty of male investors know and love. That's the good news. The bad news is they expect men will have the expertise in this field. Anand loved sports growing up in Manchester, England. While a student at Oxford University, she was captain of the Keble College teams for cricket and netball (sort of like basketball). Afterward, she moved to India and got a job at an agency that represented athletes in sports like cricket, golf, and field hockey. As an agent, she was frustrated by the process in which companies might hire one athlete to endorse their product but not another. It seemed random and opaque and based less on merit than on who you knew.

In 2014, then living in New York City, Anand launched Open-Sponsorship, basically as a way of answering the question: Can we make the process of buying and selling sports sponsorships easier and more efficient? Among others, her company represents Russell Westbrook and Klay Thompson, both of whom play in the NBA, and Rob Gronkowski, the former tight end for the New England Patriots. About one-fifth of the athletes signed up are women, and she's working on getting that number higher. Since the third year of operation, her company's been profitable.

Despite her successes, pitching to male investors has been a challenge. "I have to validate myself from the second I walk in the room," she says. If Anand can't do that, she's sunk. "If I walk into a male VC's office and I start pitching, 'I'm going to build a beauty brand for South Asians,' they may think, 'Oh, well, Birchbox was so successful, or Zola was successful, so you could be.' But when I go in and I'm saying, 'Okay, well, I'm going to build a business in a male-dominated industry,' that inherent bias against me being female is stronger than ever. . . . I've definitely fallen into that category of not looking the part."

This is the thing that's frustrating for Anand—in a competitive environment that is also male-dominated, it's difficult or even impossible for the woman entrepreneur to know if that rejection she just got was based on merit or based on sexism. "Let's say for the people who get rejected by VCs, I'd love to know, is it a bias of the person, or would they have said no regardless? I have no idea how you find out, but that's really important," she says. "Because it's also important not to be like, 'It didn't work out for me because I'm female.' Maybe your business just sucks. Maybe it's got nothing to do with you being female. I don't think you know that right now, and that's an issue."

Started in 1972 by the late Don Valentine, Sequoia Capital is one of Silicon Valley's legendary venture capital firms. It was an early investor in heavy hitters such as Apple, Google, YouTube, PayPal, and Cisco, claims it has helped companies now valued at over $3.3 trillion, and has expanded to China, India, and Israel.[50] In 2015, when *Bloomberg* reporter Emily Chang asked Sequoia chairman Michael Moritz why his US branch had no women partners, his answer created shockwaves.[51] He told her Sequoia was interested in hiring women but wasn't willing "to lower our standards" to do so. After a widespread public rebuke, Moritz softened his stance the next day, releasing a statement that said, "I know there are many remarkable women who would flourish in the venture business. We're working hard to find them and would be ecstatic if more joined Sequoia or other firms."[52] The following year, Sequoia hired its first US woman partner: Jess Lee, former CEO of fashion start-up Polyvore.[53] As of early 2020, the firm listed four women partners out of twenty-two.[54]

So it goes diversifying the venture capital field: pronouncements that change is important, pledges to do better, but a glacial pace.

Sixty-five percent of this country's major VC firms still lack a single woman partner, according to the nonprofit All Raise, which started in 2018 with the goal of making entrepreneurship equitable.[55] All Raise also reports that only 13 percent of decision makers in venture capital are women. One survey that looked at about fifteen hundred VC investors in the United States found that 18 percent are women.[56] Overall, 11 percent were described as white women, 6 percent as Asian women, 1 percent as Black women, and none as Latinx women. The organization Women in VC reports that the majority of women venture capitalists invest at the earliest stages of a start-up, when the bets tend to be riskier but the funding amounts are lower.[57] Women VCs who make bigger financial commitments to more established companies are in short supply.

Adding more women investors—and not just white and Asian American women with Ivy League degrees—is viewed as one way to change the industry's insular culture and practices. A reason white male investors so often fund white male entrepreneurs is because people are inclined to support other people who are like them—a tendency sociologists call "homophily." The assumption is that bringing in a diverse group of investors will increase the amount of funding to underrepresented groups. Whether that will really happen is unclear. The 2018 report from the National Women's Business Council noted that "[w]omen investors demonstrate a bias toward men business owners, so the gender gap in funding is not likely to narrow simply by having more women become venture capitalists."[58] Also, the 2016 study by the nonprofit StartOut found that being LGBT themselves did not always lead investors to fund LGBT founders.[59]

Robin Chase, who cofounded Zipcar and several other transportation companies, recalls a meeting she had about ten years ago at a venture capital firm in Cambridge, Massachusetts. She arrived early and ended up waiting some fifteen minutes in the reception area. "I was observing the interaction of the VC men as they flowed through that centralized space, and they were talking to each other, all men, and they were saying, 'Oh, did you see that deal?' and 'So-and-so's coming in at lunch' and 'Those entrepreneurs blah, blah, blah.' Then, with the woman receptionist, the conversation was, 'What's the code to the bathroom?' 'What's catered for lunch?' 'I see you have new recycling trash cans.' As I was sitting there observing these interactions, what I realized and recognized was 'Oh, yes, these male VCs are having this kind of conversation with men, and they had this kind of conversation with women.' Clearly, in their daily life and interactions, when they have a woman entrepreneur come in, they are anticipating or have experienced this lower-level conversation."

Adding a single woman investor would certainly be an accomplishment for a decent chunk of US venture capital firms, but the ideal is adding two or more. According to one report, firms with only one woman partner don't appear more likely to invest in women-led start-ups; that only happens when multiple women investors are present.[60] This result is seen elsewhere in business. Research shows, for example, that adding only one woman to a company board of directors won't shift the thinking of the group; you need three or more women for that to happen.[61] When California became, in 2018, the first state to require that the boards of publicly traded companies have female representation, it also had the idea that more is better.[62] At first, the law required one woman board member, but by 2021, boards must have two or three women, depending on the size of the board.[63]

Susan Ho, the cofounder and CEO of New York City–based travel-planning app and platform Journy, believes the pressure on a lone woman in a VC firm is heightened if she's being pitched a company whose main customers are women. Ho imagines the investor has to ask herself if it's worth "sticking my neck out for these companies that my colleagues don't get."

In 1997, Patty Abramson set up one of the nation's first venture capital funds devoted solely to investing in businesses launched by women.[64] At the time, she was frustrated that only 2 percent of venture capital dollars was going to women entrepreneurs. When her fund opened, Abramson declared to a Baltimore newspaper, "Fifteen years from now, there won't be a need for a fund like ours." Her prediction was, unfortunately, wrong (the 2 percent figure is holding steady decades later), and her fund closed after the dot-com bust, but Abramson helped usher in a string of funds operating today that are devoted to women entrepreneurs. One of them, Rethink Impact, is run by her daughter Jenny Abramson.

Cindy Gallop's frustration finding investors for her own start-up has nudged her to create the fund All the Sky that will invest solely in the sex-tech industry, primarily in companies started by women. "The most interesting things in sex tech, they are coming from female founders," she tells me. "We are finally owning our sexuality. We are finding unique ways to leverage it in business terms, because we get the enormous market that is women's needs, wants, and desires, historically deemed too embarrassing, shameful, taboo to address in business." Gallop is the founder and CEO of MakeLoveNotPorn, a New York City–based video-sharing platform.

Anna Palmer's experience as a woman founder pitching to male investors inspired her to help create a Boston-based venture capital fund called XFactor Ventures that since 2017 has invested in over forty young companies, each with at least one woman founder. All but one of the firm's twenty-two investment partners are themselves women entrepreneurs. Five years earlier, Palmer cofounded her first start-up, Fashion Project, a for-profit Boston-based company that helped nonprofits squeeze more money out of the designer-clothing donations they received. Palmer's meetings with male investors were eye-opening. "Early on, I was pretty frustrated that there was no one across the table that really understood the business I was building and the customer base. I ended up doing things like pitching the business to the [woman] assistant, or I'd pitch the business to the investor's wife on a conference call," she tells me. "Through that process, I realized that there is this huge group of businesses that probably aren't getting funded." Palmer and cofounder Christine Rizk have since sold Fashion Project to another company, and Palmer is now onto her next start-up, Dough, which helps customers shop from women-owned businesses.

XFactor is also taking aim at a practice used by many venture capital firms: relying on introductions to potential entrepreneurs from people they know and trust. This can penalize women and other underrepresented founders who have smaller or different networks. "From very early on with XFactor, we wanted to make a commitment that we didn't necessarily have to have the same level of network: 'I know somebody who knows somebody who can get you in.' We actually look very strongly at the hello@xfactor.ventures emails. If somebody emails XFactor with a business plan, somebody reviews it and makes a determination from there. We've had at least one company that we actually funded after the cold email intro," Palmer says. "I think that's pretty rare for a typical venture fund."

When venture firm First Round Capital studied ten years of its own investments in early-stage companies, it discovered that funding "somebody who knows somebody who can get you in" doesn't make much financial sense.[65] "For a long time, VC has been predicated on this idea that the best opportunities come through referrals," the firm writes, "yet companies that we discovered through other channels—Twitter, Demo Day, etc.—outperformed referred companies by 58.4%. And founders that came directly to us with their ideas did about 23% better."

Chip Hazard is the sole male investment partner at XFactor Ventures; he's also a general partner with the Boston VC firm Flybridge Capital Partners. Hazard tells me that before he helped launch

XFactor, the people he met with to discuss potential investments were 80 to 90 percent male. "If you'd asked me before XFactor, I would have told you I invest in what I see," he says. "That's just the nature of my deal flow, and so I'm not biased." Hazard now acknowledges that answer would've been naive. "We start XFactor, and all of a sudden my deal flow flips to 40/60 male/female. It turns out the venture business is just a network business." In 2018, Hazard and others experimented with a #StartWithEight campaign that asked investors to meet with eight women outside their networks during the month of March.[66] Forty-three investment firms pledged to do that. "Raising capital and recruiting talent all start with a meeting, and an opportunity to build a relationship," the leaders of the campaign wrote in a 2018 essay published on *Medium*.[67] "When most of the meetings venture capitalists take are with men, it is no surprise they don't invest in many female-led companies, appoint many women to boards, push to hire women into C-level positions, or chose female coinvestors." Hazard also tells me that he hopes several of the women entrepreneurs acting as investment partners in XFactor Ventures will move on to become full-time investors at other VC firms.

Entrepreneur Stephanie Lampkin is excited by the potential of these VC funds focused on women and other underrepresented groups, but points out a tendency to overlook some women. "I find that a lot of the funds that are female-focused, if you go through their portfolio, they primarily invest in white and Asian women. A lot of funds that are focused on minorities, if you go to their portfolio, the majority of the founders are men," says Lampkin, the founder and CEO of Bay Area–based Blendoor, a software tool that helps companies scrub unconscious bias from their hiring practices. "I don't think enough attention has been paid to Black, Native, and Latina women."

Despite these slow-but-promising improvements to venture capital, some founders have sworn off VC altogether. They've made the calculation that they're better off finding the resources they need elsewhere, that the process requires them to give up too much. The group Zebras Unite is searching for an alternative to an investing approach that it calls "masturbatory."[68] Started in 2017 and led by four women entrepreneurs—Jennifer Brandel, Astrid Scholz, Aniyia Williams, and Mara Zepeda—the group criticizes the practice of VCs pumping lots of money into a start-up and then demanding explosive growth, followed by the company's sale or going public. They complain the process can hasten a company's demise or force its founders to abandon their vision and values. Instead of idolizing unicorns, Zebras Unite is urging the support of "zebras," its name for companies with sustainable growth that balance making money and doing good.[69] These zebras, the group notes, are typically headed by women and other underrepresented founders. In a 2016 *Medium* blog post laying out its manifesto, the group writes: "Yes, we want to build businesses that succeed financially. But we also want so much more than that, and we aren't alone. Most of the founders we know, many of whom happen to be women, are driven to build companies that generate money *and* meaning. And they're in it for the long haul—not just to get their jollies, make their names, and exit."[70] In only a few years, Zebras Unite has grown to forty-five chapters on six continents.

Julie Lenzer started and grew her company without investor money, and for a while, that made her feel inadequate. "I used to feel, in my company, like I wasn't doing enough because I didn't get outside funding," says Lenzer, who left IBM in 1995 to start a Maryland-based software firm called Applied Creative Technologies, which helped manufacturers improve their operations and better control their inventory. She thinks TV shows like *Shark Tank* reinforce this thinking: "It sets up the expectation for people that the American dream is to have a company that's funded by other people, but in reality, getting outside funding is actually your last resort. Your ideal funding for any company is a paying customer. I know that there are some industries where investment is really important, where you need a lot of capital, that it's a highly competitive market and you need to grow fast or you will get washed out. I get that. But not everybody who starts a company should take outside money." After ten years, Lenzer sold the production and warehouse management system she had created. She's now the chief innovation officer at the University of Maryland in College Park.

Alison Rogers is another entrepreneur eyeing venture capital cautiously. "I'm not sure VC is right for everyone and everyone's ideas," she tells me. "The culture that I hear is 'We're going to come in and push you around, bully you around, and maybe the end product will look totally different than what you were expecting when you allowed this VC in.' That doesn't sound very appealing to me." In 2018, Rogers launched the Boston-based Coffee Cup Collective, her third start-up, a service in which subscribers get their to-go coffee served in reusable cups at participating coffee shops and then return the dirty cups to sites throughout the city. Rogers compares it to bike-sharing programs. For now, Rogers is mostly bootstrapping her venture, but the gender pay gap gives her pause. "We make less than our male counterparts," she says. "Saving up to take a plunge is harder. The barrier to entry is greater."

Shelly Bell, a serial entrepreneur and former computer scientist, has created a funding alternative that addresses several of the shortcomings of the traditional options. Her inspiration was 1920s Harlem rent parties, in which cash-strapped tenants hosted concerts in their apartments and charged entrance fees, which then helped the hosts pay rent. Bell's version is a nonprofit called Black Girl Ventures that started in Washington, DC, in 2016. She hosts competitions in multiple cities throughout the year, and each time eight Black or Brown women entrepreneurs are invited on stage to pitch their "tech-enabled" companies. (Bell gets three hundred or more applications each year, and she provides the selected candidates with coaching beforehand.) Anyone is welcome to join the audience and is asked to donate to that night's winnings; sometimes, sponsors chip in, too. The audience then votes on which pitches they prefer and which entrepreneurs should get the collected money—payouts have ranged from $500 to $5,000 and up. Almost half of the participants have gone on to connect with additional investors.

Bell tells me it's important to her that the audience, not a small team of judges, select the worthiest businesses. "If the current problem is that only a few people have the ability to make [funding] decisions, then why would we recreate that?" she asks. "I feel the audience can be just as or even more critical than if experts were judging."

. . . . . .

Arlan Hamilton tells me that she already feels she's achieved what she set out to do: she's proved that high-quality start-ups led by women, people of color, and LGBTQ founders are plentiful and worthy of investment. While about 10 percent of the more than 130 companies in Backstage's portfolio have closed, she's proud that others have pulled in more than $50 million from other sources, showing that other investors believe in their potential, too. She predicts one or two of these companies will be valued at half a billion dollars or even a billion dollars in the near future.

Hamilton readily admits she's in this to earn lots of money for herself and the entrepreneurs she invests in, noting how powerful it is to bring wealth to people in groups that historically haven't had it. "I think Backstage is part of a movement," Hamilton has posted.[71] "I think we are part of a community of people who have long been overlooked, undervalued and underestimated, and they're not standing for it anymore."

CHAPTER 4

YOU CAN'T BE WHAT
YOU CAN'T SEE

The power of role models

ON A RAINY MORNING in December 2018, at a coworking space next to the mall in Stonecrest, Georgia, a dozen girls were at work on a challenge: Santa has put on extra weight and can no longer fit in the chimney, so he needs to find a way to drop presents from his sleigh without breaking them. Each girl had twenty minutes to devise a packing method that would protect a fragile present—simulated in this case by a raw egg—using only wrapping paper, tissue paper, tape, and ribbon. When time was up, their instructor held each package high above her head and dropped it to the floor. Only two of the twelve eggs survived the drop intact.

Stephanie Ivery, the instructor, used the egg challenge to show the girls, ages eight to seventeen, what an engineer does: define a problem, research it, sketch out solutions, build prototypes, run tests, repeat. She told them these are the same steps used by one of the country's most noted electrical engineers, Carol Espy-Wilson, a University of Maryland professor and the first African American woman to earn a PhD in electrical engineering from MIT. Espy-Wilson is known for her work in speech recognition and enhancement and founded a software company, OmniSpeech, that improves voice quality for mobile devices.[1] Ivery told the girls that a high school engineering program was important to Espy-Wilson's success, as well as her own. In Ivery's case, precollege programs from the National Society of Black Engineers and others prepared her to be a chemist for L'Oreal and an engineer for Panasonic, jobs she did before becoming a teacher.

"I always want the girls to be able to see themselves doing amazing things to enhance our lives in the very near future, if not now," Ivery told me later. "That is why it is so important to teach and expose them to women and their stories."

The idea for the gathering came from Carolina Mincey, an executive assistant for the DeKalb County Sheriff's Office. In 2017, Mincey, who also owns an event-planning business, decided to build an Atlanta-area nonprofit that would expose girls, including her own daughter, to careers and hobbies in which women are underrepresented. She settled on three—entrepreneurship, STEM (science, technology, engineering, math), and golf—and called the effort Inspiring Greatness in You. Once a month during the school year, the nonprofit puts on Saturday morning events open to girls and their mothers, where they can do experiments, study successful women, discuss careers and businesses they might open one day, and work on their golf skills.

Mincey recruited Deborah Davis, a former pro golfer who played on the LPGA Futures Tour, to teach the girls the game. Why golf? Davis thinks the sport can help women build companies and advance careers. The golf course, she told me, is where networks are formed, deals are discussed, and women earn credibility from male executives. Davis doesn't even think you have to master golf to get these benefits—you just need to learn the etiquette and be comfortable on the course. Figuring out how to move a golf club wouldn't hurt. On the morning I visited, I watched Davis pull aside two of the moms to point out that they should place their upper arms over, not alongside, their breasts when swinging. Davis laments that most male golf instructors either don't know this tip or are too embarrassed to share it. Turning to the girls, Davis explained the kinds of golf-related businesses they might pursue one day, including course designer and shop owner, and noted that the wooden golf tee was invented by a Black man named George Franklin Grant in 1899.

One of the mothers, Sham McLendon, told me her then eleven-year-old daughter, Morgan, has always had an enterprising streak—she made and sold slime to classmates—and her mom hopes the Inspiring Greatness program will help her hold on to that. McLendon developed an interest in computers in elementary school, studied them in college, and has been in the army for more than a dozen years, focusing on information technology. McLendon knows how difficult it can be to enter and stay in male-dominated fields, and thinks organizations like this will help Morgan do that.

Morgan told me she loves makeup and helping people feel good about themselves, and so she might open a cosmetology business one day. As she examined the swag each girl received at the end of the event—candy, a bottle of nail polish, and unicorn-themed hand sanitizer—I asked her what she gets out of this group. "It makes me think I can do anything," she says.

Ask people to name an entrepreneur, and you'll probably hear Bill Gates or Steve Jobs, Elon Musk or Jeff Bezos. When pollsters quizzed British kids ages eleven to eighteen if they could identify a single woman entrepreneur, only 19 percent said yes, and the children were almost four times as likely to picture a man instead of a woman when hearing the word "entrepreneur."[2]

Do a Google image search for "famous entrepreneur" and you'll find that the first few dozen results are dominated by white men. The rare female images belong to Oprah Winfrey and Spanx creator Sara Blakely.

Take a business course, and odds are the case studies you'll read will feature white men. A review of best-selling business school case studies from 2009 to 2015 found that only 11 percent have a woman protagonist.[3] And at Harvard Business School, less than 5 percent of the case studies depict Black leaders, men or women.[4]

Watch a movie or TV show, and you'll be hard-pressed to find women building or running companies. Researchers from the University of Southern California discovered that when small business owners appeared in films rated PG-13, PG, and G, only 5 percent were played by women characters.[5] For corporate executives featured in family movies, a mere 3 percent were played by female characters.

"The entrepreneur is very much depicted as a thirty-five-year-old white male," says Maura McAdam, a professor at Dublin City University in Ireland and noted scholar on entrepreneurship and gender. "Anybody else that does not fit into that is considered the 'other' or what we would say in research terms, the 'interloper in the field.'" McAdam tells me she's taught women and men in several countries, including Saudi Arabia, and whenever she asks her students to name entrepreneurial role models, they typically list white American men. "What happens for people that do not fit with that image? One of my concerns is that they self-select out."

Any entrepreneur from an underrepresented group faces competing, almost impossible-to-satisfy requirements: "You have to have novelty in the field, you have to be doing something unique, you have to disrupt," McAdam says. "Then, one of the issues for women and minority groups is that you also have to fit in. That, unfortunately, is fit in with the stereotypical image of who the entrepreneur is. That's something for us to think about. In order to have what we refer to as an entrepreneurial legitimate identity, there is this paradox of fitting in but also standing out."

McAdam says her women entrepreneurship students often come across as conflicted or even timid when talking about their business ventures. "I mentor quite a few young female entrepreneurs," she tells me. "They talk about their 'little project' or 'this little thing we're working on.' When they introduce themselves to people, they very rarely say, 'I'm an entrepreneur.' Very rarely. Their male counterparts are right up there introducing themselves as entrepreneurs."

Plenty of research shows that the traits most often associated with entrepreneurial triumph are stereotypically masculine: aggression, competitiveness, a willingness to take risks, independence.[6] When men exhibit these traits, it's considered desirable. When women do, it's not. As researcher Lakshmi Balachandra and her colleagues note in their 2017 study, "[W]omen entrepreneurs may face a catch 22. If they conform to the femininity expected of their gender stereotype, they will fail to be viewed as competent and successful entrepreneurs.

However, if they behave in the masculine ways expected of successful entrepreneurs, they will fail to conform to their gender stereotype and violate gender norms."[7]

Amelia DeSorrento, who cofounded and was COO of a software start-up called Hatch Apps and now works in banking in Washington, DC, says it's human nature for people to be affected by these stereotypes: "If you see twenty people who look like Mark Zuckerberg and five people who don't, it's hard not to more easily attach certain attributes to the person that most resembles whatever it is you think makes for a great entrepreneur, or a great salesperson, a great engineer, a great whatever."

DeSorrento tells me about a time when she was participating in an incubator, and a well-known advocate for women in business was visiting. "She was like, 'I would love to hear the sixty-second elevator pitch for each of your companies.' It was me and five or six other founders, and they were all men. She . . . pointed to each person and said, 'I'd love to hear it.' I was sitting in the middle of the group, and she just skipped me. She thought I must have been an employee. This is a woman who campaigns for women in tech." DeSorrento was angry in the moment but later realized there was no point in being mad. The woman wasn't trying to be malicious. She was just someone who'd been exposed to a lot of stereotypes—and who hasn't? Here she was, an advocate for women entrepreneurs, and the lack of role models had colored even her view of what a real entrepreneur should look like.

Male first-year college students are more than twice as likely as their female counterparts to pick "business owner/entrepreneur" as their intended occupation, according to 2017 research out of UCLA.[8] Surely one big reason for that is this: Young men can find plenty of role models who look like them. Young women can't.

Psychology tells us that we need role models to show us what's possible. They let us imagine certain pursuits for ourselves. Researchers have explored how important it is that a role model is of the same gender, especially when someone is pursuing a path considered to be nontraditional for their gender. A 2018 study by two German researchers found that female undergrads studying business felt more confident about their entrepreneurial abilities when they had a woman entrepreneur as a role model.[9] The findings support the old maxim: you can't be what you can't see.

How rare is it to see women business leaders presented as successful real humans in the popular press? When Audrey Gelman, former CEO and cofounder of women's coworking space The Wing, appeared on the October 2019 cover of *Inc.* magazine, she became the first-ever visibly pregnant CEO to grace the cover of *any* business magazine.[10]

One way students find role models is through the case studies used in business schools. In addition to the shortage of female protagonists in these texts, when women do appear, they're often depicted as inferior. Two Canadian researchers showed in a 2018 study that women protagonists in business school case studies are presented as less visionary, less action-oriented, less willing to take risks, and more emotional than men.[11] The researchers see this affecting both female and male students, influencing how they'll perceive themselves and future colleagues and bosses. "We argue," the researchers write, "that case studies contain a 'hidden curriculum' that presents and reinforces implicit assumptions and stereotypes about women's fitness to lead."

Role models can do as much good for adults as for young people. Rita Childers and Candi Haas, cofounders of the St. Louis company Core + Rind, which makes a vegan cheese-like sauce sold around the country, have discovered that meeting entrepreneurs like themselves makes a difference. "The support of other women in business is one of the most beneficial things, especially when you're feeling lost in your decisions as an entrepreneur," Childers says. "I feel freer talking to a woman entrepreneur. We've all been in the same boat where we are not taken as seriously. It's almost like we have to work harder, and we do work harder, to get where we're at." Haas seconds this idea: "To see the example of other women leading amazing businesses, having that awesome example to look up to, and then hopefully to morph ourselves into women that other new budding entrepreneurs can look up to, it's just a good process."

· · · · · ·

STEM fields, especially computer science, are fertile ground for entrepreneurs. It's the ideal background for someone who wants to launch the next Facebook or Uber. But girls don't pursue these fields at the same rate that boys do. "In middle school, for example, 31 percent of girls believe that jobs requiring coding and programming are 'not for them.' In high school, that percentage jumps up to 40. By the time they're in college, 58 percent of girls count themselves out of these jobs," according to 2018 research commissioned by Microsoft.[12] The researchers note that girls having role models like themselves could potentially change these numbers: "Unfortunately, most girls don't have any female role models in STEM to look up to. So it's no surprise that, when asked to describe a typical scientist, engineer, mathematician, or computer programmer, 30 percent of girls say that they envision a man in these roles. As do almost 40 percent of adult women—and 43 percent of women in STEM and tech fields." A mere 1 percent of women undergraduates major in computer and information sciences, according to the 2012 report by the American Association of University Women.[13]

The Los Angeles–based Technovation Girls is among several nonprofits aiming to change those numbers. Designed for girls ages ten to eighteen in more than a hundred countries, Technovation teaches them how to create a mobile app that solves a problem in their community and then build a business around the app. The program, launched in 2010, reports that more than a quarter of its graduates end up majoring in computer science in college—a remarkable feat for such a male-dominated major—and most express increased interest in entrepreneurship and business leadership.[14] There are also options like SheHeroes, which exposes kids to women role models with nontraditional careers, and Girls Who Code and Black Girls CODE, which teach computer science.

The Microsoft-commissioned research found that participating in these activities can influence a girl's educational choices for years. Seventy-four percent of middle school girls in STEM clubs report that they'll likely study computer science in high school, compared to only 48 percent of those who aren't in such clubs.[15] And high school girls in STEM clubs are over 2.5 times more likely to report that they'll focus on computer science in college.

Briana Berger participated in Technovation in 2016. While there, she created a driver fatigue app called SleepBeep, an idea she got after seeing a truck veer off the side of a North Carolina mountain be-cause the driver had fallen asleep. SleepBeep helps drivers figure out if they're alert enough to stay on the road and looks for signs of fatigue like the car speeding up and slowing down in short intervals. The app earned her a semifinalist spot in a Technovation competition in Silicon Valley, but is on hold as she focuses on earning an undergrad degree in computer science at Stanford.

Originally from Gainesville, Florida, Berger was interested in technology at an early age. For her sixth birthday, she received a pink toy computer. Not long after, she started creating simple websites. By middle school, an aunt working in information security introduced her to coding. "Computer science, at that age, was able to make me feel like I could just go develop an app and create a company," says Berger.

She saw that most of her female peers didn't share her enthusiasm: "A lot of girls are just afraid of trying things that are too risky, and they're afraid of the unknown. They're like, 'Oh, well, that's more of a guy thing. I don't really want to try that because it seems like, what if I do it wrong? Then everybody's going to look at me.'" Berger never felt that fear, but she did experience the stares and comments that come with being one of the few girls interested in computers. One time a boy spotted her in the front row of a coding session and proclaimed, "Wow, I didn't expect there to be any girls in the class."

By age sixteen, Berger had started a coding group for girls at her school to show them that instead of playing with an app or playing with dolls, they could create them. "You can make those dolls. You can make that app," she says. "I think that's something that girls really need to learn when they're younger." The group she created in 2016, called coderGirls, has since grown into an international nonprofit aimed at girls in kindergarten to twelfth grade, with chapters as far away as Nepal and Ukraine.

Berger says she wanted to make coderGirls free of boys so that the female participants wouldn't be the only girl in the room and could see plenty of peer role models. "I feel comforted being with other girls, because it creates a camaraderie," Berger says. And she believes girls in this kind of setting gain a confidence that will aid them if they end up in male-dominated college classrooms and workplaces.

Not everybody thinks girls-only is the way to go. Vicky Wu Davis's Boston-based nonprofit, Youth CITIES, offers ten-week bootcamps that guide middle and high school students to develop and launch a business idea and build entrepreneurial leadership skills. She wants the group of participants to be half girls, half boys, and from a range of economic backgrounds. Davis tells me she tends to get enough male applicants but has to do active recruitment—lobbying teachers and guidance counselors, giving talks at schools—to ensure that girls will show up. When she presents at schools, Davis says, it helps that the girls can see her and learn that a woman of color is an entrepreneur. (Davis founded a language-learning company and a video game technology firm.)

As for why she likes a coed setting, Davis says the girls need to find out what it's like to work with and sometimes lead the boys. If it's girls-only, she says, "All of their confidence is in this sort of female-only camaraderie, and in reality we work in the coed world." Meanwhile, the boys will be better prepared for a future with strong women bosses and colleagues. Davis continues, "A lot of people often talk about needing strong female models for young girls, which I absolutely agree with. One thing that is not talked about enough is that you need strong female role models for young boys, too. If a boy sees more girls doing amazing things, then whatever stereotype, from whatever source that it came from, will start to go away."

Cindy Gallop extends this thinking to grown-ups. "Men need great female role models as much as women do," says the founder and CEO of MakeLoveNotPorn. "If we want men to lead in a different way, to operate in a different way, they need to have a completely different form of leadership behavior role-modeled by women. I very much appreciate the fact that I know—because they write to me and they tell me on social media—I have a lot of male fans who absolutely regard me as a role model for them, and I love that."

· · · · · ·

As a child, Nabiha Saklayen imagined a series of careers for herself: scientist, fashion designer, author, engineer, singer, songwriter. She credits her mother, a teacher, for supporting each newly hatched plan: "In every phase, she basically said, 'Great. Let's do that. What do you need to make that happen?' We would go out and buy whatever books I wanted, go to the museum, go watch a show. That, I think, always gave me this silent confidence that whatever I wanted to do was great, and I should pursue it." Growing up in Saudi Arabia, Bangladesh, Germany, and Sri Lanka, she was exposed to many ideas and people. Science was an enduring passion, and she idolized physicist and chemist Marie Curie, though she didn't know of any living female scientists as a child.

In 2008, Saklayen moved to Atlanta to pursue an undergraduate degree in physics at Emory University. Next she headed to Harvard to get a PhD, also in physics. It was there that she bonded with a lab mate, Marinna Madrid, who was studying applied physics. After a few years' work, the two discovered that cheap lasers could be used to deliver gene-editing tools to cells in ways that could treat diseases. Soon their work attracted the attention of experts in the field who told them their discovery could have a huge impact and that they should consider commercializing it.

Saklayen was intrigued by the suggestion, but of all the careers she'd considered, entrepreneur wasn't one of them. "I didn't even know how to process what it would mean to be an entrepreneur," she says. "I had one example of an entrepreneur that I'd met. I remember thinking of her in that moment. I'm like, 'Wow, yes, well, Liz did something like this, finished her PhD and started a company with her technology, so this is not absolutely crazy. I could potentially do this, too.' That was very helpful for me. I called her, I got coffee with her to talk about what it's like, and she gave me very valuable feedback. That was the only example of somebody in my network that I knew who had gone down that path."

Meanwhile, Saklayen was debating the start-up idea with Madrid, her lab mate. "Over several months," Saklayen tells me, "we were discussing, what does this mean? How does it affect our life plan? How should we structure this?" Finally, she says, they committed "to take that leap of faith together."

In 2017, while still Harvard students, Saklayen and Madrid applied to a start-up challenge in San Francisco as a way of testing their business idea, which they called Cellino Biotech. They won the $10,000 top prize. Saklayen says, "That was a huge breakthrough moment for us, because we realized we had a concept that other people were very drawn to and they were excited about the possibilities of this technology." Saklayen and Madrid quickly decided to expand their team to include someone who could "engineer a product that we could sell" and brought on a male cofounder, Matthias Wagner.

In the years since, the Cambridge, Massachusetts–based Cellino, with Saklayen as CEO, has continued to earn praise for its contributions to the field of cell engineering and has raised over $4 million. Hoping to help others find a role model, Saklayen cocreated a volunteer project called I Am a Scientist. It provides free materials to middle- and high-school teachers illustrating a diverse mix of people working in STEM. Saklayen still thinks about what might have happened if she hadn't met her role model, Liz O'Day, who founded the drug discovery start-up Olaris in 2014, one year after finishing her PhD in biological and biomedical sciences at Harvard. "There's an alternate world where I hadn't met Liz, and people weren't telling me to be an entrepreneur, and I didn't know what that would have looked like," Saklayen says. "I would have imagined, maybe, 'I can't do it,' or 'it's too much effort,' or 'I don't know who to talk to to get feedback.' That would have been very sad, because we wouldn't have maximized my technology and brought it to the world to make an impact in a big way."

CHAPTER 5

SLEAZY TEXTS, LATE-NIGHT MEETINGS

A #MeToo reckoning

FOR MONTHS SUSAN HO grappled with what to do: tell the world about the powerful investor who'd made unwelcome sexual come-ons to her and her cofounder, or keep quiet. She'd heard that the guy had behaved in disgusting ways with other women entrepreneurs and wanted to stop him for good. But she knew that speaking out came with great risks. It could scare off other investors and earn her a reputation as someone who's overly sensitive.

At the time Ho and cofounder Leiti Hsu were building a platform and app called Journy that would serve as a modern travel agent. For a small fee, the company would quiz travelers on their likes and dislikes and then create a personalized itinerary stuffed with recommendations on where to eat and what to do. Ho and Hsu were heavily invested, emotionally and otherwise, in the company's success, and understood they'd be putting it all at risk if they started talking publicly about what the investor had done. They understood that many women before them, in all roles and industries, had been sexually harassed by men but said nothing, making the difficult decision that they had to tolerate such treatment.

"I had this very real fear that if my cofounder and I go on the record and speak out against this venture capitalist, that we might not ever be able to raise venture capital funding for our company again," Ho tells me. "On the other side of that, there is the incredibly real fact—not a fear, a fact—that this guy for the last ten years has been systematically sexually harassing female Asian founders in tech. So what do you do?"

In the summer of 2017—after high-profile sexual harassment cases at Uber and elsewhere, but still three months before the Harvey Weinstein scandal emerged and intensified the #MeToo movement[1]—Ho decided it was time. "I got to the point where I realized I wouldn't be able to live with myself as a female businesswoman, as a female entrepreneur, if I didn't say something," Ho explains. She talked with reporter Reed Albergotti of the tech industry news site *The Information* and agreed to have her name published; Hsu did the same. On June 22, 2017, *The Information* published an article detailing their stories and the stories of four other women, all accusing prominent Silicon Valley venture capitalist Justin Caldbeck of sexual harassment.[2] In the article Ho recounted being approached in 2015 by Caldbeck, known for leading investments in top-shelf companies like Grubhub and TaskRabbit and cofounder of the investment firm Binary Capital. Caldbeck told Ho he was about to fund another travel start-up and wanted to discuss a possible partnership. They met for drinks to talk about it, and a few hours later, at around 1 a.m., he sent her text messages asking if they could get together again that night. Ho ignored the message until the next morning, when she texted him that "1 am on a weeknight is so past my bedtime." Caldbeck came back with "Well, I gotta try and change that, LOL." (Ho had shown the reporter her WhatsApp messages to back up her story.)

Ho later wrote on *Medium* about the uncomfortable relationship that developed between Caldbeck and her: "It's difficult to describe the subtle ways sexism and harassment occurs. In our messages he would write things like 'Hey you,' or when I brought up a good point, 'You are aggressive as shit. I kind of like it.' They all carry a patronizing tone that transforms your intelligence or success into something that is merely a source of attraction."[3]

In 2016, Ho and Hsu connected with Caldbeck at a hotel bar in New York City to discuss fundraising for Journy. At this meeting

Caldbeck grabbed Hsu's thigh under the table. A few hours later, at 3 a.m., Caldbeck sent Hsu a text message asking her to call him. Hsu ignored the request.

Ho thinks Caldbeck's behavior toward other women was more egregious than what she experienced. The four other women appearing in *The Information* said Caldbeck tried to sleep with them or sent sexually explicit text messages. Three of these women asked to remain anonymous, fearing a backlash from Caldbeck and other investors. The reporter noted that other women have said they abandoned their start-ups or never launched in the first place after experiencing this kind of harassment from investors. Caldbeck initially denied the stories, and his firm released a statement saying that Caldbeck had done nothing illegal and had only occasionally flirted with or dated women he met while doing business.

On the morning *The Information* article was published, Ho was walking to work in New York City and reading it on her phone. "I remember standing on the street corner for about thirty minutes, just frozen. I thought, 'Wow, why is everyone so quiet?' You would expect somebody to retweet this article by now. Holy crap."

Eventually Ho heard from a friend who'd been contacted by an employee at a major venture capital firm. He wanted to pass along a message: "Can you please tell your friend Susan that I really respect what she did?"

Ho says, "I shot back, 'Why can't he just retweet it?' My friend goes, 'He's afraid to.'"

The day after *The Information* story broke, Reid Hoffman, a venture capitalist and the cofounder of LinkedIn, wrote a post on LinkedIn that called Caldbeck's behavior "immoral and outrageous," pushed back against investors who consider these acts simple flirtation or harmless banter, and questioned why the news was being met with "a lack of outrage and commentary."[4] Hoffman wrote, "Folks may think: well, that's bad behavior but not my problem. If you think that, and work here in venture, think again. We all need to solve this problem. If you stay silent, if you don't act, then you allow this problem to perpetuate."

Ho was both relieved and frustrated by the support that followed. "It wasn't until Reid Hoffman came out and said something that the rest of Silicon Valley fell in line and echoed that sentiment," she tells me. "Hopefully, at some point, the voices of half a dozen women are enough. We don't need a man to jump in for people to take this seriously."

She adds, "The fact that people were so afraid to say something shows you just how deep the problem runs in Silicon Valley. I think the issue why everyone was quiet is because many people, in some way or another, were complicit and knew about this guy's behavior and knew of other people who behaved this way: 'We're doing deals with them, wanting to continue to do deals with them, and we're afraid to say something.'" It's only when people realize that the story isn't going away, that the accused investors have damaged their own reputations, that they feel okay about burning that particular bridge, Ho tells me. And only at that point do they feel comfortable offering public support. "That's kind of how it played out," Ho says.

Caldbeck's initial denial of the harassment morphed into an apology, plus an announcement that he'd take an indefinite leave of absence from his venture firm.[5] Eventually, Caldbeck resigned and Binary Capital collapsed—leaving some to cheer that there were real consequences for sexual harassment.[6] In a June 2017 statement, Caldbeck wrote: "The gap of influence between male venture capitalists and female entrepreneurs is frightening and I hate that my behavior played a role in perpetrating a gender-hostile environment. It is outrageous and unethical for any person to leverage a position of power in exchange for sexual gain, it is clear to me now that that is exactly what I've done."[7]

He wasn't the only investor to have a #MeToo reckoning in 2017. After the *New York Times* reported that at least one entrepreneur was accusing Dave McClure, cofounder of the venture capital firm and accelerator 500 Startups, of sexual harassment, he published an essay on *Medium* called "I'm a Creep. I'm Sorry."[8] He wrote: "I made advances towards multiple women in work-related situations, where it was clearly inappropriate. I put people in compromising situations, and I selfishly took advantage of those situations where I should have known better." In his apology, McClure noted that he'd given up day-to-day management of 500 Startups. While McClure and other investors suffered consequences for their behavior, it often proved temporary. In 2019, *Bloomberg* reported that McClure was attempting to raise a $100 million fund that would buy stakes in smaller venture capital funds.[9] By that time, his "I'm a Creep. I'm Sorry." essay had been deleted from *Medium*.

The women I interviewed told me these cases merely scratch the surface, and there are many men whose bad behavior is still hidden. According to a 2018 survey of women founders by *Inc.* and *Fast Company* magazines, 53 percent of respondents experienced harassment or discrimination while running their companies.[10] The worst offenders were investors, bankers, and vendors, though some bad treatment also came from employees. Almost none of the women surveyed said they took formal action. Instead they ended their professional relationship with the harasser or confided in their peers.

One of the country's top accelerators for young companies, Y Combinator in Silicon Valley, found that investors had been harassing women entrepreneurs in its program. According to its own 2018 survey, one out of five women faced unwelcome sexual contact, sexual overtures, or a sexual quid pro quo.[11]

None of this is unique to the entrepreneurial space. A 2016 report from the US Equal Employment Opportunity Commission notes that 60 percent of women experience unwanted sexual attention or coercion, sexually crude conduct, or sexist comments in the workplace.[12] And the decision to keep quiet is pervasive. About three out of four employees who experience sexual and other kinds of harassment never talk to a supervisor about the episode, according to the same report.[13] These workers worry that their stories won't be believed, that they'll be blamed for inviting the behavior, that they'll face social or professional retaliation, or that higher-ups will do nothing. The EEOC identified the kinds of workplaces that are ripe for harassment—and the start-up scene checks many of the boxes: The workers are homogeneous (remember that 88 percent of decision makers at US venture capital firms are men), and there are significant power disparities.[14] Alcohol use is tolerated and even encouraged (beer on tap in coworking spaces and late-day meetings are common). And the workplaces are decentralized and isolated (start-up founders are often toiling away in basements, borrowed offices, hotels, and airports, and working late hours).

Women in male-dominated workplaces often find themselves being the only woman in a room—researchers call them "Onlys." A 2019 study by LeanIn.Org and McKinsey & Company found that one in five working women is an Only, and they're nearly twice as likely as women who work with other women to have been sexually harassed during their career.[15] They're also more likely to face microaggressions.

So it's no surprise that women entrepreneurs report a steady stream of repulsive comments, creepy texts, forced kisses, and worse, all of which impose an enormous emotional tax and generate genuine safety fears. It distracts women from dedicating themselves fully to innovating and using their unique point of view that has been missing for too long from business circles.

In 2014, two years after graduating from Florida International University with a degree in finance and international business, Logan Cohen built a company called Küdzoo. With cofounder Trevor Wilkins, they created an app that rewards students for their grades, community service, and other achievements with giveaways such as gift cards, concert tickets, scholarships, and mentor introductions. (Wilkins left his daily role in the company in 2017.) Cohen says growing and funding the New York City–based business has been challenging, in part because she's a first-time founder from a small town in Pennsylvania who didn't attend an Ivy League school. At times this has left her feeling inadequate, like an impostor. Still, the app is now used by more than half a million students across the country, and Cohen has raised just over $2 million and found investors she calls "fantastic allies, middle-aged white dudes who are just so supportive and amazing." But there have been other guys with different intentions.

"I remember pitching once, and an investor said, 'I'm sorry. It's hard to concentrate with anyone that's bigger than a C cup.' I was just disgusted," Cohen says. "I just said, 'That's completely irrelevant,' and looked at him. He said, 'Oh, take a joke.' Then, I wound up leaving. I didn't storm out but didn't entertain it, not even with a fake laugh."

Another time an investor told her, "Your card says CEO, but you're like a Barbie. Who really runs this company?" Cohen says, "It's one thing that that line is so inappropriate, but it was almost like he was saying it like that's what I wanted to hear, or being a Barbie was more valuable to me than looking like a CEO, which is really warped."

When these things have happened with other investors in the room, Cohen says, they've kept quiet. "There was no one chiming in and saying, 'Yes,' and cheering him on, but the silence itself is saying that's okay. Once, when someone was just blatantly being inappropriate, one of the partners who walked us out to the elevator apologized. That was nice, but [it was not done] in front of the other partners."

When she told a male friend, also an entrepreneur, about these comments, he suggested that perhaps Cohen was "too pretty" and should consider wearing glasses.

The sexually suggestive comments have led Cohen to scrutinize invitations and modify her own behavior: "You ask to meet [an investor], and then you find out that they didn't give you the office address. One time, it was a home address, and I said, 'Oh, it's not the right place.' He's like, 'No, come up.' I was like, 'Oh, no, there's a coffee spot down here. I can meet you here.' He said, 'Oh, wow, really by the books.' I was thinking, 'Great, I think I lost this deal on having an attitude.' I don't know—maybe he had a home office, but I was alone. I just don't want to do it. It's the little things like that. Nothing extremely inappropriate happened, but it's still stuff that women need to think about that I don't think a male entrepreneur is [thinking]. Maybe a male would have gone right up and closed the deal."

It's urgent, Cohen tells me, to share these stories and send the message that these behaviors and comments aren't normal. None of it has led her to quit. "I am so strange and maybe stubborn, but it actually fed into 'I need to make this work,' because my goal, of course, is to grow Küdzoo." And Cohen already has her next chapter planned out.

"I cannot wait to become an investor. I don't want to say solely invest in women, but a large percent of my portfolio would be women-led companies, for sure." She considers it a win that, in her estimation, 85 percent of the meetings she's had while fundraising have fully focused on her company—not her looks, not sexist comments. I point out to her that 15 percent is not insignificant. Cohen agrees.

During the decade that Amy Spurling worked as a CFO and COO for tech start-ups in Boston and Phoenix, she raised over $200 million from investors and took two companies through exits. Despite her financial successes, the experience interacting with Silicon Valley investors wasn't positive. She was on the receiving end of sleazy texts inviting her to a hotel room and requests to visit a strip club and have "dinner in a low-cut shirt."[16] An investor who learned she's married to a woman wanted to know her dating history and if it's ever included men. Spurling says she was cautioned against making a stink about this behavior, that doing so would get her blacklisted. Now Spurling is raising money for her own start-up. In 2018, she cofounded Compt, whose software allows companies to offer personalized perk programs for their employees (gym reimbursement for one, continuing ed classes for another). She says these programs can help companies hire and retain top talent, especially in competitive industries. Spurling serves as CEO of the Boston start-up.

As she surveys the current investor scene, Spurling sees improvement in behavior, perhaps due to a #MeToo-sparked awareness. She also notices geographic differences in the ways investors treat women entrepreneurs. "Women are not getting funded to the level we should be in Boston, but it's not a sexual predator kind of situation that I've seen in the past on the West Coast," Spurling tells me. "It is different here. It's much more subversive. It's more dismissive."

Spurling is advocating for a Massachusetts bill that would hold accountable any investor who sexually harasses or discriminates against entrepreneurs. State legislators proposed the bill in 2019, and, as of this writing, it's still being considered.[17] "I do think that legislating it is going to be required to see change," she says. "You need to put protections in place to ensure that that doesn't continue. Otherwise it's a never-ending, continually fulfilling prophecy."

. . . . . .

Some women founders are taking their own measures to protect themselves. For Karin Lachmi, it means never going to a meeting without bringing a trusted man.

Lachmi is an Israeli-born neuroscientist whose earlier work on brain and breast cancer helped her see that life sciences researchers needed better tools to read and learn from existing studies. So, in 2013, she cofounded Bioz, an artificial intelligence–powered search engine that sifts through millions of scientific articles and then guides researchers as they design their next experiment. Her Los Altos, California–based company, where she's the chief scientific officer, has raised $11 million from investors, and its search engine is used by over 2 million researchers around the world. Lachmi has spoken out about the treatment she's had to endure from investors: One man, more than double her age, asked her "when was the last time you kissed a stranger" and then forcibly stuck his tongue into her mouth. Another investor asked her to join him for a meeting in a Jacuzzi. She says it's difficult to talk about these experiences publicly, but feels she has to for the #MeToo movement to continue its impact. "I have a daughter and a son," she explains. "I know that if my daughter will start a company one day, she will need to deal with similar situations. It is our responsibility to make sure that our kids will not need to deal with such situations."

During the early days of a start-up, Lachmi says, an entrepreneur is especially vulnerable. "You're almost desperate for any meeting, any connection, anything, and you're willing to maybe take more risks and expose yourself to a potentially bad situation. On the other hand, when taking into consideration the statistics today for women entrepreneurs, and no matter how much you protect yourself, you will probably be exposed to some level of sexual harassment or assault. It can be a minor or even a major situation, but something will happen along the way and you will most likely be alone to deal with it."

Lachmi tells me she felt unprotected and was constantly fearful that she might be harassed or assaulted by the men she was meeting with— and in such a male-dominated landscape, almost all the meetings were with men—so she scrutinized every encounter: What did that investor really mean? Should I take the meeting? Is it safe to meet him there? At that time? Will it be dark out? What should I wear? Should I be scared? "All of these questions and fears are things that I doubt our male colleagues consider or experience when scheduling a meeting with an investor. For us women, these concerns are on our minds all of the time. This is unfortunately what it feels like to live in fear."

Eventually, Lachmi instituted a rule: no outside meetings by herself. Instead, she only goes if accompanied by a trusted male colleague or friend—typically it's her cofounder and the company CEO, Daniel Levitt. "This is how I protect myself," she says. "This is not the solution that I would have wished for, as it is far from ideal. However, I didn't want to put myself anymore in that position of risk." I ask Lachmi if this approach, while safer, is too inefficient. Founders of new companies are usually strapped for time and short on help. Why send two executives to a meeting when one would do? "What's the alternative? The alternative is to either be worried all of the time that something might happen, or to not take the meeting at all—both losing propositions." Lachmi admits that she'll sometimes bow out of a meeting and let her cofounder go alone, but she hates missing out on the opportunity to talk about her company and grow her network.

Like Lachmi, Niki Bayat also scrutinizes meeting invitations. In 2016, while working on her PhD in chemical engineering, Bayat cofounded a company based on her own invention: a gel that becomes solid at body temperature and "melts" at cold temperatures. Bayat calls it "reverse chocolate." Originally she was investigating the material as a remedy for glaucoma, which her father suffers from, but now her company, the Los Angeles–based AesculaTech, is pursuing a treatment for dry eye syndrome, in which the gel acts as a tear-duct plug.

In the early days of her company, Bayat, the CEO, tells me that she found some meetings with male investors unnerving. Several invited her to addresses that she assumed were offices, but turned out to be homes or questionable locations. While her male cofounder was still a part of the company, she'd receive requests to meet only with her. "Some of them kept asking for a meeting, and the moment that I said that my cofounder was going to be in the meeting as well, they kept canceling." Bayat says women founders she's friends with have traded stories of men who called themselves investors but appeared more interested in dating than discussing term sheets. "The female founder community is very tight, so we share all these stories."

Bayat is frustrated by this distraction. "As an entrepreneur, you have so much stuff to think about every day," she says. "Every day my mind is just jumping from this subject to the other one. How are we going to do that? How are we going to do this? The last thing that you want is to be wary of the meeting that you want to go to."

Bayat has also experienced unwanted attention from—for lack of a better word—fans. In 2018, she was named to *MIT Technology Review*'s prestigious 35 Innovators Under 35 list, and her photo and accomplishments were circulated widely by the magazine, her grad school, and others. "In three days I received thousands of email and LinkedIn notifications," she says. "It was crazy—my phone flashing all the time." A few positive notes came from potential investors and collaborators, but the majority were worthless comments from men. Bayat had to hire three people to read and sort through her messages.

Shayna Brown tells me it's meetings with clients and colleagues that can be problematic. After growing up in a musical household, Brown started an audio post-production company in Austin, Texas, by maxing out her credit cards. It was 2013. At the time she had a four-year-old son and wanted the scheduling flexibility that would come with running her own business. Chez Boom Audio has flourished, doing work for movies and TV shows such as *12 Years a Slave* and *Parks and Recreation*, as well as audiobooks for authors like Neil Gaiman and Karl Rove. "The disadvantages of being a woman in this industry—other than being underestimated, not being taken seriously, the constant condescension—is a lack of network," Brown says. "There's lots of post-production get-togethers, but it's a guy's world, and I can't really show up to drink beers with them. That's a social norm that is hard to break. It's also hard on the other side with my husband. Like, 'This engineer invited me out for drinks.' Well, how do I handle that?" Once, a potential client asked to meet Brown at a bar. She remembers him saying, "Hey, I've got this big project, I want to run it by you, get some numbers from you, to see how we can incorporate your services."

She abruptly ended the meeting when it was clear he was interested in something other than business. For a time, Brown swore off meetings after 5 p.m. alone with men—even though the decision created "a big disadvantage" for her business—but now she takes those get-togethers, with some stipulations: "I make sure it's public places and I don't linger beyond the purpose of the meeting."

Trish Fontanilla is a consultant on customer experience and other topics who's been part of Boston's entrepreneurial scene for over a decade. She jokes that she was the "faux founder" of the video-messaging start-up Vsnap, because she was the first hire there and helped it get off the ground. With workdays at early-stage start-ups often ending around 10 p.m., Fontanilla says invitations to chat after work can be fraught. "I teach networking classes for people going into start-ups and entrepreneurs. Without a doubt, I always have women come up to me and say, 'I was trying to meet with this connection,' or 'I was trying to meet with a vendor or a potential customer, and they thought it was a date instead of a business meeting.' . . . Sad to say, I don't have any revolutionary advice for them, except for 'don't do drinks alone, ever.' It's hard for a lot of them because they're working and taking classes." Fontanilla recommends 7:30 a.m. coffee chats or lunch meetings, keeping communication formal, and never using emojis. "I tell them that they have to be the person that sets the standards in the relationship. If they don't, and if they show any kind of, I don't want to say weakness, but if they show any kind of 'This could go another way,' then it will pretty much always be misinterpreted."

Sexual harassment and assault are part of women's reality long before they enter the workforce. An average of one in five women will be sexually assaulted in college.[18] Sophia Yen, the doctor who cofounded the birth-control-delivery company Pandia Health, believes this trauma can influence all areas of a woman's life—including what kind of career she pursues and whether she aspires to start her own business. "You can envision that if you're sexually assaulted and you are in computer science, where it's like 75 to 90 percent men, that you are not going to want to be in that environment. Then women switch to the more soft majors, where there's 70 to 90 percent women, such as in the department of English. That can explain why women aren't going into tech."

This is significant because STEM fields can be particularly fruitful for start-ups and are the darlings of investors. Experience working at a tech company is "a major determinant" in an entrepreneur's success, according to digitalundivided's 2016 ProjectDiane report.[19] After studying ten years of its own investments, VC firm First Round Capital discovered that the start-ups with at least one founder formerly employed by Amazon, Apple, Facebook, Google, Microsoft, or Twitter performed 160 percent better than other start-ups.[20] The First Round investors suspect the networks and skills you build while working at these companies has something to do with it.

The importance of tech knowledge and work experience is troubling news for women college students aspiring to be entrepreneurs. The tech workforces at giants like Facebook and Google are still dominated by white or Asian men.[21] Men are more likely to pursue a STEM major.[22] In computer science, only 19 percent of the bachelor's degrees and 20 percent of the doctorate degrees in 2016 were awarded to women.[23] In engineering, women got 21 percent of the bachelor's degrees and 24 percent of the doctorate degrees. There are fewer women faculty in STEM classrooms as well. The atmosphere can feel discouraging or even threatening for women students.

Alice Zhang has worked in the Bay Area start-up space for over five years. She's the CEO and cofounder of Verge Genomics, which combines human genomics and artificial intelligence to help discover new drugs, and which has received $36 million from investors. Zhang tells me the sexual misconduct accusations against high-profile investors like Justin Caldbeck were no surprise to her. These stories had been circulating in the entrepreneurial community for years, especially as warnings to other women. And there are whispered stories about men whose names have not yet been made public, because the women who've been harassed or assaulted want to keep quiet.

Karin Lachmi points to herself as an example. She's spoken out about the fact that an investor forcibly stuck his tongue into her mouth and kissed her, but she hasn't said who did it. "I don't feel like a hero in choosing to not expose him," she says. "I didn't want to be alone in bearing the weight of doing so, but I felt that I needed to share my experience and drive change by speaking up."

Zhang understands why some women won't name their attackers. "There are women who don't feel there are good systems in place for reporting things that happened," she says. "And more often than not, [the behavior is] not outright illegal, or things like assault. Sometimes they're really in between."

One way to address the underreporting is a so-called decency pledge, which some venture capital firms began drafting in 2017.[24] These pledges set out acceptable behavior between investors and entrepreneurs and the steps that should be taken if there are violations. Importantly, some programs encourage colleagues who witness something to speak up and report the offense, so the burden isn't always with the person who's been harassed. This is exactly what the EEOC recommended in its 2016 report, highlighting bystander intervention training as a promising way to prevent harassment in the workplace.[25]

Venture capitalists are also beginning to feel pressure from the pension funds and other deep-pocketed folks who supply the money they invest. In 2019, the *Financial Times* reported that "#MeToo clauses" are being added to agreements, requiring that any sexual harassment complaints be disclosed.[26]

Another crucial and obvious fix would be to hire more women investors. Someone like Caldbeck might have been called out earlier if he'd been working alongside women colleagues.

Uncovering repeat offenders would also make a big difference. The San Francisco nonprofit Callisto has built a program that does just that; currently, it's offered on college campuses, though in 2018 and 2019 it was tested in the start-up community. Founder Jess Ladd, who was sexually assaulted while a college student, designed the program so that victims can create secure, time-stamped records of their sexual assaults. They can leave it at that step or submit the perpetrator's identity to the program. If any new reports come in about the same perpetrator, each survivor is contacted by a legal counselor to discuss options.

Zhang says this ability to connect victims is especially powerful, something she's seen in her own life. Once an investor acted "pretty creepy" to her. Zhang's first thought was that she had done something wrong: "Instead of immediately blaming the other party, if there's something weird that happens, my first reaction is to turn inward and to ask, 'Okay, what did I do wrong in this case? How can I be better? Should I change my behavior?' There's always the question of, maybe a little bit of guilt, maybe I induced this or encouraged this type of behavior." About a year later, during conversations with four friends who are also founders, she learned that the same investor was a repeat offender. "When you find out that four other women are experiencing the same thing, you're like, 'Okay, it's not just me.'"

For all the good that's emerged from the #MeToo movement, there have been unintended consequences. A group of researchers at the University of Colorado's Leeds School of Business found that while incidents of blatant sexual harassment appear to have dropped since 2016, there's been a jump in hostility toward women in work situations.[27] "It's not that the need to subjugate women goes away," study coauthor Stefanie K. Johnson told the *Boston Globe* in 2019. "I just think it takes a different form."[28] A 2019 survey by LeanIn.Org found that 60 percent of male managers now say they're uncomfortable mentoring or being alone with women.[29] And some male senior executives on Wall Street reportedly have stopped having business dinners with women thirty-five or younger, refuse to sit next to women colleagues on planes, and are bowing out of meetings with women in rooms without a window to see in, according to a 2018 report in *Bloomberg*.[30]

Zhang has wondered what a #MeToo backlash would mean for her business. "Are people going to be more reluctant to get those after-work drinks? Is that now viewed as inappropriate?" she asks. "In terms of business development in pharma, so much of the deals are done because you go to dinner with them and you grab drinks with them afterwards."

Susan Ho feared that speaking out about Caldbeck's harassment might hurt her company, but that hasn't happened. "I remember having my first drinks meeting with a VC after all this stuff happened. I remember high-fiving the guy to be like, 'Hey, see, we can sit down and have a meeting over drinks and not have to be weird. This is okay.' That was welcoming." In November 2018, Journy announced it had raised $3.15 million in funding, more than a year after the article in *The Information.*

"The great thing that came out of it is some amazing, amazing relationships with other women who had gone through the same thing," Ho says. One woman in particular has become a valuable adviser. "I wouldn't have met her if it weren't for this bonding experience of being sexually harassed by the same guy."

Ho says that from what she's heard, there have been fewer instances of bad actors since the #MeToo movement took off. "Everyone is just a little bit more aware. But is it where I would like things to be? No, not quite."

CHAPTER 6

THE BIG EFFECT
OF LITTLE INSULTS

The microaggression problem

IN 1970, a professor named Chester Pierce wrote an essay about the steady stream of indignities, offhand put-downs, and belittling comments that he and other Black people faced daily at the hands of the white majority.[1] He gave the phenomenon a name: "microaggressions." Even at supposedly enlightened Harvard, where he taught psychiatry and education, Pierce experienced the phenomenon daily.

"The enormity of the complications they cause can be appreciated only when one considers that these subtle blows are delivered incessantly," Pierce wrote.[2] "Even though any single negotiation of offense can in justice be considered of itself to be relatively innocuous, the cumulative effect to the victim and to the victimizer is of an unimaginable magnitude."

By coming across as casual, possibly inadvertent, or even complimentary, a microaggression had the effect of putting the recipient on the defensive. To respond to a microaggression was to appear difficult. To respond was to look as if you couldn't take a joke. Pierce noted the way white people liked to congratulate Black people on the tremendous progress that had been made in race relations.[3] "To the perception of the white offender," he wrote, "this is true and reasonable. From the vantage point of the black offended, however, this is both untrue and unreasonable. If the black offended then indicates in any manner whatsoever that he is not convinced that congratulations are in order, he is gruffly perceived as at best an ingrate or at worst an ignoramus." Pierce offered a typical encounter from his own life:

I notice in a class I teach that after each session a white, not a black, will come up to me and tell me how the class should be structured or how the chairs should be placed or how there should be extra meetings outside the classroom, etc. The student is on the initiative and sees as his usual prerogative with a black that he must instruct me and order me about and curb my own inclinations and independence. One could argue that I am hypersensitive, if not paranoid, about what must not be an unusual kind of student-faculty dialogue. This I concede. What I cannot explain, but what I know every black will understand, is that it is not what the student says in this dialogue, it is how he approaches me, how he talks to me, how he seems to regard me. I was patronized.[4]

Three years later, in 1973, economist Mary Rowe was hired by MIT to work in its administration. Among other things, she was tasked with investigating ways of improving the workplace environment at the school for underrepresented groups: women, people of color, gays and lesbians, people with disabilities. She assumed she'd be working on large issues—like the way MIT's pension plan at the time paid out benefits unequally for men and women—but noted that people often would come to her about seemingly minor problems. Things like being left out of introductions, being mistaken for someone of the same race, hearing jokes about women's bodies.

Rowe began to document these "apparently" little things and published a series of papers describing what she'd found. "I would always use the word 'apparently' because my little thing might be your major event, and vice versa," Rowe tells me. She called her early work "The Saturn's Rings Phenomenon." Just as billions of tiny particles circle Saturn, these "minutiae of discrimination" can surround a person, and while any single incident might seem insignificant, encounter enough of them and you're overwhelmed.[5] "Faced with a micro-aggression," Rowe wrote, "the victim may not be certain of the motives of the aggressor and may be unwilling to start a fight where none was meant. Under conditions of uncertainty about motives most victims are again in the position of sometimes not getting angry when they should (which perpetuates the injuries and may weaken the victim's self-image), or protesting sometimes when no injury was *consciously* intended even though it actually occurred."

Building on Pierce's work, Rowe coined the term "microinequities" to describe what she calls "a much larger universe of unfair behavior." Some of these behaviors are aggressive and hostile; many are not. They're often unintentional, the result of unconscious bias or just carelessness. Microinequities can be experienced by anyone low in the hierarchy in any given situation—even by heterosexual white men working in fields, like nursing, traditionally held by women.

"They're of enormous importance in derailing people or hurting them or keeping them awake at night," Rowe tells me.

It's been fifty years since Pierce and Rowe began writing about the subject, and yet there's little sign that the problem has abated.

"Having a male cofounder, you can see how people treat you differently just because you're a woman," says Rebecca Liebman, the CEO of LearnLux, which provides online education and coaching in personal finance to companies' employees. She and her brother Michael cofounded the Boston-based company in 2015 when she was twenty-two and he was nineteen. Since then, they've raised $2 million from investors such as Ashton Kutcher's fund Sound Ventures and Salesforce CEO Marc Benioff. "I find it really fascinating. I speak at a ton of events and people say, 'Is your age a deterrent?' and I say, 'No, it's not age, it's gender.' Because there's a ton of pattern recognition for young men being successful. It doesn't matter how young you are. But there's no pattern recognition for a young woman being successful."

In other words, when people see a young male entrepreneur, they assume he's the next Mark Zuckerberg or Bill Gates, both of whom cofounded their famous companies at age nineteen.[6] When they see a young woman, they imagine she's there to take notes. "I think when I meet someone, they automatically assume I'm the secretary," Liebman says. "If you meet a young man, you just assume that he's the founder, but if you meet a young woman, you're like, 'Oh, how long have you been with the company?' And it's like, 'I started it.'"

Liebman notices that people even use different words with her. "I can be in a meeting with Michael or without, I'll pitch something, and someone might say, 'Oh, that's cute.' And Michael will be like, 'You would just never say it's cute to run a multimillion-dollar venture company to a twenty-year-old man.' But it's fine to say it to a woman. Why? There's just wording that people use. There's the overt sexism, but then there's also just the subtle sexism that's almost harder to solve, because a lot of people are just unaware. They don't know what they're saying."

For women entrepreneurs like Liebman, who have a male cofounder, or those who have a husband who's also in business, the experience of microaggressions becomes that much more acute—these women can set their experiences side by side with a man's and see the differences in real time. Amelia DeSorrento, the cofounder and former COO of software start-up Hatch Apps, remembers attending a professional event with her then fiancé, the cofounder of a different start-up. They were approached by a man who's well known in their local entrepreneurial scene, whom she'd already met several times and with whom she'd had discussions about business. But instead of addressing DeSorrento, he spoke to her fiancé: "He says, 'Things must be going really well for you and your business because you have this woman following you around all night.'" DeSorrento and her fiancé just looked at each other. DeSorrento thought, how do you even respond to something like that?

"I think he thought he was making a joke," DeSorrento says. "This is somebody who calls me 'kiddo.' It just doesn't make me feel great and empowered when people speak to me that way. The things that are super frustrating about being a female founder is that sexism can be in the context of a joke, or comments that are just a little bit off-putting. Things like, 'When will you have kids?'" Another man once commented to her that it must be "pretty cool" to manage men.

"It's weird stuff that's just awkward and a little bit disempowering," she says. "You're not able to put your finger on it and call it sexism.

A lot of times I sit down and think, 'Am I crazy? Am I really just an aggressive and obnoxious bitch?' Maybe it's not sexism. Maybe it's some other thing that's totally separate. Malicious sexism would be a lot easier to deal with. When I've experienced overt sexism, it's really easy to sit people down and say, 'Oh, my God. Please don't ever say that again.'"

While working on her doctorate in public health at Harvard, Tariana V. Little built an app called FooFii that helps people who need food find resources. Little, who finished her degree in 2020, was inspired by her own family's experience with food insecurity. This is her second company. The first is the Boston-based media agency EmVision Productions, which she cofounded with her husband in 2013. Little tells me their identities—he's German American and she has Dominican, German, and Mexican heritage—often lead people to assume he's leading the operation, even though she's the CEO. "It can be difficult because here's this tall white male, and that is the stereotype of a business owner, and so I feel like I have to assert myself more, justify more who I am and what my role is."

Little has also learned, for her own sanity, to let it slide sometimes. "If I were to intervene every time, it would be really taxing and annoying," she says. "I had to learn how to prioritize when to call it out and when to not. It's unfortunate that women have to be in this predicament."

Natalya Bailey, the cofounder and CEO of Accion Systems, a Boston start-up developing microsized engines for satellites that has raised over $15 million in funding, recalls the time she showed up at a conference but wasn't initially allowed into the auditorium. A man told her, "There's a space conference going on. I don't know what you're doing here, but you're not going in there."

Bailey was the keynote speaker.

Women at work are nearly twice as likely as men to experience four or more kinds of microaggressions—such as having your competence or judgment questioned, or being interrupted—according to a 2019 report from LeanIn.Org and McKinsey & Company.[7] But other aspects of a woman's identity can intensify the experience. "Black women," the researchers write, "are the most likely to have their judgment questioned in their area of expertise and be asked to prove their competence. Lesbian women, bisexual women, and women with disabilities are far more likely than other women to hear demeaning remarks about themselves or others like them."

Scholars use the term double jeopardy to describe the increased discrimination that women of color experience because of both their gender and their race or ethnicity. In a 2006 study, two University of Toronto researchers saw this play out in the workplace, with women of color subjected to more harassment than either white women or men of color.[8] A dozen years later, *Harvard Business Review* summarized the experiences of fifty-nine Black women executives, who described being both highly visible, as the only Black woman in the room, and invisible, in that their skills were often overlooked.[9] One reported that her boss once invited her subordinate, a white male, to his home for dinner but didn't invite her, even though she lived only a few miles away. Another commented on the perilous line Black women must walk in order to be perceived in the proper way: "We have to have the right balance of being friendly and nice but not having that be viewed as soft and sexy. I don't even have the right adjectives to use to really describe this balance that is required for us. Not edgy but not without edge; soft but not too soft."

Rachel Lee has experienced this sense of invisibility. "As a woman of color who is LGBTQ, I have to work hard, and I have to work harder than most to even be seen," says Lee, whose St. Louis firm, Heartwork Videos, takes raw surgery footage and produces educational videos.

Stephanie Lampkin, the founder and CEO of Bay Area–based Blendoor, a software tool that helps companies scrub unconscious bias from their hiring practices, says the extra hurdle of being part of more than one underrepresented group is something that's too often overlooked: "I think, by nature of the culture of this country, talking about gender is a lot easier than talking about race." She points to the fact that while all women struggle to raise venture capital, white women still end up collecting significantly more than Black women and other women of color. These funding disparities exist, Lampkin says, "even though Black women are one of the fastest-growing demographics of entrepreneurs in the United States—probably by nature of the fact that they're not getting respected in corporate America. It's an interesting phenomenon, and I don't think enough attention has been paid to it."

In a podcast interview in 2017, Jennifer Hyman, CEO and cofounder of designer-clothing rental service Rent the Runway, talked about how women are sometimes treated as if they're pursuing a hobby instead of running a business.[10] "This is just adorable," one investor told her after a pitch meeting early in the company's history. "You must be so excited, you're going to have all these amazing dresses to wear all the time, it's going to be so fun for you." The company he was belittling went on to become a unicorn in 2019, ten years after it launched.[11]

Mothers encounter their own category of dismissive comments. Many articles about women entrepreneurs who happen to have kids will include the label "mompreneur." Not only is it a double standard—we don't hear much about "dadpreneurs"—it has the effect of implying that women are only halfway devoted to their companies, that they're managing a business while simultaneously balancing a toddler on their hip. In 2018, the United Kingdom's All Party Parliamentary Group for Entrepreneurship published a report suggesting that terms like "mumpreneur" and "lipstick entrepreneur" perpetuate a stereotype of women focused on small-scale lifestyle businesses.[12] The labels aren't just insulting—the report claims they contribute to women and girls being less likely to aspire to easier-to-scale businesses in technology and other STEM fields. A 2015 report called "Shattering Stereotypes" from the UK's nonprofit Centre for Entrepreneurs likewise derides what it calls specialized labels or even "epithets" such as mompreneur.[13] "The mere existence and continued use of feminised descriptions of entrepreneurship fuels the perception that entrepreneurial activity is a largely male preserve," the researchers write.

Robin Chase lived through this in 2000 when she cofounded Zipcar with Antje Danielson. This was a serious business with revolutionary potential, but media reports at the time often declared in their headlines that the car-sharing company was "founded by two moms"—as if they'd dreamed up the idea in between batches of cookies.

"It drove me out of my mind," Chase tells me, "because my cofounder had a PhD in geochemistry. I had this MBA and had been working in business. It was an incredibly irritating headline to me every time I saw it."

Mina Yoo, the Seattle-based founder and CEO of Heroclip, which produces a redesigned carabiner to help people hold things, and the coauthor of *Be an InventHer: An Everywoman's Guide to Creating the Next Big Thing*, says the conversation in business settings will always come around to her kids—and who's watching them. "Every panel I go to, usually a young woman will say, 'Oh, my God, Mina. You've done so well. How do you juggle everything with your kids?' It was every single time. Having been an academic, I did an informal survey of ten male entrepreneurs over text and I found out that nobody—and these are people who often give talks—nobody ever gets that question. So I think there's still the social expectation that the woman is the primary caretaker. Even at trade shows, people will say, 'Who's taking care of your kids?' and I'm like, 'Probably the same person who is taking care of your kids,' like my spouse and child care."

Despite the research done by Pierce and Rowe, the term "microaggressions" mostly lingered unnoticed by the public, but the concept lived on in the daily experience of women, people of color, and other marginalized groups. Then in 2007, Columbia University psychology professor Derald Wing Sue and his colleagues published a research paper in the *American Psychologist* that detailed his years of research on the topic.[14] He expanded that work into a 2010 book called *Microaggressions in Everyday Life: Race, Gender, and Sexual Orientation*. Sue's work coincided with the term being launched into the public imagination. Newspaper and magazine articles analyzed the phenomenon, and the idea spread across the internet. In 2017, Merriam-Webster added "microaggressions" to the dictionary.[15] Ordinary people flocked to sites that collect examples of microaggressions, such as the Everyday

Sexism Project, which according to its own description "exists to cat-alogue instances of sexism experienced on a day to day basis. They might be serious or minor, outrageously offensive or so niggling and normalised that you don't even feel able to protest."[16] The site in-cludes plenty of examples like these:

- We had some angel investors and business experts come and critique our presentations in my business class. The concept I'm working on with my group is for a company that sells menstrual products (pads and tampons). After I gave my pitch, one of the investors suggested I have one of the men in the group give the final presentation instead of me, as "the ideas will be received much better from a man. When it's you I'm just like ugh another woman talking about periods." When I asked him to elaborate, he said "Periods make people uncomfortable and having a man talk will automatically put everyone at ease." Then he told me, "It's not your fault, it's biological. Women just aren't able to project their voices like men can."
- I'm an entrepreneur, and I have three partners, the three of them guys. . . . One of them just won't stop telling me that I should smile less, or that I can't touch someone that I know, or that I cannot say hello the way I do because in his eyes I "look unprofessional" or I look "like a baby girl." Some-times I think that this fellow wants a cutesy good-looking and keep-her-mouth-shut assistant. Even though I am the CEO of my own company.

Of course, no idea enters the public consciousness without a back-lash. Critics have pointed out that there is no real science behind microaggressions, that they are largely based on anecdotal evidence. They point out that just about anyone ends up on the wrong side of an obnoxious comment from time to time, and it's just a matter of how you react—do you let it affect you, or do you let it roll off your back?[17] They argue that by giving the phenomenon a name, we are in fact giving people an excuse to claim victimhood and lay all their failures at the feet of an imagined "aggressor." Among the critics are Bradley Campbell and Jason Manning, a pair of sociologists who in 2014 published a paper called "Microaggression and Moral Culture" in the journal *Comparative Sociology*.[18] They subsequently turned their research into a 2018 book: *The Rise of Victimhood Culture: Microaggressions, Safe Spaces, and the New Culture Wars*.

Campbell and Manning complain about the airing of grievances brought about by the microaggression phenomenon, saying it's akin to gossip and analogous to the way "small children often bring their complaints to adults."[19] "The result is a culture of victimhood in which individuals and groups display high sensitivity to slight, have a tendency to handle conflicts through complaints to third parties, and seek to cultivate an image of being victims who deserve assistance."[20]

Campbell and Manning have a curious obsession with people's tendency to report microaggressions to third parties. They think people complain publicly about these incidents to elevate their own moral status—that is, something bad happened to me and therefore I am morally superior to the person who did it to me.[21] But the primary quality of a microaggression isn't that it gets reported to others. The problem with microaggressions is the implicit bias they reveal. If someone tells an entrepreneur that her business idea is cute, or that she ought to be more perky during a presentation, then that person has revealed that they don't fully value that entrepreneur, that they view women as somehow "less than." And those attitudes, even if they're inadvertent, can have real-world consequences. For those on the receiving end, it means their business idea might not get a fair hearing or might not get funded.

Figuring out the right response to belittling comments is hard. Should you say nothing? React harshly? Minmin Yen, cofounder and CEO of PhagePro, a Boston start-up developing a cholera intervention based on a kind of virus that destroys bacteria, gets advice on how to deal with these comments from older mentors who are Asian American. "One of them is more like the peaceful type of strategy, which is [to] use it as a chance to just raise their awareness," she says. "That's the strategy that I've been adopting for myself as well, to stay focused, to not take offense, to use it as an opportunity."

But when she talks to her contemporaries, especially people of color, Yen gets a range of recommendations. "It's these people who are like, 'No, we have to be very angry. The pendulum has swung our way towards our voices coming out now, especially in the past years.' Then there are some who are like, 'Well, that's just the way that it is. We just have to figure out a way to work around it. We just have to be twice as good or three times as good to be recognized. We can't mess up,' and stuff like that. It's quite sad, I would say, to hear other people's experiences through it. We all go through it in some manner."

More than twenty years ago, Julie Lenzer founded Applied Creative Technologies, a software firm that was focused on manufacturing companies and inventory control. She still remembers her first meeting with the man who would wind up as her longest-term client. He took one look at her and said, "What's she doing in here?" "I'll never forget that," Lenzer says. "I'm like, 'I'm here because the person that you have designing your system right now didn't do the job, and let me tell you what I think.'"

It can wear you down, this routine of perpetually having to prove yourself. But in the end, it might be the only antidote. "I've seen my share of people thinking that I couldn't do it because I was a girl," says Lenzer. "In my mind, I've always just said, 'You're an idiot. You're stupid. You don't know.' Then I'd go and show that I do know what I'm talking about."

CHAPTER 7

OWNING THE ROOM

How confidence is found (and faked)

KATHRYN FINNEY INTRODUCED herself to the 570 graduating students at
Mount Holyoke College, a women's liberal arts school in central Massachusetts, as a forty-one-year-old "quirky Black girl" who loves three
things: family and friends, filling out forms, and fashion—especially
hair.[1] "To paraphrase Dolly Parton, the bigger the hair, the closer to
the stars," she told them. "But many moons ago, I actually hid my love
of fashion. I actually hid myself."

Finney told the graduates that she grew up in the 1990s in Minneapolis, where she was the only Black girl in her high school honors
classes. She challenged a popular upperclassman for a seat on the student council and won—and became a target of bullying as a result. She
reacted by trying to make herself invisible, hoping the bullies would
move on. She hid her big hair under a hat. She traded her quirky,
fashionable clothes for anonymous grunge. One day her father called
her out. "You are a big girl," he told her. "You have a big personality.
You come in a room and you fill it up. You can't even hide even if you
wanted to. So stop. Give them something to look at."

Finney urged the graduates to follow her dad's advice. "As women,
we're told to make ourselves small, to shrink ourselves, that by somehow making ourselves invisible and small, we're going to protect the
very fragile egos of others," she told them. "There is nothing more
powerful, nothing, than a woman, especially a Black woman, a woman

of color, knowing and owning her personhood." The crowd erupted in cheers.

It was May 2017, and Finney, wearing a traditional black cap and gown, had just received an honorary doctorate for her work supporting women of color entrepreneurs.[2] A serial entrepreneur herself, Finney joined a line of Mount Holyoke honorary degree recipients that dates back to 1894 and includes FDR's Secretary of Labor Frances Perkins (the first woman appointed to a US presidential cabinet), civil rights activist Rosa Parks, social worker Jane Addams (the first US woman to win the Nobel Peace Prize), poet and civil rights activist Maya Angelou, and anesthesiologist Virginia Apgar (new parents will know her as the inventor of the Apgar Score).[3] What do they all have in common? They shook up the status quo.

Finney's Newark, New Jersey–based nonprofit, digitalundivided, conducted the first comprehensive analysis of entrepreneurs who are Black and Latinx women—how many there are, where they live, where they went to school, and how much money they've raised. Or, more accurately, how *little* money they've raised. "We went to go look for data and there was absolutely no data," Finney tells me. "Fortunately, I had a really expensive Ivy League education that I hadn't been using for a while, and went and did research. My background was as a trained epidemiologist." Named ProjectDiane, after civil rights activist and Freedom Rider Diane Nash, the initiative first released its findings on Black women in 2016 and on Latinx women in 2018. "It's really hard to solve a problem you can't quantify. It's very easy to ignore a problem that hasn't been quantified. Once we quantified it, it was really difficult for people to not pay attention to it," Finney says.

Finney and her team could identify only thirty-four Black women entrepreneurs and fifty-eight Latinx women entrepreneurs who, by the end of 2017, had raised at least $1 million in venture funding.[4] Not in one year. For *all time*. Black women took in a mere 0.0006 percent of all venture funding from 2009 to 2017. On one count, the data made Finney hopeful: the number of Black women–led start-ups more than doubled from 2016 to 2017.

Since 2016, Finney has run an incubator program called BIG that supports Black and Latinx women launching new companies. A dozen or so participants at a time have met in Newark or Atlanta for several months of training and mentorship. Much of the instruction focuses on confidence—building "inner power" and getting women comfortable advocating for their businesses and themselves, especially in settings where they might be the only woman of color.

They'll need that confidence, Finney says, when investors start asking them about their personal lives, questioning their credentials, and wondering why they're pursuing entrepreneurship in the first place. "The hour meeting you have with a VC, they're going to try to take up forty-five to fifty minutes of it with you explaining why you are there, because they're so fascinated by the fact that you're in the room. How do you turn that around so that it's only twenty minutes that you're spending versus forty-five minutes, so you could spend the rest of the forty minutes talking about your business?" Finney and her crew prepare the entrepreneurs to change the topic of conversation, multiple times if necessary. "There's a lot of mental gymnastics," she says. "It's exhausting."

One of the most frequently cited hurdles among the women founders I interviewed was a lack of confidence. They had nagging thoughts that their businesses wouldn't take off, that they lacked work experience or skills or education, that they wouldn't be able to convince enough people to buy into their ideas. They assumed some of this self-doubt came from within, but recognized that a lifetime of dismissals, insults, and lowered expectations was also to blame. (As consultant-author Avivah Wittenberg-Cox once tweeted, "Stick #men into a system designed and run by women and then measure their confidence.")[5] Several described to me feeling like impostors or frauds when they, for example, made it into an exclusive accelerator program. Impostor syndrome—first identified in the 1970s as an issue for professional women but now considered to strike most people at some point in their careers—describes the feeling that your success isn't deserved, and that you'll be revealed as incompetent.[6] "I think the number-one thing is that women are afraid," says Fran Biderman-Gross, who's spent almost three decades growing her New York City–based branding and marketing agency, Advantages.

"We have an idea, and then the world tells us to be afraid that we're not going to get this and we're not going to get that."

People who brim with self-confidence, writes one research team, "show conviction in their ability to make decisions, organize and execute action plans, carry out new tasks, and give opinions; they persist in difficult tasks when failure seems certain and recover confidence in their abilities rapidly after a failure."[7] It's easy to see why this trait would benefit entrepreneurs as they blaze new paths and encounter rejection and defeat. The question is, do women have enough of it?

Finney's BIG incubator program concludes with an evening event in which founders offer a five-minute pitch to a crowd of investors, mentors, families, and friends. I attended one of these events in late 2018 in an industrial-looking building in Atlanta's Tech Square neighborhood, which claims to have the Southeast's highest density of start-ups, corporate innovation programs, and academic researchers.[8] That night, eleven participants showed off a range of companies, including a broker of surplus and imperfect fruits and vegetables, a league for multiplayer video game competitions, and a genderless makeup brand. The mood was celebratory: a DJ played hip-hop, attendees helped themselves to a buffet, kids of incubator participants darted in and out, and Finney led everyone in a dance to the viral-hit children's song "Baby Shark."

Jasmine Edwards took the stage to pitch her start-up, i-Subz, a platform that matches people looking for substitute-teaching jobs with public schools that serve low-income students. Edwards had spent time as a substitute teacher, part of what she calls the original gig economy. She saw firsthand that it's difficult to apply for these positions, it's hard to get paid quickly, and schools struggle with the screening and placement process. She believes teacher absenteeism hurts at-risk students the most, and thinks her approach to finding and placing quality subs can reduce the chance that these students will fall behind or drop out. "I want to make sure that students are continually learning," Edwards told me when we spoke in 2019. "It's not 'watch movie day.' It's not 'we're not doing anything, I'm here to babysit.'"

Edwards has a master's degree in entrepreneurship from the University of South Florida. She joined the BIG incubator in 2018, the same year she launched i-Subz. "When I first got into the program, I was talking to one of the employees, who was telling me, 'You are here for a reason and you belong. You have something great inside of you.' I was never in a tech space that said that I belonged there, so it made me tear up and it made me kind of break down. I've had many more breakdowns since then.

"What I learned is that in order to be a founder, if you're going to stand in a room and tell people about your business confidently, you have to be confident yourself. You have to be able to say to yourself, 'I belong in any room that I am standing in. I am here for a reason.' If people cannot believe that you are confident about yourself, how can they believe that you are confident about your business? Some people might say that you don't know what you're doing, or they might blow you off or not call you again or not even pay attention, but you still have to go forth. It took me at least six to seven months to start developing that confidence muscle." Edwards credits the incubator's support network, reading books such as *The Art of Possibility* by Rosamund Stone Zander and Benjamin Zander, and hearing successful businesswomen talk about their own courage.

"Confidence," Edwards adds, "is also showing up for yourself. Meaning that I had to actually get in my car and drive up to Atlanta if I wanted to learn how to build my business." Edwards lives in Tampa, Florida, and commuted about seven hours one way to attend the BIG incubator sessions. At home she left her husband and three young children (their blended family also includes three older children). "It was hard financially, it was hard mentally," she says of the experience. "If you want to better yourself, sometimes you really have to dig in and go through some difficult things to get the gold out, and I decided that's exactly what I was ready for. I did the work."

The future for i-Subz looked bright after Edwards left the BIG incubator. She successfully pitched at several competitions and participated in a New Orleans–based accelerator. She raised $43,000. But in March 2020, after a two-year run, Edwards had to close the company. "I put all my resources, my personal finances in, as much as possible, and we just couldn't go anymore," she tells me. "I couldn't raise anymore. There are so many [investors] who are popping up with funds, anywhere between $500,000 and $1.5 million. I couldn't even get $100,000 two years in, after proof, after accolades, after winning awards. We have been in *Forbes*, we have data and the things that we were doing on the ground, but that still didn't convince people to say, 'You're a hard worker. We see that you're up to something good. We're going to take a chance on you.' It's just hard. It's really hard."

Edwards tells me the experience has both humbled and strengthened her. "I really thought I was going to win with this venture—the first excitement of the press and the excitement of winning things and excitement of getting your first few customers. But then the reality set in that you don't have funding and you have to close. At the same time, I'm still confident, because I gave it everything that I had as a founder." Edwards says it's likely she'll launch another business. "I'm not sure when. I need some time to step back and really analyze and see what my next thing will be."

Kathryn Finney announced in May 2020 that she's departing digitalundivided to write a business book. The BIG incubator she's leaving behind is dramatically different from one she participated in in New York City earlier in her career. Finney calls it "probably one of the worst experiences of my life." At the time, Finney was running The Budget Fashionista, which she launched in 2004 and grew into a multimedia fashion and lifestyle company that she sold ten years later. She was one of four women in the incubator, and the only Black woman, out of forty-five participants. "We were all treated horribly and marginalized and patted on the head," Finney recalls. "I was met with such resistance. I was met with no expectations. Not low, but none." Finney says the program's leader told her that "he'd never heard of anyone investing in a Black woman, so my likelihood of raising money was zero."

Finney says the treatment shook her. "I never doubted my ability, because I knew I could do it. What I doubted was my role in the tech space—what place did I have in this space and where would I fit in. When you are a high-achieving person, there is nothing more frustrating than to have people not think you can achieve because of purely arbitrary reasons, not any of your own doing, just 'you're Black and you're a woman, so you can't do anything.'"

Finney adds, "You're going to be asked to crush yourself. You're going to be asked to be less than who you are for other people to feel better about themselves. That's what I was asked in high school. That's what was happening in the incubator program. I even had experiences recently where people have asked me to be less of who I am so that others don't feel threatened." In particular, Finney's heard the admonishment "You're too strong. You're too aggressive." Her response? "Are you saying that I know what I'm talking about and I'm very direct with you? Well, that's not the same as being aggressive. Because I'm a confident Black woman, someone who's not supposed to be confident, because it's coming from me, you're reading it as arrogance or aggressiveness. If it was coming from a white man, he's like, 'Oh my god, he's brilliant. He's such a visionary. He's all these sort of things.' We're not allowed to have that same sort of belief in ourselves.

"As women, and in particular in this historical moment we're in now, we just can't afford to do that anymore. We cannot afford to be less than who we are. We have to be our full self."

Jodyanne Kirkwood, who teaches at the University of Otago in New Zealand, wanted to learn more about women's confidence, so she interviewed entrepreneurs, both female and male, working in her country.[9] "Women exhibit a lack of self-confidence in their own abilities as entrepreneurs compared to men," she writes in her 2009 study, adding that women even hesitate to call themselves "entrepreneurs." Kirkwood explains that for some women, as their businesses grow, so does their belief in their entrepreneurial know-how. But for others, their confidence doesn't improve, and this stunts their companies' goals and fundraising.

A 2019 survey commissioned by the United Kingdom's economic and finance ministry found that only 39 percent of UK women say they're confident they have the skills to launch a business, while

55 percent of men think they do.[10] "This is a perceived gap in ability, rather than an actual gap in skill sets," the researchers write. "In addition, many of the women we interviewed often credited other people for their success and dismissed their own achievements." This was something I found in my interviews as well—many of the entrepreneurs I talked to say men take credit, whereas women point to collaborators or say they were just part of a team.

Researchers have also examined what's called entrepreneurial self-efficacy, the belief that you have the talent and skills needed to start and grow a successful company. If you have entrepreneurial self-efficacy, you're more likely to start a new business. Here, too, the news is not good for women. One 2007 study conducted in the United States found that middle and high school girls and women in MBA programs have significantly lower levels of entrepreneurial self-efficacy than their male peers.[11] The researchers note that "differing expectations imposed by society may well shape self-efficacy at an early age, long before actual experiences take place."

Beyond the start-up world, researchers have been trying to figure out what confidence looks like in any workplace and if women come up short. In their 2014 book *The Confidence Code: The Science and Art of Self-Assurance—What Women Should Know*, journalists Katty Kay and Claire Shipman detail research showing that women often underestimate their skills, doubt their work is as good as men's, question if they're ready for promotions, and believe they deserve less pay than men.[12] Kay and Shipman build the case that if women adopt men's swagger and fearlessness, they'd get promoted more and grab more leadership positions.[13] Facebook executive Sheryl Sandberg's 2013 book *Lean In: Women, Work, and the Will to Lead* advances a similar message.

But the diagnosis and prescription are not so simple. Laura Guillén, a professor of people management and organization at ESADE in Barcelona, notes that some studies show women and men having similar levels of self-confidence but that projecting self-assurance can be risky for women.[14] After surveying employees at a global, male-dominated tech company, Guillén and two fellow researchers found that men who appear self-confident gain influence at work.[15] But for women to achieve influence, they have to be seen as confident *plus* caring and warm. "Popular messaging about how women must change to appear more self-confident as a key to their success isn't just false. It also reflects how the burden of managing a gender-diverse workplace is placed on the female employees themselves," Guillén writes in *Harvard Business Review* in 2018. "Where their male colleagues are allowed to focus on their own objectives, women who are expected to care for others are shouldering an unfair load."

When Melissa James interviewed to be the office manager at a biotech start-up in Boston, she was one year out of college and not sure what her next move would be. In her eyes, the interview was a flop. "I was definitely sure I didn't get this job," she tells me. "I didn't have any relevant skills. I walked from their office to my car. By the time I got to my car, I got a call from the recruiter that was handling my position, and she was like, 'Oh, my God, Melissa. You nailed it. You got the job. They want you to start on Monday.' I was like, 'What? No way.' Definitely I didn't feel like I nailed it."

Even after James started her new job, she felt inadequate compared to her colleagues. She was the first in her family to go to college and had graduated from the University of Massachusetts Amherst. Most of her coworkers came from MIT and Harvard. "I always felt like I just have to keep up with them and show them that I could work hard. Then maybe they wouldn't realize that I wasn't as smart as them," James tells me. Despite all this, she loved the job and flourished there. Her boss made it clear that he wanted her to grow and gave her challenging assignments, particularly dealing with hiring. After two years she left to do diversity recruitment for Google in Cambridge, Massachusetts. "I didn't realize I was smart until I got my job at Google. Then everybody thought you were smart, and everybody wanted to hear what you had to say. Without that confidence, I don't know—I probably would have gone so much further had I realized that early on."

In 2014, after a year at Google, James struck out on her own. She founded The Tech Connection, a Boston-based firm that helps tech companies recruit diverse talent, while preparing candidates for these positions. She wanted to help hiring managers evaluate job seekers based on their transferable skills and grit, rather than simply what school they attended and where they've interned.

James credits her work at the biotech start-up for teaching her business skills. "It was like going to a boot camp for two years. It was amazing to learn so much. If not for that experience, I don't think I would have felt comfortable starting my own company," she says. "It took a long time for me to build that kind of confidence. I think a lot of people end up fearing that they're not going to be smart, that the market won't like their idea."

James was able to build her confidence over a few years. Other women find it elusive even after decades. Shelby Scarbrough has every right to be proud, even cocky, about her accomplishments. She's worked as a protocol officer at the US Department of State and a presidential trip coordinator in the White House. She planned events in the Vatican, Buckingham Palace, and the Kremlin, and had a lead role in the Washington, DC, state funeral of President Reagan. Tapping that expertise, in 1990 she opened Practical Protocol, which manages events and offers protocol training for high-profile clients. For almost two decades, she owned ten Burger King restaurants in Northern Virginia with her now ex-husband. Nonetheless, Scarbrough tells me, "I'm always feeling like I don't know enough. I've been doing this stuff for a long time, and I always still feel like a student. I never feel like I'm quite ready for the big league."

Scarbrough, now based outside San Francisco, has seen how women entrepreneurs' lack of confidence holds them back. To combat this, she's helped create a women-only angel investor group called nCourage Entrepreneurs. "This is hard-earned money, and we're trying to put it to good use to help other women," she says.

Julie Lenzer sees self-doubt in women founders—but in male founders, too. "We all suffer from impostor syndrome at one time or another. Women are more open with it, I think," says Lenzer. "When I was growing my company, I was a part of Vistage, which is a CEO peer roundtable. I was one of two women in my group. I started to build relationships with the men in the group, and that's when I started to realize that they had those same thoughts and feelings of being an impostor. They just hide it better. They don't talk about it as much. They see it as weakness. They are socialized differently growing up. They're better at 'fake it until you make it.'"

Some women entrepreneurs are actively copying this style. At a *Forbes* event I attended in 2018, Jessica O. Matthews, founder and CEO of clean-energy company Uncharted Power and a dual citizen of Nigeria and the United States, shared her fundraising strategy: "When I was raising my round [from investors], I literally stood in front of the mirror every single day and said, 'Jessica, don't be afraid to dream like a white man.' I would say, 'Be like Chad. Be like Brad. You can do it.' I had to practice saying, 'I will build the next billion-dollar tech company.' Because it's honestly almost delusional if you can't see the exact steps to get there, but then you speak it into existence." Fellow panelist Jean Brownhill, founder and CEO of contractor-recommendation site Sweeten, added, "Mine was Timmy. I looked in the mirror and I'm like, 'What would Timmy do?'"

Men's confidence may not always be earned, but it comes with perks anyway. In a 2012 study of MBA students, researchers discovered that men tend to overestimate their own abilities, while women are more accurate.[16] In the quest for dollars, this bravado rewards male entrepreneurs. The research is striking: a 2019 report by the Kauffman Foundation notes that entrepreneurs in accelerator programs, regardless of their gender, typically reach 10 percent of their fundraising targets over three years, but the goals that women founders start with are significantly lower than those of their male counterparts.[17] According to a 2018 Boston Consulting Group analysis of participants in the global MassChallenge accelerator program, "Male founders are more likely to make bold projections and assumptions in their pitches. One investor told us, 'Men often overpitch and oversell.' Women, by contrast, are generally more conservative in their projections and may simply be asking for less than men."[18] This may be one reason women entrepreneurs receive only a tiny slice of venture capital dollars, and it's also a missed opportunity for investors: the researchers note that "businesses founded by women ultimately deliver higher revenue— more than twice as much per dollar invested—than those founded by men, making women-owned companies better investments for financial backers."

Susan Lyne, president and managing partner of the venture capital firm BBG Ventures, told an audience at a 2017 South by Southwest event: "I see men pitch unicorns and women pitch businesses."[19]

"Men tend to pitch these ridiculous scenarios, billion-dollar scenarios," says serial entrepreneur Heidi E. Lehmann. "They will promise this enormous exit. And they will go in and sell it [to investors]. Whereas women will put financials together that are more accurate, but very conservative or err on the side of caution, because they want to feel confident that they're right." Lehmann, who's now the chief commercial officer of wearable health diagnostics start-up Kenzen, based in New York City, points out that there's a danger to pitching an extremely detailed business idea, versus pitching yourself as a go-getter entrepreneur: "Investors know that the business you think you're starting initially, once you get into the market, that business is going to change a variety of times. It just will. They're looking for an individual that is confident and can sell anything. They want to feel like, if you started to sell doorknobs, but then your business turned into light fixtures, that you're going to be able to go and make that work. I think women come in and have a very specific scenario that they've detailed, and it's too realistic. If it changes, then what?"

Sarah E. Endline discovered that her own pitching style tended toward the timid when she participated in Springboard Enterprises' accelerator program for women-led companies in 2011. At the time, Endline was growing her New York City–based organic chocolate business called sweetriot. "When we were training to give pitches, I remember I got up and said something like, 'I did marketing at Yahoo!'" Endline was instructed to try again and envision how a male entrepreneur might pitch himself. She says, "The way a guy would say that is, 'I did marketing on the product side of Yahoo! for millions of consumers.' The bravado piece is somehow not as feminine, so there's a struggle around pitching in this really numerical, overachievement way, like, 'Yes, I made $25 million on that, and I'm going to make $100 million on this.' Women need more coaching and training on how to pitch in a man's world."

Endline sold sweetriot in 2018 and now serves as an entrepreneur-in-residence at Harvard Business School. She continues to see all the ways that women lack bravado. "Women, I would say, much more often doubt themselves, sometimes aloud, or they downplay their achievements. You've heard the whole 'I'm not ready to apply for that job yet. I don't have all these credentials.' The guy's like, 'Cool, I have a quarter of them. You want me to apply?' There's something to that."

Natalya Bailey is in the rocket industry. She's the cofounder and CEO of Accion Systems, a Boston start-up that's developing electric propulsion engines for satellites. As an MIT-trained engineer, Bailey draws from a deep well of scientific knowledge, but initially she lacked confidence in her leadership skills. So she sought out an executive coach. "Almost from the beginning, I worked with her to think about: What are my strengths? How can I play to those and still be myself, and naturally grow into a leader of the company? What are some of my weaknesses?" says Bailey. "I'm helping no one by having or dwelling on these insecurities. It's not going to help the company. It's not going to help anybody who works for us. So I should just hurry up and get over it."

In the end, a lot comes down to perception: Does an entrepreneur truly believe in the business and express that with enthusiasm and confidence? Can realistic, even modest-sounding projections captivate investors, advisers, and others? Consider one of the findings from the 2015 survey by the UK's nonprofit Centre for Entrepreneurs: 62 percent of male entrepreneurs reported that their companies are prospering, but only 42 percent of women said the same thing—yet the researchers point out that the women-owned businesses actually saw a higher profit before tax.[20]

CHAPTER 8

A SHOULDER TO LEAN ON

The search for mentors and support

FRAN DUNAWAY AND HER WIFE, Naomi Gonzalez, launched a Seattle clothing company called TomboyX as a side project, simply because, Dunaway says, "I wanted a cool shirt." In their Kickstarter campaign in 2013, they described their desire to create clothes for "women celebrating the tomboy spirit," who frequently shop in the men's department and struggle to find the right style and fit.[1] The shirt in the starring role had buttons down the front and was generously cut, with extra buttons at the bust and waist to keep everything covered up. They raised $76,166 on Kickstarter in thirty days, enough to begin full production of their line.

They had lots of enthusiasm. But they also understood that they didn't really know what they were doing. They had no expertise in the clothing industry. Dunaway was fifty-three at the time and had been working more than fifteen years in media production, on projects such as ads for political candidates and social causes. Gonzalez had a career as a massage therapist for athletes and others.

"When we started the company, we didn't know anything about building a company, and we didn't know a knit from a woven or a P&L from a balance sheet," Dunaway, the CEO, tells me. "It was important to us that we find people that could help us understand." Dunaway met two women through a women entrepreneurs' support group who would become not only important advisers but also early investors. "One had a very positive, upbeat 'you've got this, nothing can go wrong' attitude. The other had the polar opposite: 'You should think about this' and 'Have you thought about that?' and 'Everything could go wrong.' It was funny to have that balance, where we could hear both sides, so that we could then make our own decisions based on that advice and different perspectives. It's good to have someone that can walk you off the ledge when you're freaking out about something, or offer a different insight, especially if they have experience in what you need."

Before long, customers were telling Dunaway and Gonzalez that what they really wanted was a boxer brief made for women. "Turns out that our customers really rallied around the notion of underwear," Dunaway says, "so we pivoted out of cool shirts and into undergarments, and we now have swim, loungewear, and sleepwear as well." In less than ten years, TomboyX has become a massively popular gender-neutral and size-inclusive underwear company that's raised over $18 million from investors and that *Inc.* magazine named one of the fastest-growing privately held companies in the country.[2]

While Dunaway has sought out advisers for their expertise—in retail, operations, law, and so on—without regard to their gender, sexual orientation, or other identities, women have been an especially valuable resource. And Dunaway thinks Facebook executive Sheryl Sandberg played a role in this.

In 2013, the year TomboyX had its Kickstarter campaign, Sandberg released *Lean In.* She concluded the book by urging women to support each other and quash the thinking that there are limited spots at the top for successful women. "The more women help one another," Sandberg wrote, "the more we help ourselves. Acting like a coalition truly does produce results."[3]

Dunaway tells me, "I've often said that I should thank Sheryl for forcing the conversation and getting women to really think about how they're helping each other. I think that there's been a tremendous spin-off from that—networks and groups that allow women to find mentors and talk about their businesses and gather learnings from people."

Dunaway recounts the story of two close women friends who both own companies in male-dominated fields—one has a maritime training school, the other a bus company. Once, Dunaway invited them to tag along with her to an EY Entrepreneurial Winning Women event. "They were just blown away," she says. "They loved it. They couldn't believe the camaraderie and how different they felt being in a group of female entrepreneurs, because when they've been in their regular business meetings, it's a very different way you interact and engage and behave. It was just a different way of being in the world. They had never thought to seek out female groups and networks. Having done so, they found it very refreshing.

"Men have been doing it for so long, and they're so good at it, and do it in places where you don't find a lot of women like golf courses or strip clubs. I think it's important that women create their own network, and I think that the philosophy that Sheryl put out there was, we really have to work harder and better at leaving the door open behind us, and then lending a hand and helping a woman through that door. With #MeToo, women are only becoming more and more aware of the importance of taking care of each other, getting each other's back."

Entrepreneurship is hard, and there's no clearly defined path. No matter who you are, you need help—someone who can suggest ways around problems, offer insider information, and point you in new directions. Mentors who've already built companies are invaluable. Sponsors are even more so, as these people use their power and influence to help pull you up, such as by making introductions to investors and other important people and vouching for your good work and ideas. Then you need a network of peers who can lend a hand and cheer you on.

According to a 2011 global Gallup poll, women who have a mentor are almost three times more likely to say they'll launch a business than those who don't.[4] A 2011 report from Startup Genome found that entrepreneurs who seek out feedback and ideas—specifically from mentors, thought leaders, and customers—raise seven times more funding and have 3.5 times better user growth.[5] On the other hand, founders without good mentors struggle to attract funding. Small Business Administration research from 2013 found that business owners who receive three or more hours of counseling go on to have higher revenues and add more employees than those with less help.[6] A 2018 study of women's networking events found that attendees gain feelings of optimism and connectedness and actually are more likely to get a promotion and pay increase at work.[7] In her book *Outrageous Acts and Everyday Rebellions*, Gloria Steinem observed that networking is "the primary way women discover that we are not crazy, the system is. We also discover that mutual-support groups can create change where the most courageous individual woman could not."[8]

Help is needed outside of work, too: a partner who covers all the household bills until a start-up is profitable or picks up dinner and the kids. A parent who lets you move into a spare room while your company gets off the ground. Family members who encourage your business vision and don't pressure you to pursue a stable career instead. Researchers have shown that having a spouse's assistance—what they call spousal capital—can influence whether a new business thrives or tanks. A 2010 study of entrepreneurs in heterosexual marriages found that those with good spousal capital create profitable companies more quickly.[9]

We're often reluctant to admit that an entrepreneur needs help, as it contradicts the American idea of the maverick who does it all on his own. In her 2006 book *Pull: Networking and Success Since Benjamin Franklin*, historian Pamela Walker Laird explores the concept of social capital—in a nutshell, the connections that a person can use to get ahead.[10] Laird notes that since Colonial times, Americans have lauded the idea of the self-made man, either as a form of myth making or perhaps because they were simply blind to the built-in advantages some people enjoyed. She offers the case of Benjamin Franklin as he arrived in Philadelphia as a young man. The myth is that Franklin started from nothing and raised himself into prominence. But he had a brother-in-law who introduced him to the governor of Pennsylvania, and the governor subsequently connected Franklin with other well-placed friends who aided his career. As a white male in the 1720s, Franklin was among the only group of people eligible for success in the first place, and there was a far smaller pool of white men in Philadelphia at the time, perhaps fifteen hundred or so, which made it all the easier for a bright young man to get noticed. Laird notes that if

Franklin had instead grown up toward the end of the nineteenth century, he might have found himself toiling in a factory among a much larger pool of working-class kids, with little opportunity to make the acquaintance of governors and other luminaries.

But that was the old days. What about now? Our best-known self-made man of the past half century is Bill Gates—the brainy kid who dropped out of college, launched Microsoft, and changed everything. Surely he did it on his own, right? Laird demolishes that myth as well.[11] Gates grew up as the wealthy child of a prominent Seattle family and attended an elite prep school. His mother was on the board of directors of multiple corporations and the United Way, which afforded Gates contact with, among other people, executives at IBM. His father was a lawyer who helped the young man craft his software licensing agreements.

And self-made man Jeff Bezos? When he and wife MacKenzie announced their split in early 2019, there was a lot of public talk about how much money he'd lose in the divorce settlement—money that he'd generated by being the sole founder of Amazon. But then a *WIRED* article titled "MacKenzie Bezos and the Myth of the Lone Genius Founder" arrived to lay out the ways she was a crucial-but-overlooked cocreator of the e-commerce giant. The couple both gave up New York City hedge fund jobs to drive to Seattle to start the company.[12] MacKenzie played several roles in Amazon's early days, including as the bookkeeper who helped set up the freight contracts. "Empires like Amazon and Apple," according to *WIRED*, "are not created by a single man in a vacuum; they are the product of a mix of luck and contributions from an entire team—including from a founder's spouse."

In *Pull*, Laird notes that the contradiction between myth and reality is laid bare by the behavior of American businessmen throughout the twentieth century.[13] On the one hand, they lauded individualism and self-reliance, and on the other, they rapidly formed and joined professional and social associations aimed at supporting and promoting the careers of fellow members. "The dominant explanations for individual, family, community, national, and racial differences in prosperity insisted that competition, not cooperation, determined (and should determine) success," Laird writes. "Yet more and more

Americans pursued goals collectively, even those who praised only individualism."

So help is important, but gender often dictates who gets more of it. Almost half of women entrepreneurs, according to a 2014 Kauffman Foundation survey, say a challenge facing their business is the scarcity of mentors and advisers.[14] This situation is repeated for women across industries. In 2010, the Center for Talent Innovation reported that a whopping 89 percent of "highly qualified" women lack a sponsor and 68 percent have no mentor.[15] A 2009 Catalyst survey of lawyers showed that 62 percent of women of color say the lack of an influential mentor holds them back.[16]

A woman entrepreneur looking for guidance often turns to a man, since men dominate the ranks of business owners, executives, and professors. Yet a successful man seeking an apprentice isn't likely to pick a woman out of the crowd. A 2019 study from the Center for Talent Innovation found that sponsors strongly prefer protégés who share their gender or race; the researchers call it the mini-me syndrome.[17]

"I see this with a lot of my male colleagues who run companies," says Rebecca Liebman, the LearnLux cofounder and CEO. "A guy will take them under their wing because they're like, 'Oh, you remind me of me,' or 'I want you to be successful because you remind me of what I was like when I was young.' That happens a lot less with women."

I talked to W. Brad Johnson, a psychology professor at the US Naval Academy who has spent two decades studying mentors and cowrote the book *Athena Rising: How and Why Men Should Mentor Women*. Johnson acknowledges that men may harbor an unconscious bias: "Men may see women as nice, but they may not see them as super competent or as future leaders of the organization." And even if they get beyond that, a lot of men don't know how to mentor a woman. "Guys don't have a good script, sometimes, for how to have a close, collegial, even sometimes a kind of professional-intimate relationship, but nonsexual, with a woman," Johnson says.

It's the Mike Pence problem. Everybody made fun of Pence when he said he never eats one-on-one with a woman who isn't his wife, but he's not the only one. A nationwide poll in 2017 found that about a quarter of both men *and* women think private work meetings with someone of the opposite sex are inappropriate, often because they fear harassment or fear being accused of it.[18] *New Yorker* staff writer Jia Tolentino notes that men can follow Pence's lead and still get ahead in business, yet "no successful woman could ever abide by the same rule."[19]

In a cruel twist, the #MeToo movement is making things even harder for women. When Sheryl Sandberg's nonprofit, LeanIn.Org, surveyed male managers in 2018, 46 percent reported being uncomfortable in activities such as mentoring women and meeting one-on-one with women.[20] One year later, that figure had climbed to 60 percent. More than a third of male managers admitted they don't mentor or socialize with women because they fear how it would look.[21] "This is disastrous," wrote Sandberg and Procter & Gamble executive Marc Pritchard when sharing these survey results in *Fortune* in 2019. "The vast majority of managers and senior leaders are men. They have a huge role to play in supporting women's advancement at work—or hindering it. If they're reluctant even to meet one-on-one with women, there's no way women can get an equal shot at proving themselves." Another survey looking at the impact of #MeToo, this one published in *Harvard Business Review* in 2018, found that 65 percent of men say it's now "less safe" to mentor and coach women.[22]

In response, LeanIn.Org rolled out a #MentorHer campaign in 2018 to encourage men to take on the task.[23] A number of big names, such as former Disney CEO Bob Iger and National Basketball Association commissioner Adam Silver, made public pledges to mentor more women. "It makes a big difference when male leaders talk about this out loud," says Johnson. "If senior leaders are not all in on these kinds of things, you just find the change to be glacial."

If a woman goes in search of those places where mentoring and networking happen organically, she'll find that many are built by and for men. Some are literally for men only. In 2017, the Charles River Country Club in Newton, Massachusetts, spent more than $1 million renovating its facilities and added a pub and fireplace to the men's locker room.[24] It's a great spot to grab a bite, find business advice, or pass along recommendations, and it's only open to men. There's no

pub in the women's locker room. In Georgia, some of the most powerful executives in the country gather at the legendary Augusta National Golf Club, which began allowing women as members only in
2012. Out of some three hundred members, only six are reported to be
women.[25] The message to women is pretty clear—in the places where
an entrepreneur might make contacts and cut a deal, you don't belong.

If male mentors and sponsors are scarce, surely there are other options, right? It sounds straightforward, but a significant number of
the entrepreneurs I interviewed told me it can feel as if there aren't
enough advisers who are women or nonbinary to go around. Some
have never had a mentor who shares their gender.

"When I started out, it was difficult for me to get any mentorship from women," says Evy Chen, who in 2012 launched Evy Tea, a
Boston-based maker of bottled cold-brew tea. "I would reach out to all
those female entrepreneurs that I read about and they wouldn't give
me the time of the day." However, Chen is seeing improvement: "A
lot has changed in the past two years. There are so many [women's]
organizations and individuals now sharing their wisdom and building
each other up." Chen tells me she's eager to get ideas and opinions
from any source, but hearing from entrepreneurs who are women,
especially women of color, is particularly meaningful. "I was talking
to a venture capital fund, and I said, 'Can you please connect me to
female founders who have done this before?' My [male] partner was
like, 'Why would you need access to females? Males are just as good.'
I went, 'No, it's not the same.'"

Finding someone who matches your gender, as well as race, sexual
orientation, age, and other factors, appears to improve the odds that
the advice dispensed will be sensitive to the biases and other hurdles
you'll face. Women entrepreneurs, for example, have been coached by
male mentors to act assertive or cocky when presenting to investors,
but this is shaky advice. Research has shown that women who do this
can be perceived as unfeminine and unlikable.[26]

"You need to have mentors that look like you," says Melanie Igwe,
who's working on her second start-up, Drugviu, a Chicago-based

platform that crowdsources reports on drug effectiveness and side effects from people of color, and combines it with data and recommendations from the Food and Drug Administration and pharmacists. Igwe, the chief operating officer, and her cofounder, Kwaku Owusu, were inspired by the fact that clinical trials typically test medications only on white patients. They hope to recruit patients of color to participate in future clinical trials and, in the meantime, collect drug reports from ordinary users to shed light on risks that are unique to certain populations. Igwe has seen these risks firsthand: her father experienced surprising adverse reactions to his post-stroke medications.

Igwe puts her take on mentors this way: "Until there's real equality with respect to funding, to customers [whom founders can acquire], we need to be able to leverage information from [mentors] that have had to go through that experience with the lens that is similar to yours." In particular, Igwe says, advisers of color will know that the start-up world is not a meritocracy and will not give guidance based on the assumption it is. "It doesn't really matter how great your product is. It's about who you know. . . . It's about their level of comfort with you. There's some people that just may not be that comfortable with you. The sad part is that they may not even acknowledge it. They may not even know that they have an implicit bias. It's important to have mentors or advisers that have been able to navigate those waters, so that they can say, 'Hey, look, this is what you can do in these situations. If this is what's going on, maybe look at it like this.' Because when you're naive and you just think that merit is the trump card, you're going to have a difficult time in this arena."

After a six-year stint in the air force and two decades working in IT, Leigh Riley decided to start her own company. "I just walked in one day and said, 'I quit,'" she says. "It was that typical mentality of 'I'm really good at what I do technically—why can't I do this on my own? Why should I be making millions of dollars for somebody else when I could be making it for myself?'" In 2006 she opened her Northern Virginia management consulting firm, Acme Process Group, to help organizations increase their productivity. Over the years, she's had as many as ten employees and served a mix of clients, but there's one kind of customer that has been tough to secure: federal agencies. Riley has done the immense legwork to prove her company is woman-owned and that she's a disabled veteran and economically disadvantaged; federal agencies have contracting dollars they should spend with firms that meet these criteria. But when Riley and I first spoke in 2018, she told me she's struggled to pitch her company to the right people because she knows "virtually no one" in decision-making roles in these agencies.

"You have to be introduced by people," Riley says. "They don't answer the phone when you call them. They don't answer their emails. If you see them at a conference, you can say, 'Hi,' but they've got fifteen hundred other people trying to do the same thing."

Riley knows she needs to grow her network and then ask those connections to help her out. "Quite frankly, for me, that is very difficult, because I feel like I'm begging," she tells me. "I didn't grow up that way. I grew up just learning that if you work hard, you will get to where you need to go. But there're these incredible roadblocks getting into the federal workspace because, one, it's mostly run by men. Two, even though they have things in place for women, it doesn't necessarily open any doors. It's this weird paradox. I'm not sure I've got it figured out yet."

Once, Riley was getting ready to meet a contracting officer at the National Institutes of Health and found out he'd served as a marine. Her boyfriend at the time was also a marine, so he was able to feed her some lines: a few tidbits about the Marine Corps' birthday and a football game the day before. And lo and behold, it worked. The guy was very receptive and gave her great advice.

When I caught up with Riley in early 2020, she'd found another hack: she'd recently partnered with a larger firm that would bring her connections to federal agencies.

Riley tells me she's learned a lot in her decade-plus as a business owner—the importance of networks and credentials, how to find support when inevitable screwups happen—and she's eager to pay it forward. In 2020, she launched a second company, Vector Results Coaching, that helps entrepreneurs grow their businesses.

Amy Spurling, the CEO and cofounder of the Boston-based human resources start-up Compt, also recognizes the importance of a sprawling network and devotes time each week to building it. "Without a big network, there's no way I'd be able to get where I need to go. If your network is not big, you don't know who to try to pull in to be able to recruit diverse talent. Or making sure that I know enough VCs to be able to fundraise. There is no bad that comes from having a big network."

Decades of research have shown that men typically have larger, more powerful professional networks that include lots of people with authority.[27] Men are comfortable mixing business with friendship. Women, on the other hand, have smaller networks filled with people with less influence but strong social ties. Women tend to keep business and friendship separate. In a 2018 study of women executives working in Germany, researchers identified multiple reasons for this: People prefer to associate with people like themselves, making it difficult for women to enter male-dominated networks.[28] Women encounter networking venues that often feel stereotypically male—the foosball table, the cigar bar, the golf course. Women tend to be the primary caregiver in a family, which can put after-hours networking activities out of reach. Women can also cringe at the thought of tapping a connection to get ahead; it can feel to them as if they're using people.

In Lusnail Rondon Haberberger's case, networking options have included clay shooting, hunting, and golfing. After working for a decade as an engineer and project manager in several states, Haberberger opened her own electrical engineering firm, LUZCO Technologies, in St. Louis in 2017. The company, with more than twenty employees, often works on the infrastructure for Missouri's utility providers. A few years ago, a large local electrical contractor began an annual tradition of hosting a day of clay shooting at a Missouri ranch for about seventy-five clients and peers. Haberberger says that for the first two years, no women attended. In the third year, she showed up. "They were like, 'Wow.' They were very accommodating, and they taught me. The next year, one of the hosts actually brought his wife's gun that fit my body type better, and shared techniques. It's funny—it would have never crossed my mind that I was going to do that ever in my life. But I made incredible connections spending the whole day with them. It's building that relationship. People do business with people who they trust."

Haberberger tells me she's come to learn that working in a male-dominated field, she needs to adapt to her surroundings, while still remaining authentic to herself. She's had a lot of practice, as the engineering schools she attended also had few women. "My entire life has been surrounded by men."

As Vanessa Roanhorse was setting up her consulting business in Albuquerque, New Mexico, in early 2016, she sensed a void. "Starting my own company, and trying to find resources, and trying to find mentors and programs that I felt represented my story, my journey, as well as led by my personal and indigenous Navajo values, it was nearly impossible," she tells me. Roanhorse loved working with clients on economic development projects, but often felt isolated and the urge to "code switch," changing the way she acted depending on who was around. "Oftentimes, I am the only woman and most definitely the only Native American woman in any of these [client] conversations."

To break through the isolation, Roanhorse and seven other women formed a networking group for women entrepreneurs called Native Women Lead in 2017. The next year, the group held its first two-day business summit for two hundred attendees to learn about business plans, funding strategies, and branding. For Roanhorse, the emotional impact of that gathering went way beyond entrepreneurship. "Some of us broke into tears, because it was the most important sense of like, 'Wow, we're actually here in a safe space with our sisters, and we can actually breathe a sense of relief, at least for the day, that we're going to be okay.' It's more than business." Since then, participation in the group has ballooned.

Many of the entrepreneurs I interviewed told me that women-focused networking fills a need for them—they can take a break from fitting into the boys' club, they can be vulnerable, they can share stories of discrimination and harassment. For them, the gender separation is deliberate and important.

Keera Brooks's group happened almost by chance. In 2017, she attended a three-day training program in Atlanta with two dozen other women entrepreneurs. At the time, she was building her first business, a trucking logistics company. The rapport among the students was so intense that they've kept in touch ever since. "Our little cohort became very close over those three days," Brooks says. "We created our own Slack channel. We meet regularly just to get together, discuss our businesses and how we can help each other. We have a LinkedIn group where we support each other." Once they included their children in a get-together—"because all of us are challenged with the same burden of how do we work and care for our kids." Brooks also asked the other members to share their own network of contacts and compiled it all in a private database. "I organized it so that we could give each other warm introductions, we could help each other grow our businesses, and even use each other for our own businesses," says Brooks, who now owns and runs an e-commerce business called Wholesale Sugar Flowers in Jasper, Georgia. "It's almost like an Angie's List for women professionals."

Jacquie Kay remains in constant contact with twelve women with whom she worked at two world's fairs early in her career—one in Seattle in 1962 and another in New York City in 1964. "We call ourselves the World's Fair-est Ladies," Kay says with a chuckle, noting they've provided professional and personal support to each other over the decades. Kay is a two-time entrepreneur: Her first company, WPI, a global education and training firm, operated for thirty-six years. Since 2012, her Sun Walking Group/Labs in Cambridge, Massachusetts, has worked on a range of environmental and social impact projects, from developing a farming program on Native American–owned land to restoring the sea cucumber industry in the island country of Palau.

"I think a support system is very key for women, especially poor women and women of color—women who are willing to share what their issues are, and other women who are willing to listen. The old boy network does the same thing. That's how I think a lot of men have made it, through their networking," Kay explains.

Kay also wants to give her support to her local start-up scene, so she participates in the office hours at the weekly networking event for entrepreneurs called Venture Café Cambridge. Anyone needing advice can sign up for a free thirty-minute session with Kay or another one of the volunteer experts. "What I bring for the prospective client is an incredible ability to make connections, do networking, and establish relationships," Kay tells me. "I have these connections, and now I've reached the age where I know I need to give them to people. And I can place it in a framework of social impact and sustainability. I can help budding entrepreneurs, especially women, get access to systems and overcome barriers. I'm the wise owl now."

I think Venture Café's office hours program neatly solves a problem raised by several of the women entrepreneurs I interviewed: when they reach out to a man and ask for a meeting, the man sometimes falsely assumes they have romantic intentions. These office hours allow founders to meet advisers in a way that everyone's intentions are clear and in a space that feels safe.

Another option for networking and support is a coworking space tailored to women (and sometimes nonbinary people, too), which are multiplying around the country. There's Hera Hub, with locations in California and beyond, EvolveHer in Chicago; and The Coven in Minneapolis and St. Paul. Best known is The Wing, which operates in many major US cities and in London. Inspired by women's social clubs from the nineteenth and twentieth centuries, Audrey Gelman and Lauren Kassan launched The Wing in 2016 and have since raised $117.5 million in venture capital and other investments.[29]

Diverse and inclusive environments benefit everyone, so it can seem counterproductive to emphasize these women-focused spaces and events. Maura McAdam has studied networking initiatives targeted to women founders in the United Kingdom, and thinks timing is a key consideration. "We found that at the early stages of the entrepreneurial journey, they were very beneficial in terms of reducing the isolation, helping women with their confidence, teaching them how to pitch their ideas," says McAdam, the Dublin City University professor. "Then we found that when women became more established, they wanted to be in mixed networks, because they felt that that's where the real players were."

· · · · · ·

Earlier in this chapter I wrote about the 2010 study that showed that entrepreneurs with good support from their partners—called spousal capital—create profitable companies more quickly.[30] The University of Minnesota researchers behind that study made a sobering discovery: in heterosexual marriages, male entrepreneurs receive more help from their wives than female entrepreneurs do from their husbands. The researchers suggest this "may contribute to the gender gap in the success of new businesses."

During the course of my interviews, I met one entrepreneur who said her divorce was caused in part because her ex-husband didn't believe in her fledging business. For the most part, I heard from women entrepreneurs who got support from their spouses (as well as parents), which they considered crucial to their success. Neha Narkhede left a senior-level engineering position at LinkedIn in 2014 to cofound the Mountain View, California–based data-management company Confluent, now valued at $2.5 billion. She credits her husband with helping her make that leap. "I don't think that I could have pulled this off without his deep support for everything that I've had to do: quit a job and all of a sudden start a whole new company and give almost all my waking hours to it," Narkhede says. "There have been several moments of doubt and impostor syndrome kicking in, and he was the one who felt I could go on. Each one of those times, I remember he made me believe in what I've done before, the fact that I could do it again, and I should stick it through. Instead of that, if I'd heard a voice that said, 'It's not worth your time,' or 'It's time to start a family,' it would have made it much easier for me to quit."

Narkhede's husband also absorbed most household responsibilities. He does the taxes and keeps in touch with relatives. "He's taken every other worry off my plate," she tells me. "There's no other way you can devote as much time to something you've never done before and be successful at it."

In her 2017 *Harvard Business Review* article "If You Can't Find a Spouse Who Supports Your Career, Stay Single," gender-and-business consultant Avivah Wittenberg-Cox reports that in most of the heterosexual unions she's examined, husbands will back their wives' work only as long as it doesn't interfere with their own careers.[31] She's only rarely seen this kind of dynamic in same-sex couples. Wittenberg-Cox cites a survey of Harvard Business School grads that revealed that more than half of the men anticipate their careers will take priority; most of the women graduates, however, envision each spouse's career getting equal emphasis.

The average woman in the United States spends about 4 hours per day doing unpaid work, such as household chores, shopping, and caring for children or adults, while the typical man devotes 2.4 hours per day to these activities.[32] According to the Bureau of Labor Statistics, in households with a mother and father who both work full-time, the woman on average assumes 60 percent of the childcare and 60 percent of the household work.[33] Other research has found that same-sex couples typically share household chores more equally, but once children arrive, the partner who makes less income usually shoulders more of the homemaking activities.[34]

A study done for the Small Business Administration found that women with a PhD in a STEM field are significantly less likely to participate in entrepreneurship if they have a child under the age of two.[35] But having kids has no such effect on men: among men with STEM PhDs and children under two, entrepreneurship rates are just as high as with men with older kids, or no kids at all.

Narkhede tells me that she thinks a lack of support—at home, as well as in other social and professional circles—could explain why more men than women find entrepreneurial success. "You have roadblocks every other week, and it starts to feel way too hard," she says. "At some point, it's like, is it worth it or not? If your support system and the people closest to you who matter to you don't think it's worth it, it's a big deal and a big choice to make. Men don't have the choice to make. No one asks them, 'Hey, how do you do this in spite of kids and in spite of having a family?' Men have constant encouragement. I don't think we talk enough about what impact that constant encouragement and people's view of you can have on your ability to be successful."

Many of the entrepreneurs I interviewed credit their parents with nurturing traits like independence, resilience, and creativity. Vanessa Castañeda Gill marvels at the kind of preparation her mother provided for her. A financially strapped single mom with no college degree who worked days and nights, she helped a fourteen-year-old Gill navigate a diagnosis of Asperger's syndrome. "She spent so many sleepless nights researching autism, how it works, and how she was able to communicate with me better and understand me better. She made so much of an effort, even when it frustrated her like crazy. She would get things out of me and help me express my emotions, and she really understood where I was coming from." In college, Gill hatched the idea for a video game with a female protagonist who has autism, one that could help young people apply and understand social-emotional skills. Gill is now the cofounder and CEO of Los Angeles–based video game studio Social Cipher, which targets neurodiverse communities, and her mother still plays an important role: "My mom helps me every step of the way, with everything from developing my leadership and management skills to powerfully navigating the business world as a woman."

For Stephanie Kaplan Lewis, her father provided an example with the email database services company he started in the late 1990s. "In our family growing up, it was always just understood: when you graduate college, you could go work for someone else or you could start your own business. Those were both two totally acceptable paths," she says. "Even though I wasn't someone that grew up with an interest in business or entrepreneurship—really I was more interested in media and journalism—it never was crazy to me, the idea of working for yourself or starting something of your own. That contributed to feeling comfortable, taking a risk, and doing it." In 2009, while still an undergrad at Harvard, Lewis teamed up with two classmates, Annie Wang and Windsor Hanger Western, to create Her Campus, an online magazine for college women now with over four hundred campus chapters in eleven countries. Lewis, CEO and editor in chief of the Boston-based company, notes that her younger brother, Jesse, also soaked up the message. Straight out of college, he started a same-day package-delivery company called Parcel that he sold to Walmart in 2017, three years after launching it.

A 2017 study from Rutgers University found that college students are significantly more likely to think starting a business is an appealing and realistic option if they believe they have the support of their families.[36] Another study of Swedes explored why the children of entrepreneurs are more likely to be entrepreneurs themselves.[37] This particular study showed the effect with adoptive parents, pointing to the importance of nurture, not nature or any "entrepreneur gene." Its researchers also note that children appear to be more influenced by the parent who shares their gender (all the more reason to encourage more entrepreneuring mothers if you want more entrepreneuring daughters down the line). In a different study, this time quizzing US kids in grades five through twelve, over half of the children of business owners reported that they want to be an entrepreneur when they grow up, while only 35 percent of the children of nonbusiness owners said this.[38]

Sometimes the example given by parents is stronger than the actual advice. Amanat Anand grew up in India watching her parents' entrepreneurial ventures, but in her case, her parents discouraged her from following their lead. "They try to protect me from the lows of entrepreneurship," Anand says. "They're just like, 'Are you sure you want to do this now? Why not wait, get more experience before you do it?'"

Anand's mother operates a heavy-equipment dealership in India, and her experience in this male-dominated industry has colored the career advice she's given Anand. "She gets inappropriately asked out for dinner and things like that, and she's like, 'I have a husband and I have a family and kids, and why does this keep happening?' At conferences, everyone goes with their wives, and she's just assumed to be someone's wife and not one of the dealers. She gets a lot of eyebrows raised when she enters the room," Anand explains. "I've always heard her stories, and I think that's why she's always like, 'No, don't do this.'"

Despite the discouraging stories, Anand followed her mother's example and in 2015 cofounded SoaPen, a New York City–based firm that makes a soap applicator that teaches kids how to wash their hands. Why? "For me, I can't imagine not being an entrepreneur," she says.

CHAPTER 9

ENTREPRENEURSHIP'S POTENTIAL

Making it work for everyone

RENATA CAINES GREW up in Roxbury, one of Boston's poorest neighborhoods, and never had a lot of money.[1] After two years of college, she dropped out when thousands of dollars of unexpected expenses left her unable to cover tuition and other costs. She worked a series of low-paying jobs in nonprofits, focusing on social justice and youth, and took classes here and there. Then, at age twenty-eight, she pledged to spend a year going back to school full-time while still working full-time. She was prepared, she tells me, to "bang it out." Midway through, a conversation at a family gathering changed the direction of her life.

Caines says, "An uncle of mine came up to me, particularly because I'm the youngest adult in my family and I live in Massachusetts, and he said, 'I have a certain amount of capital, and it's not a lot, but it is enough for us to get going on some sort of family business to create generational wealth. I think it would be lucrative to get into the cannabis industry, because it's about to be legal here in Massachusetts. I think that's something that we can think about.'"

Caines was intrigued and started doing research. Two years earlier, in 2016, Massachusetts voters had legalized recreational marijuana, and the first retail sales were set to start in late 2018. The potential for profit appeared great for those with business sense, good timing, and a willingness to work hard. Caines wanted in, though she had some qualms.

Growing up, she'd had friends who'd sold cannabis illegally, so she knew the costs: "I have friends that have been killed over disputes or have been jailed. . . . This is an industry where so many people's lives have been ruined and destroyed. It's all well and good for me to talk to you about all of my plans, but I would be remiss without always bringing into the conversation all of the folks who still can't live in public housing with their families or can't get certain jobs because of this plant that now we're profiting off of."

The war on drugs targeted some communities and ignored others. People who are Black or Latinx make up 22 percent of the Massachusetts population, but are three-quarters of the prison population with drug offenses.[2] With statistics like this in mind, Massachusetts lawmakers set up the recreational cannabis industry with a statewide equity mandate, the first state in the nation to do so.[3] The Cannabis Control Commission promised in its mission statement to regulate the industry so there'd be "full and robust participation by minorities, women and veterans"—especially "people from communities that have previously been disproportionately harmed by marijuana prohibition and enforcement."[4]

In her business management class at Northeastern University in early 2018, Caines sketched out a plan for a transportation company that would serve marijuana growers, manufacturers, and retailers. She enlisted her mother, Ivelise Rivera, who's worked as a computer instructor at a Roxbury community center for almost two decades, as her business partner. In April 2018, Caines and Rivera applied for economic empowerment status from the Cannabis Control Commission. Massachusetts residents were given only two weeks in 2018 to apply to this program and needed to meet certain criteria, such as being Black or Latinx, living and working in a community unfairly hit by the war on drugs, or having a past drug conviction or being married to or the child of someone with a conviction.[5] Caines and her mother's economic empowerment status was approved. It comes with zero financial help, but it does move applicants to the front of the line when they're ready to seek governmental permission to set up a cannabis business.

At the suggestion of a potential investor, Caines and Rivera began considering opening a cannabis dispensary instead. It's an appealing but expensive option, with some estimating it can require as much as $1.5 million to open just one store in Boston.[6] Caines learned she'd have to secure a storefront before applying for a license, usually paying rent in the meantime, and the local and state application process can last months and months, with no guarantee of getting a "yes" at the end. Caines found one property in Boston that would have cost about $17,000 a month, but there was no way they could afford rent before their business actually opened. They eventually settled on a property occupied by a Chinese restaurant in the nearby city of Somerville; the owner agreed to rent it to them if they got approval and not charge rent in the meantime.

Figuring out the marijuana rules was overwhelming, Caines tells me, and entrepreneurs without lawyers and accountants are at a disadvantage. Most banks won't lend to marijuana businesses because the drug, as of this writing, is illegal at the federal level, so entrepreneurs who don't have their own stash of savings need the help of investors.[7] Caines tells me that investors were very interested in the fact that she has economic empowerment status, but Caines wanted to partner with someone who shared her interest in social justice. "Finding the right investors, that's definitely been a challenge," she says. "All of these funders are rich white men, and what does that mean for me and for my family?" It's common in Massachusetts and elsewhere to hear stories of predatory investors taking too much control and ownership from disadvantaged cannabis entrepreneurs.[8]

After a few false starts, Caines found what she was looking for. "I never in a million years would think that I would ever be so happy about some rich white man coming into my life," she says. "It feels so bizarre, but he is very determined. He has very much created a partnership with us. He understands that I have just as much stake in this business as he does."

As of this writing, Caines and her mother were still waiting to hear whether their application with the city of Somerville would be approved. They'd also begun looking at two other nearby cities as alternatives. And a cannabis-related transportation company is still a possibility, one that they'd use her uncle's money to help fund. After two years, Caines has learned that becoming a cannabis entrepreneur requires endurance.

Despite Massachusetts's efforts to build a fair cannabis industry, it hasn't played out that way. By March 2019, the thirteenth recreational pot dispensary in the state had opened, yet none were run by owners with economic empowerment status, and only one was woman-owned.[9] In an editorial at the time, the *Boston Globe* lamented that the process was favoring those with vast sums of money and connections, and warned that "the window of opportunity to build an equitable marijuana industry in Massachusetts" was in danger of closing. Finally, in March 2020, entrepreneurs Kevin Hart and Kobie Evans debuted their Boston dispensary, the first in the state with owners with economic empowerment status.[10] According to a 2019 report by *Marijuana Business Daily*, only 5 percent of all recreational marijuana businesses in Massachusetts (retail and otherwise) are owned by women, while a mere 1 percent are owned by people considered a racial minority.[11] You'll find a similar picture in the other states where pot is legal.

This wasn't always the case. When the US cannabis industry was just forming—California was first to legalize medical marijuana in 1996, while in 2012 Colorado and Washington were first to legalize recreational use—you could find plenty of examples of women and people of color setting up marijuana businesses.[12] But as more states changed their laws and the profit potential multiplied, deep-pocketed corporations and large investors arrived and pushed out smaller players, and the field became dominated by white men.

At a September 2019 event for cannabis entrepreneurs in Boston, I listened to former Boston city councilor Tito Jackson talk about the hurdles. Jackson, who's planning his own recreational pot dispensaries, called Massachusetts's approach to equity commendable but flawed. "This space is so hard around access to capital," he said, noting banks' refusal to loan to marijuana entrepreneurs and the lack of financial assistance from the state. Jackson thinks Illinois did better because its cannabis effort includes a $30 million low-interest loan program to assist underrepresented entrepreneurs.[13] He wants Massachusetts's equity program to have more muscle and truly lift up everyone. "I also would say I don't see enough women in this space," he told his audience. "You damn sure can't tell me . . . that women aren't as good in this space as men."

The story of the emerging cannabis industry raises many questions: Is it possible for a new industry to be built on an equitable foundation? If it can, does that mean that even older industries can be reformed? And can good intentions, good people, and good practices open up entrepreneurship so that everyone has a shot? After spending several years researching the entrepreneurial system's shortcomings and conducting over a hundred interviews, I feel hopeful that the answers to these questions are yes.

And as I mentioned in the first chapter, this isn't just about being fair. It's crucial for everyone's economic well-being. In an age when old industries and old ways of building a career have crumbled, entrepreneurship is needed to create jobs and grow the economy. It won't hurt men if women entrepreneurs do better—the opposite is true. The economy will be stronger for everyone.

But to get there, specific things need to happen. Changes need to be made to the way money is loaned and invested, and the ways investors interact with entrepreneurs and judge potential deals. The government needs to step in to make the entrepreneurial path less risky and more equitable, and address financial burdens that it helped create in the first place. Start-up ecosystems need to be built so that everyone is invited in. Allies need to open doors for entrepreneurs and block the bad behavior of others.

And the way forward must be inclusive. It can't simply benefit white women. It must deliberately reach women of color, as well as women with different abilities, nonbinary people, and so on. As sociologist Katie Wullert and her Stanford colleagues write in the *Harvard Business Review*, "[Diversity] efforts directed at women broadly tend to advance white women at the expense of women of color."[14]

Pipeline Angels is one group guarding against this phenomenon. Launched in 2011 by Natalia Oberti Noguera, the organization provides intensive training in angel investing to women and nonbinary femmes. "More white women investing in white women is not the answer," Oberti Noguera declared to great applause at a 2019 entrepreneurship event I attended. Pipeline Angels creates a welcoming space for all of its participants, with a code of conduct that bars microaggressions and other forms of harassment and a policy of alcohol-free events. Nearly four hundred angel investors in the Pipeline Angels program have invested more than $6 million in entrepreneurs who are, like them, women and nonbinary femmes.[15]

Women's wealth is climbing. Credit Suisse estimates that women in North America and Europe now hold 40 to 45 percent of wealth, because they're working more, making more money, delaying marriage and childbirth, living longer, and inheriting more.[16] This is encouraging news for capital-starved entrepreneurs, because of the ways wealthy women tend to direct their money. One study noted that more than half of women angel investors consider an entrepreneur's gender highly important when making an investment decision; only 6 percent of men do the same.[17] Women report being more interested than men in investing for social and environmental impact, though men's interest is catching up, and high-net-worth women tell researchers they're more likely than men to think investing to do good trumps accumulating wealth.[18] Meanwhile, interest in "gender-lens" investing is growing. The term, coined in 2009, applies to investing in companies that are owned or led by women, serve the needs of women, or prioritize gender equity. A 2018 report found that assets under management following this strategy climbed from $100 million to $2.4 billion in only four years.[19]

These shifts in wealth, coupled with an overhaul of venture capital and an expansion of funding alternatives, could dramatically improve the financial picture for women entrepreneurs in the coming years.

Mara Zepeda, one of the cofounders of the group Zebras Unite, which is urging a more inclusive and sustainable approach to start-ups, tells me she's excited by the proliferation of financing options. Character-based lending—in which a borrower's good name and deeds, and the financial strength of their business, are more important than their credit score—is one of her favorites. "What I'm really interested in is getting a lot more experiments going, so we can have a better sense of what works," says the Portland, Oregon–based entrepreneur. "There's going to be a different flavor of capital that works for different types of founders."

Equity crowdfunding is another option that holds promise for underrepresented entrepreneurs. Investors, who are often called mini-angel investors, buy small shares of early-stage companies that are growing but still privately owned.

While these alternatives are being tested, venture capital urgently needs a reboot. To start, a diverse group of people should be making investment decisions. The nonprofit All Raise wants to see the number of women partners at large VC firms reach 18 percent or more by 2028; in early 2020, the figure was 13 percent.[20] To reach its goal, All Raise is using tactics like coaching entry-level women employees at venture firms and publicizing job openings that are typically kept under wraps. The Dutch venture capital community has set a more aggressive goal: in 2019, more than two dozen firms in that country pledged that by 2022 their employees would number 35 percent women; they also promised that all of the companies they invest in would have management teams made up of 35 percent women.[21]

"I think the idea of looking for investment opportunities with underrepresented founders needs to be firmly put into the fabric of how you operate your business as an investor," says Boston-based venture capitalist Chip Hazard, "and at most firms that's going to happen when the firms themselves are more diverse."

When it comes to legal reforms to expressly prohibit sexual harassment by investors, California has led the way. Workplace protections against sexual harassment typically cover only employees and employers, leaving entrepreneurs vulnerable. The California law, which went into effect on January 1, 2019, covers several other business relationships besides investor and entrepreneur: elected official and lobbyist, director and actor, and producer and filmmaker.[22] In all these relationships, there is an imbalance of power, with one party holding influence, access, and money. Other states should follow California's lead.

Paying customers are another crucial way women-owned companies get cash—and this country's federal, state, and local governments are some of the richest customers around. In 1994, Congress first set a goal of spending 5 percent of federal contracting dollars with women-owned businesses.[23] It wasn't until 2015 that this goal was achieved, and the success was short-lived. It missed the goal in 2016, 2017, and 2018.[24] Local governments also struggle with this issue. The city of Boston, for instance, gave less than 1 percent of its contracts to women- and minority-owned businesses in 2018.[25]

We must do better, and there are examples of setting and meeting more aggressive goals. Philadelphia pledges to award 35 percent of its contracts to businesses owned by women or people considered minorities or with disabilities, and exceeded this goal for the first time in fiscal year 2019.[26] Dallas commits 18 to 36 percent of its contracts, depending on the goods and services, to women- and minority-owned businesses.[27] Meanwhile, New York City promises that by 2021 at least 30 percent of its contracting dollars will go to women- and minority-owned businesses.[28] "If our economy isn't inclusive, then it's not working as it should," New York City mayor Bill de Blasio has said.

Ordinary people buying from women-owned companies would make a difference, too. In March 2020, the crowd-sourced review site Yelp added a feature that lets users search for women-owned businesses and reported that a growing number of reviewers are noting if a place has a woman at the helm.[29] Shoppers can also look for products or websites carrying a seal from the Female Founder Collective (femalefoundercollective.com). This initiative, launched in 2018 by fashion designer Rebecca Minkoff, certifies that companies are women-founded and -owned. Other options include Dough (joindough.com), a shopping site that only sells items from women's companies, and The F Project (thefproject.co), a directory of consumer products made by women's ventures. "It's really about getting the consumer to think about, when they buy things, who is running this company?" says entrepreneur Sophia Yen. "If they have an opportunity to choose between a woman-run and a man-run company, maybe choose the woman-run." Programs are also singling out companies owned by Black women. The nonprofit called Buy from a Black Woman (buy fromablackwoman.org) offers a directory of businesses. In New York City there's the Uptown Underground Market (uptownunderground market.com), a series of pop-up events that sell goods only from Black women-owned businesses.

In Anchorage, Alaska, Gareth Olds's parents ran a school that trained dental assistants. For part of his childhood, his family, which included two sisters, got its health insurance through Medicaid and was on food stamps. As Olds describes it years later, this strong social safety net made his parents' entrepreneurial venture a little less risky: "They knew that if things really went poorly with the business, we'd be able to go to the doctor. If something happened, we'd be able to eat."[30] First as an economics PhD student at Brown University and then a Harvard Business School professor, Olds investigated whether his parents' experience was shared by others. Several years' worth of study showed him that public assistance programs could, in fact, encourage entrepreneurship.[31] "If you give someone a guarantee of health insurance for their children, I found a 25 percent increase in the likelihood they start a business," he explained in a Harvard Business School interview.[32] "I found about a 10 percent increase in small business formation among food stamp recipients as the program expanded in the 2000s." He notes that many new business owners who are eligible for food stamps don't end up using them, but knowing they're available makes a difference. These programs, Olds maintains, reduce the peril associated with entrepreneurship and allow people to save money they can invest in a business.[33] Before he left Harvard in 2017, Olds also found that parents of college-age children are less likely to launch a business if the tuition at their local public colleges goes up.[34]

Olds's research joins a larger conversation about the role of government in supporting entrepreneurs: Is smaller government, with fewer regulations and lower taxes, the right approach? Or is bigger government, one that provides a safety net and addresses inequities, better? In 2015, while an editor at *Harvard Business Review*, Walter Frick explored these questions in an article for *The Atlantic*.[35] He found that some tax cuts, but not all, do a good job of spurring entrepreneurship, and surprisingly, more federal regulation can lead to more new business. Food stamp programs can help aspiring entrepreneurs, but not if they require enrollees to find and keep a job (instead of allowing them time to start a business). Frick concluded that the evidence doesn't support the idea that we have to choose between either a bigger government or a more entrepreneurial economy. In some cases, he noted, a big government means *more* entrepreneurship. "When governments provide citizens with economic security, they embolden them to take more risks," Frick wrote. "Properly deployed, a robust social safety net encourages more Americans to attempt the high-wire act of entrepreneurship."

On the campaign trail in the summer of 2019, several Democratic presidential candidates rolled out government plans to spur entrepreneurship and make it more inclusive. As Elizabeth Warren tweeted in June of that year, "The racial wealth gap tilts the playing field against entrepreneurs of color, holding back our economy. The government helped create that wealth gap, and the government has an obligation to address it."[36] Warren, Pete Buttigieg, and US senator Kamala Harris all called for the creation of government funds that would invest in companies started by underrepresented founders.[37] In Warren's case, she envisioned grants to entrepreneurs of color, with the money handled by minority- and women-owned investment firms. The candidates proposed varying levels of student loan relief, too, saying the government's failure to financially support higher education led to higher tuition and thus overwhelming debt for students and parents. In turn, they explained, the debt is delaying and even preventing people from starting businesses.

Average tuition and fees at public four-year colleges have tripled since the late 1980s, while they've doubled at private nonprofit four-year schools.[38] As costs have gone up, so, too, have loan amounts. Women, who earn 57 percent of bachelor's degrees, owe almost two-thirds of the outstanding student debt in our country.[39] Black women hold the most debt of all students graduating with a bachelor's degree—$30,366 of mean cumulative debt, compared to $19,486 for white men and $21,993 for white women. Women also take longer to pay back their loans, in part because of the gender pay gap they encounter once they graduate. Not surprisingly, the weight of this debt can make the idea of a risky start-up unappealing. In one startling 2018 study, researchers found that having up to $10,000 in student loans lowers the likelihood of launching a company by 7 percent and cuts the amount of money the start-up makes by 42 percent.[40] Another 2018 study showed that student debt curtails the entrepreneurial aspirations of millennials, with the effect stronger for women than men.[41]

If the government were to cancel or refinance student debt, that would be a massive help to women entrepreneurs, especially women of color. So would broad government-subsidized childcare, considering that women continue to shoulder most of the parenting duties.[42] The 2019 survey, commissioned by the UK's economic and finance ministry found that women in that country are twice as likely as men to say family obligations are an obstacle to launching a company.[43] And for mothers already running a company, balancing family and work is the number-one barrier that limits their business growth. Fathers who are entrepreneurs, on the other hand, don't report this as a major hurdle. The researchers behind this UK survey suggest following the lead of the Netherlands, which has introduced entrepreneur-friendly policies such as a sixteen-week paid maternity leave for the self-employed.[44] They write: "Research shows that women entrepreneurs in countries with supportive work-family policies, such as the Netherlands, express more ambitious growth intentions, employ more workers and are more innovative than those in countries without such benefits."[45]

The United States is probably a long way from offering paid parental leave for all and widespread government-subsidized childcare, but there are things we could do in the meantime. To start, places where entrepreneurs of all genders learn and work—such as accelerator programs, coworking spaces, and entrepreneurship conferences—should provide care for young children. Groups like Native Women Lead are offering a wonderful example; when it held entrepreneurs' summits in 2018 and 2019 in Albuquerque, New Mexico, it provided on-site childcare.

I'm reminded of the day I met Salimata Bangoura. It was June 2019, and we were at a daylong conference just west of Boston for women entrepreneurs. We both had to sneak out early so we could pick up our kids from school. "Just when things were getting good, just when I started making connections with people, I had to leave," Bangoura told me later. "I feel like I missed out on a lot." Bangoura and I also noticed that another attendee brought an infant with her and popped in and out of the meeting room when the baby became fussy. "She spent most of the time outside," Bangoura says. "That's just so unfair."

The mother of three young children, Bangoura tells me she marvels that childcare is almost never offered at business events, even those catering to women, and that speakers at these events tend to avoid talking about their kids. Once, she attended a panel discussion at a major marketing firm, with about a half-dozen panelists debating what brings women joy. "Not one person talked about children. It's like, I get it, right? You don't have to talk about kids. But it's almost as if it's taboo. . . . It's almost as if women are expected, when you enter the world of business, to shut that part of yourself down."

Bangoura is fixated on the lives of busy working parents because they are her core customer. In 2017, while pursuing her MBA in entrepreneurship at Babson College, she launched Dugu, a Natick, Massachusetts–based company that delivers West African fusion meals to customers' homes and workplaces. Dugu will also drop off meals at a preschool, so parents can pick up their children and dinner at the same time.

When the start-up ecosystem you've spent several years building ends up being "very male, very pale," you've got a problem. That's what Cheryl Watkins-Moore says happened in St. Louis.

After several corporate headquarters such as Southwestern Bell, McDonnell Douglas, and General Dynamics departed Missouri's second-largest city in the 1990s, leaders in academia, business, and philanthropy banded together to figure out what might replace them.[46] They realized entrepreneurial activity was lacking, and the area's universities were engaging in valuable research, especially in plant and life sciences, but not enough was being commercialized. So in the early 2000s, they set out to create a start-up community focused on bioscience. Eventually they built a two-hundred-acre innovation district in midtown St. Louis, put together pools of money to invest in start-ups, and assembled other key resources for entrepreneurs.

"As the community started humming around 2008, what they started to see is a lot of interest but very little diversity," Watkins-Moore tells me. "It was very male, very pale, very disconcerting. What studies show is that you need all types of individuals together when you're talking about reaching high levels of innovation. Not just from one race or gender, but different thoughts, experiences, ages, all of that. That's what was lacking at that time." She credits the leaders of this emerging start-up community for recognizing that something was amiss. "It was like, 'Wait a minute, we need to do something very differently. . . . This is not what we're trying to accomplish here.'"

Watkins-Moore, a surgeon by training who spent years working in the corporate world, joined the effort in 2011. First she served as an entrepreneur-in-residence for BioGenerator, which creates and invests in bioscience start-ups in St. Louis, while working on her own health-care software company. But soon after she moved to her current role: heading up the entrepreneurial inclusion efforts for BioSTL, the nonprofit that supports the city's bioscience sector. She was eager to take up the cause; she says, "I saw the challenges and issues I was experiencing as a woman of color leading a start-up in our ecosystem." Throughout the year, Watkins-Moore organizes events that highlight diverse examples of successful founders, and lines up resources for underrepresented entrepreneurs—in one option, participants get free help securing a patent or creating a prototype. Since 2014, inclusion participants in BioSTL's programs have raised $50 million for their business ventures. There are also internships that expose high school students of color to start-ups and STEM fields. Another program offers one or two years of on-the-job training as a VC analyst; the hope is that a diverse mix of program graduates will go on to work at venture capital firms. "To start to change investment decisions," Watkins-Moore explains, "you've got to start changing who sits around those tables." When I visited the city's innovation district in 2018, I saw a bustling area. There are now more than 400 companies and 5,800 employees, plus lots of coworking and shared lab spaces, where deteriorating empty warehouses once stood.[47]

What St. Louis has done is build an entrepreneurial ecosystem, offering founders the work space, money, education, support, employees, and collaboration needed to start and grow companies. Done right, these ecosystems can make sure women and other underrepresented entrepreneurs are included.

Incubators and accelerators are a key ingredient of these ecosystems, as they offer early-stage entrepreneurs resources like intensive coaching, work space, and financial support. According to a 2016 report by the Initiative for a Competitive Inner City, high-tech incubators and accelerators have been dominated by white male entrepreneurs.[48] Program leaders often recruit participants through their own networks or unintentionally set up the offerings so they glorify bro culture. Sometimes they exclude people with childcare responsibilities. Fortunately, there are practical remedies—from allowing founders to participate remotely, to bringing in a diverse group of judges and mentors. MassChallenge has shown how powerful one tweak can be. One of the largest accelerators in the world, with programs in the United States and three other countries, MassChallenge gives participating start-ups a chance to battle for a share of up to $3 million in annual awards.[49] It began in Boston in 2010, and in its early years, most of the participating start-ups were led by all-male teams. But in 2018, more women were added to the panels that choose which start-ups to accept into the program, and for the first time, more than half of the 128 teams in the Boston cohort had at least one woman cofounder.[50]

Building incubators and accelerators targeted to underrepresented groups is another option. In 2012, Babson College in Wellesley, Massachusetts, launched the Women Innovating Now Lab, which offers five months of free business instruction, coaching, and networking to women entrepreneurs, in either Boston or Miami.[51] Serial entrepreneur

Heatherjean MacNeil, one of the accelerator's cofounders and its former global director, tells me the team designed it to prepare women entrepreneurs for roadblocks unique to them. For example, because research shows that investors ask entrepreneurs different kinds of questions depending on the entrepreneur's gender, participants are coached to anticipate these questions. "Women are faced with the pressure to create and build businesses that align with this meta-narrative of being Mark Zuckerberg: coming up with really big ideas, raising large amounts of funding, growing big teams, and just doing it in a way that's embedded in masculine business practices," MacNeil explains. "But I think women are natural entrepreneurs. I think business can be done differently, can look differently, when there's an opportunity to really explore what that looks like outside of these masculinized norms." MacNeil adds that fostering a sense of community is important for the accelerator. "Each cohort felt like such a strong-knit family, a lot of cross-collaboration going on between businesses, a lot of support—even down to like, 'I'll pick up your kids from daycare.'"

Creating an inclusive ecosystem will require some effort and resources. But cities and regions have shown repeatedly that they're capable of ambitious efforts. When Amazon announced in 2017 that it was looking for a North American location for its second headquarters—promising to spend more than $5 billion on the project and produce up to fifty thousand jobs—more than two hundred cities and regions submitted bids to the company.[52] These communities dangled billions of dollars' worth of tax credits and other incentives and promised help in creating everything from education programs to a corporate helipad.[53] I agree with the many who complained that these incentives were unwarranted considering Amazon's wealth and power and suggested the effort would be better directed to women and other underrepresented entrepreneurs. In a 2018 interview with *Forbes*, AOL cofounder Steve Case had his own message for the regions that attempted to lure Amazon: "Take half the energy and half the capital you are willing to devote to Amazon and put it towards your startup sector—that will bear far greater fruit over the next 10 to 20 years."[54]

· · · · · ·

When I attended one of her talks in 2019, Kathryn Finney told the audience about a conversation she had with a friend who was feeling political angst and wanted to do something constructive. She recalled telling him: "You are a white male in tech who went to an Ivy League school. You are going to get into doors I will never, ever get into. We went to the same school—it doesn't matter. You're going to get seats at tables that people are not going to ever invite me, or someone who looks like me or another woman, to, so use your power. You have power. If you want to make things better, when you get invited to that investor, and you know there's not going to be any color, no women, take one with you. And don't just say, 'Sit here,' but say, 'She has an amazing company. I think you should look at investing in her.' You can do that, you have the power."

Finney, the founder of digitalundivided, which runs an incubator for Black and Latinx women entrepreneurs, says being a sponsor is one of the most important things allies can do, even more important than mentoring. It means making key introductions, actively lobbying on someone's behalf, and vouching for their talent and ideas.

In her speech, Finney said: "There is a privileged position that comes when you are white. And if you're a white male, it's a particularly privileged position. Your word is worth more than my words in certain circles. . . . People give you power. So use it."

Finney makes a crucial point. Underrepresented entrepreneurs can't fix a broken entrepreneurial system on their own. Leaning in doesn't address institutional hurdles or unconscious biases. We all need to play a role.

Being a sponsor typically assumes you have some social capital. But there is another tactic that anyone can deploy. Mary Rowe, the MIT researcher who's spent decades studying microinequities, tells me her research has shown that their opposite, which she calls microaffirmations, can be hugely powerful. There are many ways to practice microaffirmations: Offer congratulations when someone succeeds and be ready to listen when someone fails. Broadcast someone's good work and make sure they get credit for it. Give someone space to talk and prevent interruptions. Extend to someone an opportunity that would ordinarily be out of reach. You do these things consistently, a little here and a little there, sometimes privately and sometimes publicly. Rowe says the person receiving the microaffirmation may feel more confident and perform better. And if one person in a group uses microaffirmations, those around them are likely to copy the practice.

Rowe says we can also build a more inclusive climate by mobilizing bystanders. In other words, people who witness inappropriate behavior need to speak up and take action. Rowe acknowledges that a new entrepreneur eager for a first investment might have a difficult time calling out an investor. So in that case the investor's peers need to mobilize. "The best constraints on the bad behavior of powerful people are other powerful people," Rowe says. "The best teachers of good behavior to powerful people in any context are other powerful people."

Caro Berry makes enamel pins, patches, and other items with sayings like "All Black Everything" and "Pastel Punk" and sells them online under the name Pretty in Punk. "I've been contacted on a fairly regular basis since I started the business by those who want to sell my wares in their store or feature me in a magazine's article," Berry, who's based in Germany, writes in a November 2017 blog post.[55] "The emails almost always start the same: *'we love the feminist angle,'* as if to warm me up, followed by *'we want to curate a selection of female artists,' 'we want to empower women,' 'we want to create a space for women,'* and so on. Hm. In the 20+ months I've run this business I have never once referred to myself as female or a woman. Why? Because I am neither."

Berry goes on to explain that they're nonbinary, yet people repeatedly assume they're a cisgender woman and rarely ask if that's so. They write:

> I feel awkward and embarrassed, like every other time I'm misgendered, but I'm also upset. I'm upset because for a second I feel validated, welcomed, wanted. Perhaps the magazine or store is in another country or on another continent, enabling me to feel even more accomplished in what I have built. But this feeling disappears quickly as I come to realise I don't fit the stipulated requirements

and therefore don't belong in their carefully curated collection of creatives. I'm upset because all of the reasons these individuals list as to why they want a female- or women-only space are ALL applicable to me and every other gender deviant out there! It's not women vs. men it's ALL OF US vs. the patriarchy!

Mason Aid tells me they've experienced a similar situation navigating entrepreneur groups geared toward women. Aid is a nonbinary person raised as female and identifying as more masculine. Since 2017, Aid's been building a Columbia, Missouri–based consulting firm that helps companies and other groups create more inclusive environments. They've found networking with and learning from women's entrepreneurship groups valuable and share similar experiences with the members. "I do have the struggles that come with being assigned female at birth," Aid says. "When you look at the mindset with work: apologizing too much, and not being as assertive. I was socialized that way as well." But at times these groups can make Aid feel invalidated or like an outsider. Even a simple greeting such as "Hey, ladies," though well intentioned, sends an unwelcoming message.

Aid has been able to use these experiences in their work, as several clients have been women entrepreneurs who are targeting a female customer. Aid helps these companies figure out if reaching out to a broader audience would make more sense and how to do that effectively. Aid notes that as Generation Z grows up, these considerations will become more urgent. According to Pew Research Center, more than one-third of Gen Z (born 1997 to 2012) personally knows someone who uses gender-neutral pronouns.[56] In comparison, only 12 percent of baby boomers and 16 percent of Generation X report the same thing.

Aid's and Berry's experiences reveal the complexities of creating investment funds or accelerator programs or networking events geared toward women entrepreneurs. There are a lot of benefits to be had: Women entrepreneurs can learn about opportunities unique to them. They can champion business ideas, such as women's health products, that other groups may dismiss. They can discuss sensitive topics like sexual harassment. They can find camaraderie and safety that may be missing from other spaces. On the other hand, these women-focused initiatives run the risk of isolating women and excluding gender-expansive people. And they're often built on the assumption that women are a homogeneous group, when a woman's race, socioeconomic background, and other identities can lead to markedly different entrepreneurial experiences.

Aid says efforts to include nonbinary people have been uneven: "I see it in the women's groups I'm part of. Much more space is given for masculine people who were assigned female at birth than for feminine people who were assigned male at birth. That is problematic."

Derrick Reyes, the CEO and cofounder of New York City–based Queerly Health, a digital platform that connects people who are LGBTQ+ with health and wellness providers, has attended events and joined networks promoted to women in tech or entrepreneurial women. "I know that not every phase of the start-up journey is made for people who identify the way that I do, whether that's as a queer person or a nonbinary person or an Afro-Latinx person or any other marginalized identity that belongs to me. I sometimes will enter spaces and wonder, 'Is this for me? Is this for people like me?' I ended up just deciding that if I was there, then it was for me and people like me. I try not to ask myself if I belong anymore. I just say that I do, and I try to make sure to hold the door open for other people of marginalized identities, so that they know this is also for them."

An entrepreneurs' breakfast celebrating Women's History Month in Boston led me to Katie Burkhart in March 2019. Despite the morning's focus on women, Burkhart told me later that she would like to see us move away from gender-segregated events. "I would really like the opportunity to be at the table with everybody else. I don't really want my own table," says Burkhart, who owns the Boston-based branding firm Matter 7 and is developing two other companies. "I want to be able to go to an entrepreneur competition and win the competition, not the women's competition—like somehow we aren't qualified to play in the game with everybody else."

Venture capitalist Maia Heymann, based in Cambridge, Massachusetts, also sees that solutions designed for women have the potential to feel condescending. "I sometimes bristle at this notion that women need help, like 'Got to give the women extra help, they can't do it on their own.' Of course, that's not what anyone intends, but there is the possibility of a subtle undertone of 'They need help.'" What women need, Heymann says, is for barriers of bias to be removed so that they can raise capital and compete.

Instead of women-focused networking events, what entrepreneur Melonee Wise would prefer are smaller gatherings in which the invite list is carefully curated to bring together people who would benefit from meeting each other but who wouldn't ordinarily cross paths. Wise, the CEO of Fetch Robotics, says this approach would avoid a common pitfall of women's events: people of other genders tend to stay away. "What you end up with is a whole bunch of people in a sub-population who are brought together, who already know each other because there's so few of us, and we don't actually get the valuable networking we're looking for."

Barbara Clarke, a Boston-based angel investor who's funded over sixty companies, also prefers mixed-gender events—but ones where all feel comfortable and included. "I want to know that when I go to the bathroom in between sessions that there is going to be a line at the women's room. It's not just going to be all men," she tells me. Clarke declined an invitation to an entrepreneur's event at a local casino because she predicted it would be dominated by men and fueled by alcohol. "How is that going to end? Is that going to end well? I'll probably be like one of three women. . . . I don't think that that's going to be a really fun place for me to be."

Clarke's experience recalls the now-famous story of venture capitalist Chris Sacca's penchant for hosting meetings with entrepreneurs in his hot tub. In her book *Brotopia: Breaking Up the Boys' Club of Silicon Valley*, journalist Emily Chang recounts an interview she did with Sacca in 2015 in which he bragged about these meetings at his home near Lake Tahoe, California, and how they helped him evaluate an entrepreneur's character and endurance.[57] Chang writes: "What he did not seem to grasp—perhaps because he suffers from the same blind spot as so many other men in the industry—was any awareness that the demographic of people who might be comfortable sharing a hot tub with a potential investor might be rather narrow."

The value of separating genders has long been debated. Women's colleges, first founded in the United States in the mid-nineteenth century, maintain that they're still relevant and necessary today, despite women's advancements in education and the workplace.[58] In fact, these colleges reported an enrollment spike after the 2016 election of Donald Trump and the #MeToo movement.[59] Kimberly Wright Cassidy, the president of Bryn Mawr College outside Philadelphia, has written about "a culture of enlarged expectations of and opportunities for women" that is found on these campuses.[60] She also points to one survey that revealed that alumnae of women's colleges are more likely to earn an advanced degree than other grads.[61]

Like women's colleges, historically black colleges and universities (HBCUs) have been championed for the ways they challenge and prepare their students. Digitalundivided's 2018 ProjectDiane report notes that more Black women undergrads from Howard University, an HBCU in Washington, DC, go on to launch a start-up than Black women undergrads from Harvard.[62] The researchers write: "The larger population of Black women at Howard may be a factor in the university's ability to outperform Harvard, however Harvard has significantly more resources than Howard and a strong, long-term history of producing founders of extremely successful start-ups (Microsoft, Facebook)." Also worth noting: first-year women students at HBCUs report more than twice the interest in being an entrepreneur than all women students at all colleges, according to 2017 research out of UCLA.[63]

The gender segregation debate also pops up in the entertainment world: Should we still celebrate actors and actresses separately, as the Oscars, Emmys, and Tonys have done for decades? In 2019, the nonbinary star of *Billions*, Asia Kate Dillon, urged the Television Academy to scrub gendered acting categories from the Emmys.[64] "If we separated categories by the colors of eyes, hair or skin, people would go, 'This is unacceptable,'" Dillon has said. "That's how I feel about gender categories. At this point, it feels unacceptable and unnecessary and archaic." However, supporters of the distinct awards note that having a single category, especially in male-dominated fields, would often mean women would get iced out. They point to the Oscars director category, which has always been gender-neutral.[65] Only five women have ever been nominated, and only one woman has ever won.

If things are to get better, how long might it take? According to a 2019 Bank of America survey, about a third of women entrepreneurs believe women will eventually achieve equal access to capital, and on average they estimate it will take fourteen years of changes in our society for it to happen.[66] Yet about one-quarter think it'll never happen. The bank's survey the previous year found that women entrepreneurs believe gender-blind financing will most help achieve that goal, followed by education and government-funded programs.[67]

Fourteen years sounds a whole lot better than another recent prediction. In 2019, the World Economic Forum estimated it will take 208 years for the United States, at its current pace, to close its gender gap.[68] This prediction considers workforce, politics, education, and health. Canada, in comparison, will require fifty-one years.

We need to act with more urgency and refuse to accept our current pace as adequate.

For a long time we've known that the entrepreneurial system favors some and thwarts others. On the federal level alone, there have been at least five decades' worth of investigations and pledges to do better—from President Jimmy Carter's 1977 Task Force on Women Business Owners, which promised "to mitigate conditions and practices that place women at a competitive disadvantage," to the 2019 launch of a bipartisan Senate Entrepreneurship Caucus (complete with a Women's Entrepreneurship Roundtable) to investigate how to encourage more start-ups and remove roadblocks.[69] We've learned a lot in those five decades, and progress has been made. But the progress must accelerate.

When I reach New Orleans entrepreneur Emery Whalen by phone, she tells me that she thinks there's been an increased awareness of "the realities of being a woman in business." She attributes this partly to the #MeToo movement, partly to a new willingness to talk openly about the hurdles women face. "It feels like there is always a wave," she tells me. "Everybody is paying attention. It's very exciting, and then there's a bit of a pendulum swing, or just a return to the status quo. . . . I don't want the conversation to end."

Whalen got into the restaurant industry in 2010 as a hostess. Eight years later, she and chef Brian Landry launched a company, QED Hospitality, that operates restaurants, bars, and cafés in boutique hotels in New Orleans and Nashville. Whalen is one of many restaurant workers who were inspired by #MeToo and Time's Up and are seeking ways to make their industry safer and more equitable.

"I would like the conversation to be more about progress and change," Whalen says. "My wish is for focused, action-biased conversations and endeavors. It's not just constant conversation, which I do think is important. It is a conversation towards something, towards an end goal. I think by creating and holding those kinds of spaces, where it's less about shame and blame and more about 'now what?' you'll have more people participating."

My "now what?" includes new funding options, new government policies, and new ecosystems, all of which would be a massive help. But beyond that, we need to see a wholesale shift in people's attitudes about what makes a good entrepreneur and who gets to do it. Almost sixty years ago, Betty Friedan wrote in *The Feminine Mystique* about how people's entrenched attitudes get chipped away, bit by bit—it happens with individual women doing things they "ought not" to do.[70] "Every girl who manages to stick it out through law school or medical school, who finishes her M.A. or Ph.D. and goes on to use it, helps others move on," Friedan wrote. "Every woman who fights the remaining barriers to full equality which are masked by the feminine mystique makes it easier for the next woman." And that's how I came to think of the women I met while researching this book. In her own way, every woman I interviewed is doing what Friedan urged—putting herself forward, struggling through, reaching boundaries, and smashing through them. The best thing the rest of us can do is to listen to their stories, learn from them, and understand that the way things are is not the way things have to be.

ACKNOWLEDGMENTS

THANK YOU TO the one-hundred-plus women and nonbinary founders who shared their stories for this book. You generously offered your expertise, opinions, and time, and tolerated my nosy questions and sometimes endless emails. While not all of you are named in the book, you were crucial in helping me understand entrepreneurship's problems and potential.

Several entrepreneurs and their allies were immensely generous in making introductions and inviting me into their networks. Thank you, Fran Biderman-Gross, Sarah Burgaud, Amy Choi, Sarah E. Endline, Christina Harbridge, Susan Towers, Cheryl Watkins-Moore, and Sophia Yen.

I had the joy of working with two Beacon Press editors, one former, one current. Thank you, Rakia Clark, for your early and steadfast enthusiasm, and Amy Caldwell, for your expert editing and wise guidance. Thanks to the rest of the wonderful Beacon team: Melissa Nasson, Sanj Kharbanda, Emily Powers, Pamela MacColl, Susan Lumenello, Beth Collins, Jane Gebhart, Kim Arney, and Nicole-Anne Keyton.

My agent, Carly Watters, took an immediate interest in my project, suggested important additions, and never wavered as an advocate. Thank you for standing by my side.

Thanks to my super-talented and tireless research assistants—Chloe Vassot, Anushree Nande, Anna Sims, and Emeralde Jensen-Roberts—and fact checker Matt Mahoney. I could not have pulled this off without your help.

Thank you to the friends and colleagues who guided me along the way and provided a sympathetic ear: Sandi Goldfarb, Doug Most,

Veronica Chao, Neil Swidey, Shirley Leung, Shira Springer, Linda K. Wertheimer, and Holly Lebowitz Rossi.

Thanks to my Emerson College colleagues who offered support, encouragement, and time away from teaching, especially Rob Sabal, Kim McLarin, Maria Koundoura, Roy Kamada, Megan Marshall, Mako Yoshikawa, Lu Ann Reeb, Angela Siew, Lisa Diercks, John Rodzvilla, Benoit Denizet-Lewis, David Emblidge, and Delia Cabe. Also, I appreciate Emerson's Faculty Advancement Fund Grant, which helped cover my reporting costs.

Finally, thank you to my parents, sister, husband, and son for your enduring love. My two guys, especially, helped this project become a reality.

NOTES

INTRODUCTION

1. Christina Cauterucci, "Attitude Problem," *Slate*, November 21, 2019, https://slate.com/news-and-politics/2019/11/elizabeth-warren-likable-presidential -candidate.html.

2. Justin Baragona, "CNN Political Analyst: 'There's a Hectoring Quality' with Elizabeth Warren," *Daily Beast*, November 21, 2019, https://www.thedailybeast .com/cnn-political-analyst-david-gergen-theres-a-hectoring-quality-with-elizabeth -warren.

3. Cauterucci, "Attitude Problem."

4. "Women in the U.S. Congress 2020," Center for American Women and Politics, Eagleton Institute of Politics, Rutgers University, https://www.cawp.rutgers .edu/women-us-congress-2020, accessed April 9, 2020.

CHAPTER 1: ENTREPRENEURSHIP'S MERITOCRACY MYTH

1. "Forbes Lists: All," *Forbes*, https://www.forbes.com/lists/list-directory/#369039 ab274d, accessed December 7, 2019.

2. "America's Most Innovative Leaders," *Forbes*, September 2019, https://www .forbes.com/lists/innovative-leaders/#29eceo9d26aa.

3. Kristen Clarke (@KristenClarkeJD), "This is inexcusable in 2019. Forbes issues list of America's 100 'most innovative leaders' and *99* of them are men . . . ," Twitter, September 8, 2019, 10:16 a.m., https://twitter.com/KristenClarkeJD/status /1170702337570160640; Maria (@depprayon14), "You need to fire your editors now. Maybe replace them with women? This list is truly astonishing . . . ," Twitter, September 7, 2019, 4:58 p.m., https://twitter.com/depprayon14/status/1170441255 861522432.

4. Farhad Manjoo, "Unicorn: A Fitting Label for Its Time and Place," *New York Times*, July 5, 2015, https://bits.blogs.nytimes.com/2015/07/05/unicorns-a-fitting -word-for-its-time-and-place/; Aileen Lee (@aileenlee), "At a board retreat where the recent 100 list of innovators is being dissected as an example of how privilege can be blinding . . . ," Twitter, September 14, 2019, 2:35 p.m., https://twitter.com /aileenlee/status/1172941878238408704.

5. Randall Lane, "Opportunity Missed: Reflecting on the Lack of Women on Our Most Innovative Leaders List," *Forbes*, September 8, 2019, https://www.forbes .com/sites/randalllane/2019/09/08/opportunity-missed-reflecting-on-the-lack -of-women-on-our-most-innovative-leaders-list/#75b9c40e1c6b; Randall Lane (@RandallLane), "Following up on our mistakes on the innovators list below, I've

asked @CarolineLHoward to lead a task force . . . ," Twitter, September 9, 2019, 5:34 p.m., https://twitter.com/RandallLane/status/1171175020992876544.

6. Lauren Hodges and Mary Louise Kelly, "Female CEOs Blast 'Forbes' List of Innovative Leaders That Includes Only One Woman," National Public Radio, September 11, 2019, https://www.npr.org/2019/09/11/759899375/female-ceos -blast-forbes-list-of-innovative-leaders-that-includes-only-one-woman.

7. Richard Peterson, "Few Females Hold CEO Positions at IPOs," S&P Global Market Intelligence, February 11, 2016, https://www.spglobal.com/market intelligence/en/news-insights/blog/few-females-hold-ceo-positions-at-ipos.

8. "The Global Unicorn Club," CB Insights, last updated January 2020, https:// www.cbinsights.com/research-unicorn-companies, accessed February 10, 2020.

9. *The 2019 State of Women-Owned Business Report* (American Express, 2019), 3, https://about.americanexpress.com/files/doc_library/file/2019-state-of-women -owned-businesses-report.pdf.

10. *The 2018 State of Women-Owned Business Report* (American Express, 2018), 10, https://about.americanexpress.com/files/doc_library/file/2018-state-of-women -owned-businesses-report.pdf.

11. "Women Entrepreneurs Are Key to Accelerating Growth," Ewing Marion Kauffman Foundation Policy Brief, July 20, 2015, 1; Maura McAdam, *Female Entrepreneurship* (London: Routledge, 2013), 11, 62.

12. "The VC Female Founders Dashboard," PitchBook, February 28, 2019, updated April 6, 2020, https://pitchbook.com/news/articles/the-vc-female-founders -dashboard.

13. William Aulet and Fiona E. Murray, *A Tale of Two Entrepreneurs: Understanding Differences in the Types of Entrepreneurship in the Economy* (Kansas City, MO: Ewing Marion Kauffman Foundation, May 1, 2013), 2–3, http://dx.doi.org/10.2139 /ssrn.2259740.

14. John Haltiwanger, Ron S. Jarmin, and Javier Miranda, "Who Creates Jobs? Small Versus Large Versus Young," *Review of Economics and Statistics* 95, no. 2 (May 2013): 347–48, http://www.mitpressjournals.org/doi/pdf/10.1162/REST_a_00288; Tim Kane, *The Importance of Startups in Job Creation and Job Destruction* (Kansas City, MO: Ewing Marion Kauffman Foundation, July 2010), https://www.kauffman .org/-/media/kauffman_org/research-reports-and-covers/2010/07/firm_formation _importance_of_startups.pdf.

15. E. J. Reedy, *Making Entrepreneurial Growth Vibrant Again* (Kansas City, MO: Ewing Marion Kauffman Foundation, July 28, 2015), https://www.kauffman.org /what-we-do/research/2015/07/making-entrepreneurial-growth-vibrant-again.

16. *Global Economic Prospects, January 2020: Slow Growth, Policy Challenges* (Washington, DC: World Bank, 2020), xvii, doi:10.1596/978-1-4648-1468-6.

17. Petr Sedláček, "Startups and Young Firms in the Economy: Trends, the Great Recession, and a Look Ahead," Ewing Marion Kauffman Foundation's New Entrepreneurial Growth Agenda, 2015, https://www.kauffman.org/neg/section -3#startupsandyoungfirmsintheeconomy.

18. Evan Absher, "Mayors and Entrepreneurs Should See Each Other as Allies," Ewing Marion Kauffman Foundation, August 22, 2019, https://www .kauffman.org/currents/2019/08/mayors-and-entrepreneurs-are-allies.

19. Jenna Temkin, "How a Rural Virginian Town Is Using Entrepreneurship to Boost Its Local Economy," Brookings Institute, August 1, 2019, https://www .brookings.edu/blog/the-avenue/2019/08/01/how-a-rural-virginian-town-is-using -entrepreneurship-to-boost-its-local-economy.

20. Lesa Mitchell, *Overcoming the Gender Gap: Women Entrepreneurs as Economic Drivers* (Kansas City, MO: Ewing Marion Kauffman Foundation, September 2011), 2, https://www.kauffman.org/-/media/kauffman_org/research-reports-and-covers /2011/09/growing_the_economy_women_entrepreneurs.pdf.

21. Ruta Aidis, Julie Weeks, and Katrin Anacker, *2015 Global Women Entrepreneur Leaders Scorecard: Executive Summary* (ACG, 2015), 7, http://i.dell.com/sites /doccontent/corporate/secure/en/Documents/2015-GWEL-Scorecard-Executive -Summary.pdf.

22. Carolyn Y. Johnson, "Bias in Biotech Funding Has Blocked Companies Led by Women," *Washington Post*, January 29, 2020, https://www.washingtonpost.com /science/2020/01/29/bias-biotech-funding-has-blocked-women-led-companies.

23. Shalini Unnikrishnan and Cherie Blair, "Want to Boost the Global Economy by $5 Trillion? Support Women as Entrepreneurs," Boston Consulting Group, July 30, 2019, https://www.bcg.com/publications/2019/boost-global -economy-5-trillion-dollar-support-women-entrepreneurs.aspx.

24. Unnikrishnan and Blair, "Want to Boost the Global Economy by $5 Trillion?"

25. Katie Abouzahr et al., "Why Women-Owned Startups Are a Better Bet," Boston Consulting Group, June 6, 2018, https://www.bcg.com/publications/2018 /why-women-owned-startups-are-better-bet.aspx.

26. *First Round: 10 Year Project* (First Round Capital, 2015), http://10years.first round.com.

27. *All In: Women in the VC Ecosystem* (PitchBook and All Raise, 2019), 6, https:// pitchbook.com/news/reports/2019-pitchbook-all-raise-all-in-women-in-the-vc -ecosystem.

28. Caroline Castrillon, "Why Women-Led Companies Are Better for Employees," *Forbes*, March 24, 2019, https://www.forbes.com/sites/carolinecastrillon /2019/03/24/why-women-led-companies-are-better-for-employees/#5d20dc373264.

29. Anthony P. Carnevale et al., *Born to Win, Schooled to Lose: Why Equally Talented Students Don't Get Equal Chances to Be All They Can Be* (Washington, DC: Georgetown University Center on Education and the Workforce, 2019), https:// cew.georgetown.edu/cew-reports/schooled2lose.

30. Allison Clift-Jennings, "Filament Personal Update," Jura, December 31, 2016, https://jura.io/update.

31. Dell Gines, *Black Women Business Startups* (Kansas City, MO: Federal Reserve Bank of Kansas City, 2018), 14–18, https://www.kansascityfed.org/~/media /files/community/blackwomenbusinessesreport.pdf; *2018 State of Women-Owned Business*, 4.

32. *2019 State of Women-Owned Business*, 4–5.

33. Rose Eveleth, "How Self-Tracking Apps Exclude Women," *Atlantic*, December 15, 2014, https://www.theatlantic.com/technology/archive/2014/12/how -self-tracking-apps-exclude-women/383673.

34. Eveleth, "How Self-Tracking Apps"; Caroline Criado-Perez, "The Deadly Truth about a World Built for Men—from Stab Vests to Car Crashes," *Guardian*, February 23, 2019, https://www.theguardian.com/lifeandstyle/2019/feb/23/truth -world-built-for-men-car-crashes.

35. Ruth Hailu, "Fitbits and Other Wearables May Not Accurately Track Heart Rates in People of Color," *STAT*, July 24, 2019, https://www.statnews.com/2019/07 /24/fitbit-accuracy-dark-skin/; Sidney Fussell, "Why Can't This Soap Dispenser Identify Dark Skin?," *Gizmodo*, August 17, 2017, https://gizmodo.com/why-cant -this-soap-dispenser-identify-dark-skin-1797931773.

36. Nicole Yi, "This Discreet Alarm for Women Looks Like Jewelry—but Can Actually Save Your Life," *PopSugar*, February 20, 2018, https://www.popsugar.com /news/InvisaWear-Smart-Jewelry-Review-44584710.

37. Mary Ann Azevedo, "JUUL Lands $12.8B from Big Tobacco as Vaping Grows Up, Sells Out," *Crunchbase News*, September 20, 2018, https://news .crunchbase.com/news/juul-lands-12–8b-from-big-tobacco-as-vaping-grows-up -sells-out.

38. Emma Hinchliffe, "Funding for Female Founders Stalled at 2.2% of VC Dollars in 2018," *Fortune*, January 28, 2019, https://fortune.com/2019/01/28 /funding-female-founders-2018.

39. David Gelles, "Juicero, Start-Up with a $700 Juicer and Top Investors, Shuts Down," *New York Times*, September 1, 2017, https://www.nytimes.com/2017 /09/01/technology/juicero-start-up-shuts-down.html.

40. Lauren Hirsch and Lauren Thomas, "Untuckit, the Company Known for Its Untucked Shirts, Is Looking to Raise Money at a Valuation Greater Than $600 Million," CNBC, December 6, 2018, https://www.cnbc.com/2018/12/06/untuckit -eyes-valuation-greater-than-600-million.html.

41. Christine Flammia, "Don't Waste Money on an 'Untucked' Shirt. Just Un-Tuck Your Damn Shirt," *Esquire*, April 2, 2018, https://www.esquire.com/style /mens-fashion/a19655853/untucked-mens-shirt-untuckit.

42. Ilana Yurkiewicz, "Study Shows Gender Bias in Science Is Real. Here's Why It Matters," *Scientific American*, September 23, 2012, https://blogs.scientific american.com/unofficial-prognosis/study-shows-gender-bias-in-science-is-real -heres-why-it-matters/; Jenna Goudreau, "13 Subtle Ways Women Are Treated Differently at Work," *Business Insider*, June 27, 2014, https://www.businessinsider .com/subtle-ways-women-treated-differently-work-2014–6.

43. Ashleigh Shelby Rosette and Robert W. Livingston, "Failure Is Not an Option for Black Women: Effects of Organizational Performance on Leaders with Single Versus Dual-Subordinate Identities," *Journal of Experimental Social Psychology* 48, no. 5 (2012): 1162–67, https://doi.org/10.1016/j.jesp.2012.05.002.

44. Matt Phillips, "Elon Musk Rejects 'Boring, Bonehead Questions,' and Tesla's Stock Slides," *New York Times*, May 3, 2018, https://www.nytimes.com/2018/05 /03/business/tesla-elon-musk.html.

45. Mihir Zaveri, "Elon Musk Walks Back 'Pedo Guy' Attack on Thai Cave Diver," *New York Times*, July 18, 2018, https://www.nytimes.com/2018/07/18 /business/elon-musk-vern-unsworth-pedo-guy.html.

46. "Elon Musk Settles SEC Fraud Charges; Tesla Charged With and Resolves Securities Law Charge," US Securities and Exchange Commission Press Release, September 29, 2018, https://www.sec.gov/news/press-release/2018–226.

47. David Gelles et al., "Elon Musk Details 'Excruciating' Personal Toll of Tesla Turmoil," *New York Times*, August 16, 2018, https://www.nytimes.com/2018 /08/16/business/elon-musk-interview-tesla.html.

48. Marina Koren, "What If a Female CEO Acted Like Elon Musk," *Atlantic*, August 17, 2018, https://www.theatlantic.com/science/archive/2018/08/elon-musk -new-york-times-interview-ceo/567835.

49. Amy Nelson, "A Female Founder's Take on the Tears of Elon Musk," *Forbes*, August 21, 2018, https://www.forbes.com/sites/amynelson1/2018/08/21/a -female-founders-take-on-the-tears-of-elon-musk/#5367f7183a4e.

50. Yasmin Khorram, "Judge Refuses to Push Back Elizabeth Holmes' Thera-nos Trial Despite Coronavirus Concerns," CNBC, April 1, 2020, https://www.cnbc.com/2020/04/01/judge-refuses-to-delay-holmes-theranos-trial-despite-coronavirus-concerns.html.

51. Tanya Tarr, "Here Are the Real Lessons Learned from Elizabeth Holmes's Failure," *Forbes*, March 26, 2019, https://www.forbes.com/sites/tanyatarr/2019/03/26/here-are-the-real-lessons-learned-from-elizabeth-holmess-failure/#630a72f4198b.

52. Mitchell, *Overcoming the Gender Gap*, 9–10.

53. Renee Morad, "How Gender Equality Is a Growth Engine for the Global Economy," NBC News: Know Your Value, January 29, 2019, https://www.nbcnews.com/know-your-value/feature/how-gender-equality-growth-engine-global-economy-ncna963591.

54. Economist Intelligence Unit, "Closing the Wealth Gap: How Women Leverage Entrepreneurship and Cultural Change to Generate Wealth," RBC Wealth Management, 2018, https://www.rbcwealthmanagement.com/us/en/research-insights/closing-the-wealth-gap-how-women-leverage-entrepreneurship-and-cultural-change-to-generate-wealth/detail.

CHAPTER 2: CENTURIES OF SECOND-CLASS STATUS

1. US House Committee on Small Business, *New Economic Realities: The Role of Women Entrepreneurs: Hearings before the Committee on Small Business*, 100th Cong., 2d sess., serial no. 100–53 (Washington, DC: Government Printing Office, 1988), 11–13, https://files.eric.ed.gov/fulltext/ED304524.pdf.

2. "Lillian Lincoln Lambert, MBA 1969," Harvard Business School Alumni Stories, January 1, 2003, https://www.alumni.hbs.edu/stories/Pages/story-bulletin.aspx?num=2017.

3. "50 Years of Women in the MBA Program," Harvard Business School, https://www.hbs.edu/women50, accessed December 3, 2019.

4. US House Committee on Small Business, *Selected Documents Pertaining to the Women's Business Ownership Act of 1988 (Public Law 100–533)*, 100th Cong., 2d sess. (Washington, DC: Government Printing Office, 1988), 1–7, 35–44.

5. House Committee, *New Economic Realities*, 3–4.

6. House Committee, *New Economic Realities*, 69–70.

7. House Committee, *New Economic Realities*, 8–10.

8. House Committee, *New Economic Realities*, 42–44.

9. House Committee, *New Economic Realities*, 65–66.

10. House Committee, *Selected Documents*, 52; "Contracting Guide," US Small Business Administration, https://www.sba.gov/federal-contracting/contracting-guide, accessed December 3, 2019.

11. House Committee, *Selected Documents*, 53.

12. "Women-Owned Small Business Federal Contracting program," US Small Business Administration, https://www.sba.gov/federal-contracting/contracting-assistance-programs/women-owned-small-business-federal-contracting-program, accessed December 6, 2019.

13. House Committee, *New Economic Realities*, 35–36, 56.

14. House Committee, *New Economic Realities*, 45–55.

15. House Committee, *Selected Documents*, 2, 6.

16. House Committee, *Selected Documents*, 3–17.

17. House Committee, *Selected Documents*, 4.

18. Regina Blaszczyk, "Women in Business: A Historical Perspective," Smithsonian Institution's National Museum of American History, 2002, https://amhistory.si.edu/archives/wib-tour/historical.pdf.

19. "Women Now Seen as Equally as or More Competent Than Men," American Psychological Association, July 18, 2019, https://www.apa.org/news/press/releases/2019/07/women-equally-more-competent; "Do you think married women whose husbands make enough to support them . . . USROPER.45–050.R01," Fortune/Roper Survey, September 1945 (Ithaca, NY: Cornell University, Roper Center for Public Opinion Research), accessed November 14, 2019.

20. Markus C. Becker, Thorbjorn Knudsen, and Richard Swedberg, eds., *The Entrepreneur: Classic Texts by Joseph A. Schumpeter* (Stanford, CA: Stanford University Press, 2011), 21.

21. Virginia G. Drachman, *Enterprising Women: 250 Years of American Business* (Chapel Hill: University of North Carolina Press, 2002), 1–5, 112.

22. "Women and the Law," Women, Enterprise & Society at Harvard Business School, 2010, https://www.library.hbs.edu/hc/wes/collections/women_law/; "Marriage and Coverture," Women, Enterprise & Society at Harvard Business School, 2010, https://www.library.hbs.edu/hc/wes/collections/women_law/marriage_coverture.

23. Lee Virginia Chambers-Schiller, *Liberty, a Better Husband: Single Women in America; the Generations of 1780–1840* (New Haven, CT: Yale University Press, 1984), 3.

24. Catherine Allgor, "Coverture: The Word You Probably Don't Know but Should," National Women's History Museum, September 4, 2012, https://www.womenshistory.org/articles/coverture-word-you-probably-dont-know-should.

25. "Declaration of Sentiments," National Park Service's Women's Rights National Historical Park, https://www.nps.gov/wori/learn/historyculture/declaration-of-sentiments.htm, accessed December 6, 2019.

26. "Women and the Law"; "Marriage and Coverture."

27. B. Zorina Khan, "Married Women's Property Laws and Female Commercial Activity: Evidence from United States Patent Records, 1790–1895," *Journal of Economic History* 56, no. 2 (1996): 356, http://www.jstor.org/stable/2123970.

28. Allgor, "Coverture."

29. Sven Beckert and Seth Rockman, eds., *Slavery's Capitalism: A New History of American Economic Development* (Philadelphia: University of Pennsylvania Press, 2016), 1–19.

30. "Dress from the Pre-Revolutionary War-Era Added to Smithsonian Costume Collection," National Museum of American History Press, April 23, 2008, https://americanhistory.si.edu/press/releases/dress-pre-revolutionary-war-era-added-smithsonian-costume-collection.

31. Harriot Horry Ravenel, *Eliza Pinckney* (New York: Charles Scribner's Sons, 1896), 4.

32. Cokie Roberts, *Founding Mothers: The Women Who Raised Our Nation* (New York: William Morrow, 2004), 2.

33. Ravenel, *Pinckney*, 7, 102–4.

34. Ravenel, *Pinckney*, 104.

35. Ravenel, *Pinckney*, 106–7.

36. Ward L. Miner, *William Goddard: Newspaperman* (Durham, NC: Duke University Press, 1962), 194. Miner writes: "The 1790 census records her as owning four slaves and having one 'other free person' in her household."

37. "March Highlight: Mary Katherine Goddard," Declaration Resources Project: Harvard University, March 4, 2016, https://declaration.fas.harvard.edu/blog/march-goddard.

38. Caroline Bird, *Enterprising Women* (New York: W. W. Norton, 1976), 6.

39. Abbey Teller and Christina Park, "Women in Postal History: Mary Katherine Goddard," Smithsonian National Postal Museum, https://postalmuseum.si.edu/WomenHistory/women_history/history_goddard.html, accessed December 3, 2019.

40. Drachman, *Enterprising Women*, 14–18.

41. Drachman, *Enterprising Women*, 14–18.

42. Teller and Park, "Mary Katherine Goddard."

43. Miner, *William Goddard*, 194.

44. One example of Goddard not being identified as someone who enslaved people is her biography in the Maryland Women's Hall of Fame: https://msa.maryland.gov/msa/educ/exhibits/womenshall/html/goddard.html.

45. Edith Sparks, *Boss Lady: How Three Women Entrepreneurs Built Successful Big Businesses in the Mid-Twentieth Century* (Chapel Hill: University of North Carolina Press, 2017), 8.

46. Drachman, *Enterprising Women*, 40–45.

47. Drachman, *Enterprising Women*, 101–3; "Our History," Lane Bryant, https://www.ascenaretail.com/our-brands/lane-bryant, accessed July 20, 2019.

48. A'Lelia Bundles, *On Her Own Ground: The Life and Times of Madam C. J. Walker* (New York: Scribner, 2001), 15, 21, 25, 34, 50, 56, 84, 88, 137.

49. Bundles, *Ground*, 33, 37, 43–46, 58–61, 64.

50. Bundles, *Ground*, 58–59, 65, 68, 78, 82.

51. Bundles, *Ground*, 85, 88–89, 92–93.

52. Martha Lagace, "HBS Cases: Beauty Entrepreneur Madam Walker," Harvard Business School: Working Knowledge, June 25, 2007, https://hbswk.hbs.edu/item/hbs-cases-beauty-entrepreneur-madam-walker.

53. Bundles, *Ground*, 91.

54. Bundles, *Ground*, 96, 105, 146.

55. Bundles, *Ground*, 154.

56. Bundles, *Ground*, 101, 109.

57. Lagace, "HBS Cases."

58. Bundles, *Ground*, 117, 125, 129, 131, 136, 180, 187–88.

59. Bundles, *Ground*, 133.

60. Bundles, *Ground*, 233–49, 274, 277.

61. "Wealthiest Negress Dead," *New York Times*, May 26, 1919, 15.

62. Amisha Padnani and Jessica Bennett, "Overlooked," *New York Times*, March 8, 2018, https://www.nytimes.com/interactive/2018/obituaries/overlooked.html.

63. Lagace, "HBS Cases."

64. Bundles, *Ground*, 19; "Sundial Brands Enters Prestige Hair Category with Historic Launch of Madam C.J. Walker Beauty Culture Exclusively at Sephora," PR Newswire, February 23, 2016, https://www.prnewswire.com/news-releases/sundial-brands-enters-prestige-hair-category-with-historic-launch-of-madam-cj-walker-beauty-culture-exclusively-at-sephora-300224231.html; "Unilever to

Acquire Sundial Brands," Unilver Press Releases, November 27, 2017, https://www
.unilever.com/news/press-releases/2017/unilever-to-acquire-sundial-brands.html.

65. Joi-Marie McKenzie, "New Voices Foundation Acquires Madam C. J.
Walker's Estate to Create Think Tank for Black Women Entrepreneurs," *Essence*,
December 18, 2018, https://www.essence.com/news/new-voices-foundation-madam
-c-j-walkers-estate-think-tank-for-black-women-entreprenuers.

66. Kathy Peiss, "'Vital Industry' and Women's Ventures: Conceptualizing
Gender in Twentieth Century Business History," *Business History Review* 72, no. 2
(1998): 219, https://doi.org/10.2307/3116276.

67. Peiss, "'Vital Industry,'" 230.

68. Sparks, *Boss Lady*, 27.

69. Sparks, *Boss Lady*, 14, 26–27, 32; "Walter H. and Olive Ann Beech Collection: Biography," Wichita State University Libraries' Special Collections and University Archives, http://specialcollections.wichita.edu/collections/ms/97–02/97–2-a
.html#bio, accessed July 22, 2019.

70. Sparks, *Boss Lady*, 25–26; "Beech Collection: Biography."

71. Sparks, *Boss Lady*, 6–7, 25, 28–29; "Beech Collection: Biography."

72. Sparks, *Boss Lady*, 166–168; "Beech Collection: Biography."

73. "Women in Air Racing," Ninety-Nines, https://www.ninety-nines.org
/women-in-air-racing.htm, accessed December 4, 2019.

74. D. Cochrane and P. Ramirez, "Women in Aviation and Space History:
Amelia Earhart," Smithsonian National Air and Space Museum, https://airandspace
.si.edu/explore-and-learn/topics/women-in-aviation/earhart.cfm, accessed December 4, 2019.

75. "Mrs. Thaden Gets Harmon Air Award," *New York Times*, April 2, 1937, 25.

76. Sparks, *Boss Lady*, 167.

77. Sparks, *Boss Lady*, 29–30, 69–70; "Beech Collection: Biography."

78. Sparks, *Boss Lady*, 213–14; "Beech Collection: Biography."

79. Sparks, *Boss Lady*, 1–2.

80. Andrew R. Chow, "Overlooked No More: Bette Nesmith Graham, Who
Invented Liquid Paper," *New York Times*, July 11, 2018, https://www.nytimes.com
/2018/07/11/obituaries/bette-nesmith-graham-overlooked.html.

81. "Notice to Readers and Advertisers," *New York Times*, November 24, 1968, W4.

82. "Help Wanted—Female" and "Sales Help Wanted—Female," *New York
Times*, November 24, 1968, W4–22.

83. "Help Wanted—Male" and "Sales Help Wanted—Male," W27–60.

84. Jacqueline A. Berrien, "Statement on 50th Anniversary of the Civil Rights
Act of 1964," US Equal Employment Opportunity Commission, July 2, 2014,
https://www.eeoc.gov/eeoc/history/cra50th/index.cfm.

85. William A. Darity and Patrick L. Mason, "Evidence on Discrimination in
Employment: Codes of Color, Codes of Gender," *Journal of Economic Perspectives*
12, no. 2 (1998): 65, http://www.jstor.org/stable/2646962.

86. Nicholas Pedriana and Amanda Abraham, "Now You See Them, Now You
Don't: The Legal Field and Newspaper Desegregation of Sex-Segregated Help
Wanted Ads 1965–75," *Law & Social Inquiry* 31 (2006): 911–14, http://doi.org
/10.1111/j.1747-4469.2006.00039.x.

87. "11 Picket Times Classified Office to Protest Male-Female Labels," *New
York Times*, August 31, 1967, 66; "Highlights: 1966–1976," National Organization
for Women, https://now.org/about/history/highlights, accessed July 25, 2019.

88. Martha Weinman Lear, "The Second Feminist Wave," *New York Times Magazine*, March 10, 1968, 24.

89. Pedriana and Abraham, "Now You See Them, Now You Don't," 905, 914–19.

90. Drachman, *Enterprising Women*, 152, 156.

91. "Voices of the Past, Promise of Tomorrow: Women's Enterprise Development in the U.S.," Diane Wilkins Productions for the National Women's Business Council, Tallahassee, FL, 2006, video, 29:00.

92. House Committee, *Selected Documents*, 35–36.

93. Claudia Goldin, *Understanding the Gender Gap: An Economic History of American Women* (New York: Oxford University Press, 1990), 3.

94. "Changes in Women's Labor Force Participation in the 20th Century," Bureau of Labor Statistics, February 16, 2000, https://www.bls.gov/opub/ted/2000/feb/wk3/art03.htm; *Women in the Laborforce: A Databook, Report 1084* (Bureau of Labor Statistics Reports, December 2019), https://www.bls.gov/opub/reports/womens-databook/2019/home.htm.

95. Goldin, *Understanding the Gender Gap*, 10–13.

96. Goldin, *Understanding the Gender Gap*, 159–75.

97. Goldin, *Understanding the Gender Gap*, 27.

98. Teresa Amott and Julie Matthaei, *Race, Gender, and Work: A Multi-Cultural Economic History of Women in the United States* (Boston: South End Press, 1996), 173, 209.

99. Dawn S. Carlson, K. Michele Kacmar, and Dwayne Whitten, "What Men Think They Know about Executive Women," *Harvard Business Review*, September 2006, https://hbr.org/2006/09/what-men-think-they-know-about-executive-women.

100. Virginia Littlejohn, "Women's Business Enterprises," in *Women in Washington: Advocates for Public Policy*, ed. Irene Tinker (Beverly Hills, CA: Sage Publications, 1983), 286–87.

101. The Editors of *Working Woman* with Gay Bryant, *The Working Woman Report: Succeeding in Business in the 80s* (New York: Simon & Schuster, 1984), 284.

102. Sandra Opdycke, *The Routledge Historical Atlas of Women in America* (New York: Routledge, 2000), 74.

103. Rachel Siegel, "Yale's Classrooms Were Full of Men. Then the First Female Undergrads Enrolled," *Washington Post*, November 14, 2018, https://www.washingtonpost.com/history/2018/11/14/yales-classrooms-were-full-men-then-first-female-undergrads-enrolled.

104. Julia Hanna, "The Accidental Pioneers," Harvard Business School Alumni Stories, December 1, 2012, https://www.alumni.hbs.edu/stories/Pages/story-bulletin.aspx?num=2797.

105. Lillian Lincoln Lambert with Rosemary Brutico, *The Road to Someplace Better: From the Segregated South to Harvard Business School and Beyond* (Hoboken, NJ: John Wiley & Sons, 2010), 10, 15, 16, 64, 75, 80.

106. Wolfgang Saxon, "H. Naylor Fitzhugh, 82, Educator and Pioneer in Target Marketing," *New York Times*, July 29, 1992, 19, https://www.nytimes.com/1992/07/29/nyregion/h-naylor-fitzhugh-82-educator-and-pioneer-in-target-marketing.html.

107. Lambert, *The Road*, 89, 93.

108. Lambert, *The Road*, 96.

109. Lambert, *The Road*, 92.

110. Lambert, *The Road*, 138, 141.

111. Lambert, *The Road*, 142.

112. Lambert, *The Road*, 151.

113. Lambert, *The Road*, 172.

114. House Committee, *Selected Documents*, 34.

115. US Census Bureau, *Survey of Business Owners (SBO)—Women-Owned Firms: 2002* (Washington, DC, August 2006), 475, https://www2.census.gov/programs-surveys/sbo/tables/2002/2002-sbo-women/sbo200cswmn.pdf.

116. US Senate Committee on Small Business and Entrepreneurship, *Opportunities and Challenges for Women Entrepreneurs on the 20th Anniversary of the Women's Business Ownership Act*, 110th Cong., 2d sess., serial 44–861 (Washington, DC: Government Printing Office, September 9, 2008), https://www.govinfo.gov/content/pkg/CHRG-110shrg44861/html/CHRG-110shrg44861.htm.

CHAPTER 3: THE BOYS' CLUB

1. Arlan Hamilton's quotes and biographical information come from my April 9, 2019, phone interview with her, as well as Hamilton's October 19, 2018, keynote speech at the Vision conference in St. Louis.

2. Arlan Hamilton (@ArlanWasHere), "My name is Arlan. I'm a 37-year old Black woman from Texas . . . ," Twitter, July 14, 2018, 6:18 p.m., https://twitter.com/ArlanWasHere/status/1018258447941316608.

3. Laura Montini, "Ashton Kutcher, Ellen DeGeneres, and 8 Other Top Celebrity Startup Investors," *Inc.*, September 21, 2015, https://www.inc.com/laura-montini/ss/ashton-kutcher-and-other-top-celebrity-startup-investors.html.

4. Tom Nicholas, *VC: An American History* (Cambridge, MA: Harvard University Press, 2019), 1–2, 112, 266, 319.

5. Nicholas, *VC*, 112–13, 262, 319.

6. "The VC Female Founders Dashboard."

7. *The State of Black Women Founders: ProjectDiane 2018* (digitalundivided, 2018), 3, https://projectdiane.digitalundivided.com.

8. H. Waverly Deutsch et al., *The State of LGBT Entrepreneurship in the U.S.* (StartOut, July 2016), 3, https://startout.org/wp-content/uploads/2018/03/State_of_LGBT_Entrepreneurship.pdf.

9. *All In*, 25.

10. Richard Kerby, "Where Did You Go to School?," *Noteworthy—The Journal Blog*, July 30, 2018, https://blog.usejournal.com/where-did-you-go-to-school-bde54d846188.

11. Kerby, "Where Did You Go to School?"

12. Arlan Hamilton, "Dear White Venture Capitalists: If You're Reading This, It's (Almost!) Too Late," *Medium/Female Founders*, June 13, 2015, https://medium.com/female-founders/dear-white-venture-capitalists-if-you-re-not-actively-searching-for-and-seeding-qualified-4f382f6fd4a7.

13. Arlan Hamilton, "Why Do Investors Say 'No' More Often Than 'Yes'?," *Medium*, November 20, 2015, https://medium.com/@ArlanWasHere/why-do-investors-say-no-more-often-than-yes-753a63271016.

14. Ainsley Harris, "Arlan Hamilton's Backstage Capital Has Invested in 100 Startups with Underrepresented Founders," *Fast Company*, June 6, 2018, https://www.fastcompany.com/40580713/arlan-hamiltons-backstage-capital-has-invested-in-100-startups-with-underrepresented-founders; "The New Establishment

2019," *Vanity Fair*, https://www.vanityfair.com/new-establishment-list, accessed December 4, 2019.

15. "Arlan Hamilton on the Changing Face of Entrepreneurship," interview with *Amanpour & Co.*, March 22, 2019, video, 18:52, http://www.pbs.org/wnet /amanpour-and-company/video/arlan-hamilton-on-the-changing-face-of -entrepreneurship.

16. Christie Pitts, "Announcing Backstage Accelerator," *Medium/Green Room*, September 5, 2018, https://medium.com/greenroom/announcing-backstage -accelerator-10964b6a59ec.

17. Arlan Hamilton (@ArlanWasHere), "1/At the top of September, Back- stage announced our first Accelerator cohort . . . ," Twitter, December 13, 2018, 12:51 a.m., https://twitter.com/ArlanWasHere/status/1073092975092162560; Arlan Hamilton (@ArlanWasHere), "1/Hey everyone! Something I've been thinking about. We received +1800 applications . . . ," Twitter, November 21, 2018, 1:10 p.m., https://twitter.com/ArlanWasHere/status/1065306591505862656.

18. Arlan Hamilton (@ArlanWasHere), "The rumors are true. Today at #USOW2018 I announced that my venture capital firm @Backstage_Cap has launched . . . ," Twitter, May 5, 2018, 7:12 p.m., https://twitter.com/ArlanWas Here/status/992904943773208576; Arlan Hamilton (@ArlanWasHere), "They're calling it a 'diversity fund.' I'm calling it an IT'S ABOUT DAMN TIME fund," Twitter, May 6, 2018, 10:41 a.m., https://twitter.com/ArlanWasHere/status /993138674475843585.

19. Kia Kokalitcheva and Dan Primack, "Arlan Hamilton's Diversity-Minded Investment Fund Falls Through," *Axios*, March 19, 2019, https://www.axios.com /arlan-hamilton-diversity-minded-investment-fund-falls-through-3476dc4c-a541 -4bcd-bbe1-a038d5a18c09.html.

20. "Arlan Hamilton," *Amanpour.*

21. Arlan Hamilton (@ArlanWasHere), "Recording my debut album, 'I don't work here.' Featuring the hit singles . . . ," Twitter, January 29, 2018, 2:52 p.m., https://twitter.com/ArlanWasHere/status/958065332303876097.

22. Arlan Hamilton, "Emotions are running high . . . ," *Medium*, October 21, 2016, https://medium.com/@ArlanWasHere/emotions-are-running-high -6cb46825543.

23. Kristen Lenz and Maria Aspan, "Women Entrepreneurship Report: The 2018 State of Women and Entrepreneurship Survey," *Inc.* and *Fast Company*, Septem- ber 18, 2018, https://www.inc.com/women-entrepreneurship-report/index.html.

24. Alicia Robb, Susan Coleman, and Dane Stangler, *Sources of Economic Hope: Women's Entrepreneurship* (Ewing Marion Kauffman Foundation, November 2014), 12, https://www.kauffman.org/~/media/kauffman_org/research%20reports%20and %20covers/2014/11/sources_of_economic_hope_womens_entrepreneurship.pdf.

25. Deborah J. Vagins, "The Simple Truth about the Gender Pay Gap," Ameri- can Association of University Women, https://www.aauw.org/research/the-simple -truth-about-the-gender-pay-gap, accessed February 15, 2020.

26. *NWLC: The Lifetime Wage Gap, State by State* (Washington, DC: National Women's Law Center, November 14, 2019), https://nwlc.org/resources/the-lifetime -wage-gap-state-by-state.

27. Rachel Thomas et al., *Women in the Workplace 2019* (LeanIn.Org and Mc- Kinsey & Company, 2019), 6, https://womenintheworkplace.com.

28. Robb, Coleman, and Stangler, *Sources of Economic Hope*, 12.

29. *Women Business Owners' Access to Capital Literature Review* (Washington, DC: Library of Congress Federal Research Division and National Women's Business Council, March 1, 2018), https://s3.amazonaws.com/nwbc-prod.sba.fun/wp-content /uploads/2018/03/28215658/NWBC-Report_Understanding-the-Landscape -Access-to-Capital-for-Women-Entrepreneurs.pdf.

30. Historic.ly (@historic_ly), "None of this is true! Let's look at how each of the companies were founded!," Twitter, April 21, 2019, 11:03 am, https://twitter .com/historic_ly/status/1119980086420299777.

31. Victor Hwang, Sameeksha Desai, and Ross Baird, *Access to Capital for Entrepreneurs: Removing Barriers* (Kansas City, MO: Ewing Marion Kauffman Foundation, April 2019), 11, https://www.kauffman.org/-/media/kauffman_org /entrepreneurship-landing-page/capital-access/capitalreport_042519.pdf.

32. Aimee Groth, "Entrepreneurs Don't Have a Special Gene for Risk—They Come from Families with Money," *Quartz*, July 17, 2015, https://qz.com/455109 /entrepreneurs-dont-have-a-special-gene-for-risk-they-come-from-families-with -money.

33. Amy Traub et al., *The Asset Value of Whiteness: Understanding the Racial Wealth Gap* (Demos, February 6, 2017), https://www.demos.org/research/asset -value-whiteness-understanding-racial-wealth-gap.

34. Lisa J. Dettling et al., *Recent Trends in Wealth-Holding by Race and Ethnicity: Evidence from the Survey of Consumer Finances* (Washington, DC: Fed Notes, Board of Governors of the Federal Reserve System, September 27, 2017), https://doi.org /10.17016/2380-7172.2083.

35. Robb, Coleman, and Stangler, *Sources of Economic Hope*, 12.

36. Hwang, Desai, and Baird, *Access to Capital*, 9–11.

37. *Women Business Owners' Access to Capital*.

38. Hwang, Desai, and Baird, *Access to Capital*, 9, 12.

39. Jeffrey Sohl, "The Angel Market in 2018: More Angels Investing in More Deals at Lower Valuations," Center for Venture Research, May 9, 2019, https:// paulcollege.unh.edu/sites/default/files/resource/files/2018-analysis-report.pdf.

40. "High-Tech Heels and Flats That Feel Like Sneakers Inside: Created by Antonia Saint NY," Kickstarter, last updated July 23, 2018, https://www.kickstarter .com/projects/antoniasaintny/high-tech-heels-and-flats-that-feel-like-sneakers; "Hi-Tech Heels and Flats Feel Like Sneakers Inside: Antonia Saint NY," Indi- egogo, last updated September 3, 2017, https://www.indiegogo.com/projects/hi -tech-heels-flats-feel-like-sneakers-inside#, accessed December 5, 2019.

41. Jamie Veitch and Aoife Flood, *Women Unbound: Unleashing Female Entrepre- neurial Potential* (PwC and Crowdfunding Center, July 2017), https://www.pwc.com /gx/en/about/diversity/womenunbound.html.

42. Michael A. Johnson, Regan A. Stevenson, and Chaim R. Letwin, "A Woman's Place Is in the . . . Startup! Crowdfunder Judgements, Implicit Bias, and the Stereotype Content Model," *Journal of Business Venturing* 33, no. 6 (November 2018): 813–31, https://doi.org/10.1016/j.jbusvent.2018.04.003.

43. Dana Kanze et al., "Male and Female Entrepreneurs Get Asked Different Questions by VCs—and It Affects How Much Funding They Get," *Harvard Busi- ness Review*, June 27, 2017, https://hbr.org/2017/06/male-and-female-entrepreneurs -get-asked-different-questions-by-vcs-and-it-affects-how-much-funding-they-get; Dana Kanze et al., "We Ask Men to Win and Women Not to Lose: Closing the

Gender Gap in Startup Funding," *Academy of Management Journal* 61, no. 2 (April 20, 2018), https://doi.org/10.5465/amj.2016.1215.

44. Malin Malmstrom, Jeaneth Johansson, and Joakim Wincent, "Gender Stereotypes and Venture Support Decisions: How Governmental Venture Capitalists Socially Construct Entrepreneurs' Potential," *Entrepreneurship Theory and Practice* 41, no. 5 (September 1, 2017): 833–60, https://doi.org/10.1111%2Fetap.12275.

45. Malin Malmstrom, Jeaneth Johansson, and Joakim Wincent, "We Recorded VCs' Conversations and Analyzed How Differently They Talk About Female Entrepreneurs," *Harvard Business Review*, May 17, 2017, https://hbr.org/2017/05/we-recorded-vcs-conversations-and-analyzed-how-differently-they-talk-about-female-entrepreneurs.

46. Alison Wood Brooks et al., "Investors Prefer Entrepreneurial Ventures Pitched by Attractive Men," *PNAS* 111, no. 12 (March 25, 2014): 4427–31, https://doi.org/10.1073/pnas.1321202111.

47. Malin Malmstrom and Joakim Wincent, "Research: The Digitization of Banks Disproportionately Hurts Women Entrepreneurs," *Harvard Business Review*, September 19, 2018, https://hbr.org/2018/09/research-the-digitization-of-banks-disproportionately-hurts-women-entrepreneurs.

48. Lakshmi Balachandra et al., "Don't Pitch Like a Girl! How Gender Stereotypes Influence Investor Decisions," *Entrepreneurship Theory and Practice* 43, no. 1 (September 26, 2017): 116–37, https://doi.org/10.1177%2F1042258717728028.

49. Vera Chok, "If You Saw a Nanny in This BBC Interview, What Does That Say about You?," *Guardian*, March 13, 2017, https://www.theguardian.com/commentisfree/2017/mar/13/nanny-bbc-interview-robert-kelly-small-children.

50. "Sequoia: Companies," Sequoia Capital, https://www.sequoiacap.com/companies, accessed December 5, 2019.

51. "Sequoia's Moritz: Looking for Women to Be Partners," interview with Michael Moritz by Emily Chang, Bloomberg, December 2, 2015, video, 2:13, https://www.bloomberg.com/news/videos/2015-12-02/sequoia-s-moritz-looking-for-women-to-be-partners.

52. Jessica Guynn, "Michael Moritz Taking Heat for Comments about Hiring Women," *USA Today*, December 3, 2015, https://www.usatoday.com/story/tech/2015/12/03/michael-moritz-sequoia-capital-women-diversity-silicon-valley/76736642.

53. Lizette Chapman and Sarah McBride, "Sequoia Capital Hires Yahoo's Jess Lee as First Woman U.S. Investing Partner," *Bloomberg*, October 20, 2016, https://www.bloomberg.com/news/articles/2016-10-20/sequoia-capital-hires-yahoo-s-jess-lee-as-first-woman-u-s-investing-partner.

54. "Sequoia: People," Sequoia Capital, https://www.sequoiacap.com/people, accessed February 15, 2020.

55. Pam Kostka, "More Women Became VC Partners Than Ever Before in 2019 but 65% of Venture Firms Still Have Zero Female Partners," *Medium/All Raise*, February 7, 2020, https://medium.com/allraise/more-women-became-vc-partners-than-ever-before-in-2019-39cc6cb86955.

56. Kerby, "Where Did You Go to School?"

57. "Women in VC Homepage," Women in VC, https://www.women-vc.com, accessed December 5, 2019.

58. *Women Business Owners' Access to Capital.*

59. Deutsch et al., *The State of LGBT Entrepreneurship*, 9.

60. Gené Teare and Ned Desmond, "The First Comprehensive Study on Women in Venture Capital and Their Impact on Female Founders," *TechCrunch*, April 19, 2016, https://techcrunch.com/2016/04/19/the-first-comprehensive-study -on-women-in-venture-capital.

61. *Quick Take: Women on Corporate Boards* (Catalyst, December 21, 2018), https://www.catalyst.org/research/women-on-corporate-boards.

62. Laurel Wamsley, "California Becomes 1st State to Require Women on Corporate Boards," National Public Radio, October 1, 2018, https://www.npr.org/2018 /10/01/653318005/california-becomes-1st-state-to-require-women-on-corporate -boards.

63. California Senate Bill, Corporations: Boards of Directors, SB 826, October 1, 2018, http://leginfo.legislature.ca.gov/faces/billNavClient.xhtml?bill_id =201720180SB826.

64. Stacy Cowley, "Patty Abramson, 74, Supporter of Businesses Owned by Women, Dies," *New York Times*, September 6, 2019, updated September 10, 2019, https://www.nytimes.com/2019/09/06/business/patty-abramson-dead.html.

65. *First Round: 10 Year Project*.

66. Flybridge, "#StartWithEight: Celebrating International Women's Day with Action," *Medium*, March 5, 2018, https://medium.com/@flybridge/startwitheight -celebrating-international-womens-day-with-action-ac55babc1f3f.

67. Flybridge, "#StartWithEight."

68. "Zebras Unite: About Us," Zebras Unite, https://www.zebrasunite.com /our-story, accessed December 5, 2019; Jennifer Brandel et al., "Sex & Startups," *Medium*, February 16, 2016, https://medium.com/@sexandstartups/sex-startups -53f2f63ded49.

69. Jennifer Brandel et al., "Zebras Fix What Unicorns Break," *Medium*, March 8, 2017, https://medium.com/@sexandstartups/zebrasfix-c467e55f9d96.

70. Brandel et al., "Sex & Startups."

71. "Arlan Hamilton: Discussion," *Next Web*, November 29, 2018, https:// answers.thenextweb.com/s/arlan-hamilton-PBPer5, accessed December 5, 2019.

CHAPTER 4: YOU CAN'T BE WHAT YOU CAN'T SEE

1. Jill Hecht Maxwell, "Carol Espy-Wilson, SM '81, EE '84, PhD '87: Institute Trailblazer Innovates in Speech Enhancement," *MIT Technology Review*, October 20, 2015, https://www.technologyreview.com/s/601034/carol-espy-wilson-sm-81-ee-84-phd-87.

2. "Eight in ten young people can't name one female entrepreneur," Santander UK, February 27, 2020, https://www.santander.co.uk/about-santander/media-centre /press-releases/eight-in-ten-young-people-cant-name-one-female-entrepreneur.

3. Lesley Symons, "Only 11% of Top Business School Case Studies Have a Female Protagonist," *Harvard Business Review*, March 9, 2016, https://hbr.org/2016/03 /only-11-of-top-business-school-case-studies-have-a-female-protagonist.

4. Deirdre Fernandes, "At Harvard Business School, Diversity Remains Elusive," *Boston Globe*, June 1, 2019, https://www.bostonglobe.com/metro/2019/06/01 /harvard-business-school-diversity-remains-elusive/bpyxP4cE1iCQJdLbHQEaQI /story.html.

5. Stacy L. Smith et al., *Gender Roles & Occupations: A Look at Character Attributes and Job-Related Aspirations in Film and Television* (Los Angeles: Geena Davis Institute on Gender in Media, 2012), https://seejane.org/wp-content/uploads/full-study -gender-roles-and-occupations-v2.pdf.

6. Sarah Thébaud, "Status Beliefs and the Spirit of Capitalism: Accounting for Gender Biases in Entrepreneurship and Innovation," *Social Forces* 94, no. 1 (September 2015): 61–86, https://doi.org/10.1093/sf/sov042; Gloria L. Sweida and Rebecca J. Reichard, "Gender Stereotyping Effects on Entrepreneurial Self-Efficacy and High-Growth Entrepreneurial Intention," *Journal of Small Business and Enterprise Development* 20, no. 2 (2013): 296–313, https://doi.org/10.1108/14626001311326743.

7. Balachandra et al., "Don't Pitch Like a Girl!," 116–37.

8. Ellen Bara Stolzenberg et al., *The American Freshman: National Norms Fall 2017, Expanded Version* (Los Angeles: Higher Education Research Institute, UCLA, 2019), 50, 76, https://www.heri.ucla.edu/monographs/TheAmericanFreshman2017-Expanded.pdf.

9. Laura Aline Bechthold and Laura Rosendahl Huber, "Yes, I Can! A Field Experiment on Female Role Model Effects in Entrepreneurship," *Academy of Management Proceedings* 2018, no. 1 (2018), https://journals.aom.org/doi/abs/10.5465/AMBPP.2018.209.

10. Rasha Ali, "Business Magazine Puts First 'Visibly Pregnant CEO' on Its Cover, and It's About Time!," *USA Today*, September 18, 2019, https://www.usatoday.com/story/life/parenting/2019/09/18/business-magazine-inc-puts-pregnant-the-wing-ceo-audrey-gelman-cover/2362304001.

11. Colleen M. Sharen and Rosemary A. McGowan, "Invisible or Clichéd: How Are Women Represented in Business Cases?," *Journal of Management Education* 43, no. 2 (April 2019): 129–73, https://journals.sagepub.com/doi/abs/10.1177/1052562918812154.

12. *Closing the STEM Gap: Why STEM Classes and Careers Still Lack Girls and What We Can Do about It* (Microsoft, 2018), 6–7, https://query.prod.cms.rt.microsoft.com/cms/api/am/binary/RE1UMWz.

13. Christianne Corbett and Catherine Hill, *Graduating to a Pay Gap: The Earnings of Women and Men One Year after College Graduation* (Washington, DC: American Association of University Women, 2012), 13, https://www.aauw.org/files/2013/02/graduating-to-a-pay-gap-the-earnings-of-women-and-men-one-year-after-college-graduation.pdf.

14. "Technovation-Impact," Technovation, https://www.technovation.org/impact, accessed December 3, 2019.

15. *Closing the STEM Gap*, 11.

CHAPTER 5: SLEAZY TEXTS, LATE-NIGHT MEETINGS

1. Eric Newcomer, "Uber Fires More Than 20 Employees in Harassment Probe," *Bloomberg*, June 6, 2017, https://www.bloomberg.com/news/articles/2017-06-06/uber-said-to-fire-more-than-20-employees-in-harassment-probe; "Harvey Weinstein Timeline: How the Scandal Unfolded," BBC News, January 10, 2019, https://www.bbc.com/news/entertainment-arts-41594672.

2. Reed Albergotti, "Silicon Valley Women Tell of VC's Unwanted Advances," *Information*, June 22, 2017, https://www.theinformation.com/articles/silicon-valley-women-tell-of-vcs-unwanted-advances.

3. Susan Ho, "My Cofounder Leiti Hsu and I Are Two of Three Women Who Went on the Record to Report Justin Caldbeck," *Medium*, June 26, 2017, https://medium.com/@susanho/my-cofounder-leiti-hsu-and-i-are-two-of-three-women-who-went-on-the-record-to-report-justin-36feof50c87d.

4. Reid Hoffman, "The Human Rights of Women Entrepreneurs," LinkedIn, June 23, 2017, https://www.linkedin.com/pulse/human-rights-women -entrepreneurs-reid-hoffman.

5. Dan Primack, "Justin Caldbeck Takes Indefinite Leave of Absence from Binary Capital," *Axios*, June 23, 2017, https://www.axios.com/justin-caldbeck-takes -indefinite-leave-of-absence-from-binary-capital-1513303207–8186919a-3e39-411a -ad4f-30423b811d12.html.

6. Kate Clark, "Justin Caldbeck Sues Binary Capital Co-Founder Jonathan Teo for Breach of Contract and Fiduciary Duty, Fraud and More," *TechCrunch*, February 28, 2019, https://techcrunch.com/2019/02/28/justin-caldbeck-sues-binary-capital-co -founder-jonathan-teo-for-breach-of-contract-and-fiduciary-duty-fraud-and-more.

7. Primack, "Justin Caldbeck."

8. Katie Benner, "Women in Tech Speak Frankly on Culture of Harassment," *New York Times*, June 30, 2017, https://www.nytimes.com/2017/06/30/technology /women-entrepreneurs-speak-out-sexual-harassment.html; Dave McClure, "I'm a Creep. I'm Sorry," *Medium*, July 1, 2017, now deleted by author, archived here: https://web.archive.org/web/20171113095856/https://medium.com/@davemcclure /im-a-creep-i-m-sorry-d2c13e996ea0, accessed December 1, 2018.

9. Lizette Chapman, "After a Sex Scandal, 500 Startups and Its Former CEO Plan Their Next Acts," *Bloomberg*, March 25, 2019, https://www.bloomberg.com /news/articles/2019-03–25/after-a-sex-scandal-500-startups-and-its-former-ceo -plan-their-next-acts.

10. Kristin Lenz and Maria Aspan, "Exclusive Report: Hundreds of Female Founders Speak Out on Ambition, Politics, and #MeToo," *Inc.*, September 18, 2018, https://www.inc.com/women-entrepreneurship-report/index.html.

11. Y Combinator, "Survey of YC Female Founders on Sexual Coercion and Assault by Angel and VC Investors," *Y Combinator Blog*, October 15, 2018, https:// blog.ycombinator.com/survey-of-yc-female-founders-on-sexual-harassment -and-coercion-by-angel-and-vc-investors.

12. Chai R. Feldblum and Victoria A. Lipnic, *Select Task Force on the Study of Harassment in the Workplace* (Washington, DC: US Equal Employment Opportunity Commission, June 2016), 9–10, https://www.eeoc.gov/eeoc/task_force/harassment /upload/report.pdf.

13. Feldblum and Lipnic, *Select Task Force*, v.

14. Feldblum and Lipnic, *Select Task Force*, 25–29; *All In*, 25.

15. Thomas et al., *Women in the Workplace 2019*.

16. Amy Spurling, "Boston vs CA: Capital Raising Differences," LinkedIn, July 12, 2017, https://www.linkedin.com/pulse/boston-amazing-tech-wo-misogyny-amy -spurling.

17. "Friedman Advocates for Greater Protections against Sexual Harassment and Discrimination," CindyFriedman.org, http://cindyfriedman.org/friedman -advocates-for-greater-protections-against-sexual-harassment-and-discrimination, accessed October 18, 2019.

18. Charlene L. Muehlenhard et al., "Evaluating the One-in-Five Statistic: Women's Risk of Sexual Assault While in College," *Journal of Sex Research* 54 (2017): 549–76, https://doi.org/10.1080/00224499.2017.1295014.

19. Kathryn Finney and Marlo Rencher, *The #ProjectDiane Report: The Real Unicorns of Tech: Black Women Founders* (digitalundivided, February 2016), 8, https:// www.digitalundivided.com/project-diane-2016-report/the-projectdiane-report-the -real-unicorns-of-tech-black-women.

20. *First Round: 10 Year Project.*

21. Sara Harrison, "Five Years of Tech Diversity Reports—and Little Progress," *WIRED*, October 1, 2019, https://www.wired.com/story/five-years-tech-diversity-reports-little-progress.

22. "Bachelor's, Master's, and Doctor's Degrees Conferred by Postsecondary Institutions, by Sex of Student and Discipline Division: 2016–17," National Center for Education Statistics, https://nces.ed.gov/programs/digest/d18/tables/dt18_318.30.asp, accessed December 1, 2019.

23. *Women, Minorities, and Persons with Disabilities in Science and Engineering: 2019*, Special Report NSF 19–304 (Alexandria, VA: National Science Foundation and National Center for Science and Engineering Statistics, 2019), https://ncses.nsf.gov/pubs/nsf19304/digest/field-of-degree-women.

24. Reed Albergotti, "Venture Capitalists, Tech Leaders Back 'Decency Pledge,'" *Information*, June 24, 2017, https://www.theinformation.com/articles/venture-capitalists-tech-leaders-back-decency-pledge.

25. Feldblum and Lipnic, *Select Task Force*, 54–60.

26. Aliya Ram, "Tech Investors Include #Metoo Clauses in Start-Up Deals," *Financial Times*, March 18, 2019, https://www.ft.com/content/5d4ef400-4732-11e9-b168-96a37d002cd3.

27. Stefanie K. Johnson et al., "Has Sexual Harassment at Work Decreased Since #MeToo?," *Harvard Business Review*, July 18, 2019, https://hbr.org/2019/07/has-sexual-harassment-at-work-decreased-since-metoo.

28. Katie Johnston, "Women Facing 'Massive Increase in Hostility' in Workplace, #Metoo-Era Study Says," *Boston Globe*, September 3, 2019, https://www.bostonglobe.com/business/2019/09/03/women-are-facing-massive-increase-hostility-workplace-author-metoo-era-study-says/idjrymGJnMFvNANUO9seHM/story.html.

29. LeanIn.Org and SurveyMonkey, *Working Relationships in the #MeToo Era: Key Findings*, https://leanin.org/sexual-harassment-backlash-survey-results, accessed November 22, 2019.

30. Gillian Tán and Katia Porzecanski, "Wall Street Rule for the #Metoo Era: Avoid Women at All Cost," *Bloomberg*, December 3, 2018, https://www.bloomberg.com/news/articles/2018-12-03/a-wall-street-rule-for-the-metoo-era-avoid-women-at-all-cost.

CHAPTER 6: THE BIG EFFECT OF LITTLE INSULTS

1. Chester Pierce, "Offensive Mechanisms," in *The Black Seventies*, ed. Floyd B. Barbour (Boston: Porter Sargent Publisher, 1970), 265–82.

2. Pierce, "Offensive Mechanisms," 266.

3. Pierce, "Offensive Mechanisms," 267.

4. Pierce, "Offensive Mechanisms," 277.

5. Mary P. Rowe, "The Saturn's Rings Phenomenon," *Harvard Medical Alumni Bulletin* 50, no. 1 (September/October 1975): 14–16, http://mitsloan.mit.edu/shared/ods/documents/?DocumentID=3986.

6. Seema Jayachandran, "Founders of Successful Tech Companies Are Mostly Middle-Aged," *New York Times*, August 29, 2019, https://www.nytimes.com/2019/08/29/business/tech-start-up-founders-nest.html.

7. Thomas et al., *Women in the Workplace 2019.*

8. Jennifer L. Berdahl and Celia Moore, "Workplace Harassment: Double Jeopardy for Minority Women," *Journal of Applied Psychology* 91, no. 2 (2006):

426–27, https://pdfs.semanticscholar.org/c5cd/8934b5d10b331560b24bcc3d7dc3 c4a4818d.pdf.

9. Alexis Nicole Smith et al., "Interviews with 59 Black Female Executives Explore Intersectional Invisibility and Strategies to Overcome It," *Harvard Business Review*, May 10, 2018, https://hbr.org/2018/05/interviews-with-59-black-female -executives-explore-intersectional-invisibility-and-strategies-to-overcome-it.

10. Recode Staff, "Full Transcript: Jennifer Hyman, CEO of Rent the Runway, is creating the Spotify of women's clothes," *Vox*, February 9, 2017, https://www.vox .com/2017/2/9/14566938/full-transcript-jennifer-hyman-ceo-rent-the-runway -subscription-womens-clothes.

11. Ian Agar, "Rent the Runway scores $1B valuation with $125M fundraise," PitchBook, March 21, 2019, https://pitchbook.com/news/articles/rent-the-runway -scores-1b-valuation-with-125m-fundraise.

12. *APPG for Entrepreneurship: Women in Leadership* (London: APPG for Entrepreneurship, July 19, 2018), 17, https://appgentrepreneurship.org/research.

13. Sarah Fink, *Shattering Stereotypes: Women in Entrepreneurship* (London: Centre for Entrepreneurs and Barclays, April 2015), 9, https://centreforentrepreneurs .org/wp-content/uploads/2015/11/Shattering_Stereotypes_Women_in _Entrepreneurship.pdf.

14. Derald Wing Sue et al., "Racial Microaggressions in everyday life: implications for clinical practice," *American Psychologist* 62, no. 4 (May–June 2007): 271–86.

15. "Microaggression: A Not So Subtle Growth in Usage," Merriam-Webster .com, last modified February 2017, https://www.merriam-webster.com/words-at -play/microaggression-words-were-watching, accessed November 30, 2019.

16. "The Everyday Sexism Project: Homepage," Everyday Sexism Project, https://everydaysexism.com, accessed December 1, 2019.

17. Alex Fradera, "The Scientific Evidence for Microaggressions Is Weak and We Should Drop the Term, Argues Review Author," *British Psychological Society Research Digest*, March 16, 2017, https://digest.bps.org.uk/2017/03/16/the-scientific-evidence -for-microaggressions-is-weak-and-we-should-drop-the-term-argues-review-author.

18. Bradley Campbell and Jason Manning, "Microaggression and Moral Cultures," *Comparative Psychology* 13, no. 6 (January 2014): 692–726, https://doi.org /10.1163/15691330–12341332.

19. Campbell and Manning, "Microaggression and Moral Cultures," 6.

20. Campbell and Manning, "Microaggression and Moral Cultures," 5.

21. Campbell and Manning, "Microaggression and Moral Cultures," 22.

CHAPTER 7: OWNING THE ROOM

1. "2017 Commencement Full Ceremony," Mount Holyoke, May 21, 2017, video, 2:24:33, https://www.mtholyoke.edu/commencement/2017-commencement.

2. Keely Savoie, "Commencement 2017: The 180th Launch," Mount Holyoke News & Events, May 3, 2017, https://www.mtholyoke.edu/media/commencement -2017–180th-launch.

3. "Honorary Degree Recipients," Mount Holyoke Archives and Special Collections, https://lits.mtholyoke.edu/archives-special-collections/asc-research/asc -research-guides/honorary-degree-recipients, accessed December 1, 2019.

4. *The State of Black Women Founders: ProjectDiane 2018*, 3; *The State of Latinx Women Founders: ProjectDiane 2018* (digitalundivided, 2018), 4, https://projectdiane .digitalundivided.com/latinx.

5. Avivah Wittenberg-Cox (@A_WittenbergCox), "Agree. So tired of this '#women lack confidence' line . . . ," Twitter, September 18, 2019, 11:54 a.m., https://twitter.com/A_WittenbergCox/status/1174350921075240962.

6. Jaruwan Sakulku and James Alexander, "The Imposter Phenomenon," *International Journal of Behavioral Science* 6, no. 1 (2011): 75–97, https://www.tci-thaijo .org/index.php/IJBS/article/view/521/pdf.

7. Margarita Mayo et al., "Aligning or Inflating Your Leadership Self-Image? A Longitudinal Study of Responses to Peer Feedback in MBA Teams," *Academy of Management Learning & Education* 11, no. 4 (2012): 2, https://www.jstor.org /stable/23412349.

8. "Join Tech Square's Startup Scene," Georgia Tech Innovation Ecosystem, https://www.gatech.edu/innovation-ecosystem/startups/tech-square, accessed December 1, 2019.

9. Jodyanne Kirkwood, "Is a Lack of Self-Confidence Hindering Women Entrepreneurs?," *International Journal of Gender and Entrepreneurship* 1, no. 2 (2009): 118–33, https://doi.org/10.1108/17566260910969670.

10. *The Alison Rose Review of Female Entrepreneurship* (HM Treasury, March 8, 2019), 9, 56–60, https://cdn10.contentlive.co.uk/5317a56e21de4cdebbb8422b 2114589d:static/pdf/7525_rose_review_final.pdf.

11. Fiona Wilson, Jill Kickul, and Deborah Marlino, "Gender, Entrepreneurial Self-Efficacy, and Entrepreneurial Career Intentions: Implications for Entrepreneurship Education," *Entrepreneurship Theory and Practice* 31, no. 3 (2007): 387–406, http://w4.stern.nyu.edu/management/docs/Gender_ETP.pdf.

12. Katty Kay and Claire Shipman, *The Confidence Code: The Science and Art of Self-Assurance* (New York: Harper Business, 2014), 13–24.

13. Kay and Shipman, *Confidence Code*, 119–65.

14. Laura Guillén, "Is the Confidence Gap between Men and Women a Myth?," *Harvard Business Review*, March 26, 2018, https://hbr.org/2018/03/is-the -confidence-gap-between-men-and-women-a-myth.

15. Laura Guillén, Margarita Mayo, and Natalia Karelaia, "Appearing Self-Confident and Getting Credit for It: Why It May Be Easier for Men Than Women to Gain Influence at Work," *Human Resource Management* 57, no. 4 (July/August 2018): 839–54, https://doi.org/10.1002/hrm.21857.

16. Margarita Mayo et al., "Aligning or Inflating Your Leadership Self-Image? A Longitudinal Study of Responses to Peer Feedback in MBA Teams," *Academy of Management Learning & Education* 11, no. 4 (2012): 2, https://www.jstor.org /stable/23412349.

17. Hwang, Desai, and Baird, *Access to Capital for Entrepreneurs*, 10.

18. Abouzahr et al., "Why Women-Owned Startups Are a Better Bet."

19. Kristen Bellstrom, "Investors Explain Why 'Men Pitch Unicorns and Women Pitch Businesses,'" *Fortune*, March 15, 2017, https://fortune.com/2017/03 /15/sxsw-2017-funding-tips-women-entreprenuers.

20. Fink, *Shattering Stereotypes*, 17.

CHAPTER 8: A SHOULDER TO LEAN ON

1. "TomboyX: Staking a Claim in Women's Clothing," Kickstarter, last updated August 8, 2013, https://www.kickstarter.com/projects/tomboyx/tomboyx-staking -a-claim-in-womens-clothing, accessed February 2, 2020.

2. "2019 Inc. 5000: The Most Successful Companies in America," *Inc.*, August 14, 2019, https://www.inc.com/inc5000/2019/top-private-companies-2019 -inc5000.html.

3. Sheryl Sandberg, *Lean In: Women, Work, and the Will to Lead* (New York: Alfred A. Knopf, 2013), 164.

4. Sangeeta Bharadwaj Badal and Rajesh Srinivasan, "Mentor Support Key to Starting a Business," Gallup, November 25, 2011, https://news.gallup.com/poll /150974/mentor-%20support-key-%20starting-business.aspx.

5. Max Marmer et al., *Startup Genome Report: A New Framework for Understanding Why Startups Succeed* (Startup Genome, 2011) (edited March 2012), 5, 10, 45–48.

6. *Impact Study of Entrepreneurial Dynamics: Office of Entrepreneurial Development Resource Partners' Face-to-Face Counseling, Contract SBAHQ09C004B*, prepared by the Concentrance Consulting Group for the US Small Business Administration (Washington, DC, September 2013), 5, 38–45, https://www.sba.gov/sites/default/files /files/OED_ImpactReport_09302013_Final.pdf.

7. Shawn Achor, "Do Women's Networking Events Move the Needle on Equality?," *Harvard Business Review*, February 13, 2018, https://hbr.org/2018/02 /do-womens-networking-events-move-the-needle-on-equality.

8. Gloria Steinem, *Outrageous Acts and Everyday Rebellions*, 2d ed. (New York: Henry Holt, 1995), 214.

9. Amanda E. Matzek, Clinton G. Gudmunson, and Sharon M. Danes, "Spousal Capital as a Resource for Couples Starting a Business," *Family Relations* 59, no. 1 (February 2010): 60–73, https://doi.org/10.1111/j.1741-3729.2009.00586.x.

10. Pamela Walker Laird, *Pull: Networking and Success Since Benjamin Franklin* (Cambridge, MA: Harvard University Press, 2006), 1–14.

11. Laird, *Pull*, 159–60.

12. Louise Matsakis, "MacKenzie Bezos and the Myth of the Lone Genius Founder," *WIRED*, January 11, 2019, https://www.wired.com/story/mackenzie -bezos-amazon-lone-genius-myth.

13. Laird, *Pull*, 53.

14. Robb, Coleman, and Stangler, *Sources of Economic Hope*, 10.

15. Sylvia Ann Hewlett and DeAnne Aguirre, "When Female Networks Aren't Enough," *Harvard Business Review*, May 12, 2010, https://hbr.org/2010/05/when -female-networks-arent-eno.

16. Deepali Bagati, *Women of Color in U.S. Law Firms: Women of Color in Professional Services Series* (Catalyst, 2009), 27, https://www.catalyst.org/wp-content /uploads/2019/01/Women_of_Color_in_U.S._Law_Firms.pdf.

17. Center for Talent Innovation, *The Sponsor Dividend: Key Findings* (Center for Talent Innovation, January 8, 2019), 2, https://www.talentinnovation.org/_private /assets/TheSponsorDividend_KeyFindingsCombined-CTI.pdf.

18. Claire Cain Miller, "It's Not Just Mike Pence. Americans Are Wary of Being Alone with the Opposite Sex," *New York Times*, July 1, 2017, https://www .nytimes.com/2017/07/01/upshot/members-of-the-opposite-sex-at-work-gender -study.html.

19. Jia Tolentino, "Mike Pence's Marriage and the Beliefs That Keep Women from Power," *New Yorker*, March 31, 2017, https://www.newyorker.com/culture /jia-tolentino/mike-pences-marriage-and-the-beliefs-that-keep-women-from -power.

20. Sheryl Sandberg and Marc Pritchard, "The Number of Men Who Are Uncomfortable Mentoring Women Is Growing," *Fortune*, May 17, 2019, https://fortune.com/2019/05/17/sheryl-sandberg-lean-in-me-too.

21. LeanIn.Org and SurveyMonkey, *Working Relationships in the #MeToo Era: Key Findings*, https://leanin.org/sexual-harassment-backlash-survey-results, accessed November 22, 2019.

22. Candace Bertotti and David Maxfield, "Most People Are Supportive of #MeToo. But Will Workplaces Actually Change?," *Harvard Business Review*, July 10, 2018, https://hbr.org/2018/07/most-people-are-supportive-of-metoo-but-will-workplaces-actually-change.

23. Natalie Robehmed, "Amid #MeToo Backlash, Lean In's Sheryl Sandberg Launches #MentorHer Campaign," *Forbes*, February 6, 2018, https://www.forbes.com/sites/natalierobehmed/2018/02/06/amid-metoo-backlash-lean-ins-sheryl-sandberg-launches-mentorher-campaign/#62777d7027e4.

24. Shirley Leung, "Can a Country Club Operate a Men's Only Bar? Yes, If It's in the Locker Room," *Boston Globe*, July 24, 2018, https://www.bostonglobe.com/business/2018/07/24/can-country-club-operate-men-only-bar-yes-locker-room/iyLxpBUIlrI2VlFYOUpzmK/story.html.

25. "Forecaddie: Heidi Ueberroth is Augusta National's sixth female member," *Golfweek*, April 7, 2019, https://golfweek.usatoday.com/2019/04/07/golf-heidi-ueberroth-augusta-national-sixth-female-member-masters.

26. Catalyst, *The Double-Bind Dilemma for Women in Leadership: Damned If You Do, Doomed If You Don't* (Catalyst, July 15, 2007), 8, 11, https://www.catalyst.org/research/the-double-bind-dilemma-for-women-in-leadership-damned-if-you-do-doomed-if-you-dont.

27. Elena Greguletz, Marjo-Riitta Diehl, and Karin Kreutzer, "Why Women Build Less Effective Networks Than Men: The Role Of Structural Exclusion and Personal Hesitation," *Human Relations* 72, no. 7 (2018), https://doi.org/10.1177/0018726718804303.

28. Greguletz, Diehl, and Kreutzer, "Why Women Build Less Effective Networks Than Men."

29. Emma Hinchliffe, "The Wing's Next Move? Sequoia's Jess Lee, Time's Up Backers, and $75 Million," *Fortune*, December 19, 2018, https://fortune.com/2018/12/19/the-wing-series-c-sequoia-jess-lee.

30. Matzek, Gudmunson, and Danes, "Spousal Capital as a Resource for Couples Starting a Business," 60–73.

31. Avivah Wittenberg-Cox, "If You Can't Find a Spouse Who Supports Your Career, Stay Single," *Harvard Business Review*, October 24, 2017, https://hbr.org/2017/10/if-you-cant-find-a-spouse-who-supports-your-career-stay-single.

32. "Balancing Paid Work, Unpaid Work and Leisure," OECD, May 3, 2018, https://www.oecd.org/gender/balancing-paid-work-unpaid-work-and-leisure.htm.

33. Bureau of Labor Statistics, "Time Spent in Primary Activities by Married Mothers and Fathers by Employment Status of Self and Spouse," 2011–2015, Tables A-7A to A-7C, https://www.bls.gov/tus/tables/a7_1115.pdf, accessed November 22, 2019.

34. Claire Cain Miller, "How Same-Sex Couples Divide Chores, and What It Reveals About Modern Parenting," *New York Times*, May 16, 2018, https://www.nytimes.com/2018/05/16/upshot/same-sex-couples-divide-chores-much-more-evenly-until-they-become-parents.html.

35. *Understanding the Gender Gap in STEM Fields Entrepreneurship*, prepared by Margaret E. Blume-Kohout for the Small Business Administration Office of Advocacy (Albuquerque, NM: SBA, October 2014), 54, https://www.sba.gov/sites/default/files/Gender%20Gap%20in%20STEM%20Fields_0.pdf.

36. Tao Shen, Arturo E. Osorio, and Alexander Settles, "Does Family Support Matter? The Influence of Support Factors on Entrepreneurial Attitudes and Intentions of College Students," *Academy of Entrepreneurship Journal* 23, no. 1 (2017), https://www.abacademies.org/articles/does-family-support-matter—the-influence-of-support-factors-on-entrepreneurial-attitudes-and-intentions-of-college-students-6581.html.

37. Matthew J. Lindquist, Joeri Sol, and Mirjam Van Praag, "Why Do Entrepreneurial Parents Have Entrepreneurial Children?" (IZA Discussion Paper No. 6740, Institute for the Study of Labor, Bonn, Germany, July 2012), http://ftp.iza.org/dp6740.pdf.

38. Gallup and Operation HOPE, *2016 Gallup-HOPE Index Report: Quantifying the Economic Energy of America's Youth* (Gallup, April 5, 2017), https://news.gallup.com/reports/207899/d.aspx.

CHAPTER 9: ENTREPRENEURSHIP'S POTENTIAL

1. Boston Planning & Development Agency Research Division Analysis, *Boston in Context: Neighborhoods* (Boston: Boston Planning and Development Agency, January 2017), 28, http://www.bostonplans.org/getattachment/6f48c617-cf23-4c9f-b54b-35c8a954091c.

2. "Defining Disparities," Cannabis Control Commission, http://mass-cannabis-control.com/wp-content/uploads/2018/12/Defining-Disparities.pdf, accessed October 16, 2019.

3. Naomi Martin, "'The Window Is Closing': Why Black Entrepreneurs Are Disappointed with Mass. Marijuana Legalization," *Boston Globe*, August 30, 2019, https://www.bostonglobe.com/news/marijuana/2019/08/30/the-window-closing-why-black-entrepreneurs-are-disappointed-with-mass-marijuana-legalization/K5CsWnDG8bexG5tU8RwilL/story.html.

4. "About the Commission," Cannabis Control Commission, last modified 2019, https://mass-cannabis-control.com/about-us-2, accessed November 22, 2019.

5. "Summary of Equity Provisions," Cannabis Control Commission, http://mass-cannabis-control.com/wp-content/uploads/2018/03/UPDATED-Guidance-Summary-of-Equity-Provisions-with-6th-criterion-added-1.pdf, accessed November 22, 2019.

6. Several in the industry offer this estimate, including cannabis entrepreneur and former Boston city councilor Tito Jackson when he spoke at the All Together Now conference in Boston on September 9, 2019.

7. *Women and Minorities in the Cannabis Industry* (*Marijuana Business Daily*, 2019), 11, https://mjbizdaily.com/women-minorities-cannabis-industry.

8. Beth Healy et al., "You Can't Own More Than 3 Pot Shops, but These Companies Test the Limits—and Brag about It," *Boston Globe*, March 21, 2019, https://www.bostonglobe.com/news/special-reports/2019/03/21/seahunter/okkkbXkh38kTkH9HDiiFXL/story.html; Ted Siefer, "In Pot Chase, Social Equity Meets Economic Reality," *Commonwealth Magazine*, March 31, 2019, https://commonwealthmagazine.org/marijuana/in-pot-chase-social-equity-meets-economic-reality.

9. "Equity Is Still a Missing Piece in the Legal Marijuana Retail Puzzle," editorial, *Boston Globe*, March 23, 2019, https://www.bostonglobe.com/opinion/editorials/2019/03/23/equity-still-missing-piece-legal-marijuana-retail-puzzle/oUJAX6zn ZBPm1oeK4M2LaL/story.html.

10. Naomi Martin and Felicia Gans, "Boston's First Recreational Marijuana Store Opens, More Than 3 Years after Legalization," *Boston Globe*, March 9, 2020, https://www.bostonglobe.com/2020/03/09/marijuana/bostons-first-marijuana-store -open-monday-nearly-4-years-after-legalization/.

11. *Women and Minorities in the Cannabis Industry*, 4, 6.

12. Lissa Harris, "Women Are Disappearing from the Cannabis Industry. Why?," *Entrepreneur*, May 21, 2019, https://www.greenentrepreneur.com/article /333207; Ellen Milligan et al., "Cannabis CEOs Are White Men, Just Like in the Rest of Corporate America," *Bloomberg Businessweek*, July 16, 2019, https://www .bloomberg.com/news/articles/2019-07-16/cannabis-ceos-are-white-men-just -like-in-the-rest-of-corporate-america.

13. Jeff Smith, "Illinois Becomes 11th State to Legalize Adult-Use Marijuana; $2B Market Projected," *Marijuana Business Daily*, June 25, 2019, https://mjbizdaily .com/illinois-11th-state-to-legalize-adult-use-cannabis-2-billion-market-projected.

14. Katie Wullert, Shannon Gilmartin, and Caroline Simard, "The Mistake Companies Make When They Use Data to Plan Diversity Efforts," *Harvard Business Review*, April 16, 2019, https://hbr.org/2019/04/the-mistake-companies-make -when-they-use-data-to-plan-diversity-efforts.

15. "Pipeline Angels Homepage," Pipeline Angels, http://pipelineangels.com, accessed November 22, 2019.

16. James Davies, Anthony Shorrocks, and Rodrigo Lluberas, *Credit Suisse Global Wealth Report 2018: Women and Wealth* (Credit Suisse, October 18, 2018), 25–29, https://www.credit-suisse.com/about-us-news/en/articles/news-and-expertise /global-wealth-report-2018-women-hold-40-percent-of-global-wealth-201810.html.

17. Laura Huang et al., *The American Angel* (Wharton Entrepreneurship and Angel Capital Association, November 2017), http://docs.wixstatic.com/ugd/ecd9be _5855a9b21a8c4fc1abc89a3293abff96.pdf.

18. *Sustainable Signals: New Data from the Individual Investor* (Morgan Stanley, 2017), 8, https://www.morganstanley.com/pub/content/dam/msdotcom/ideas /sustainable-signals/pdf/Sustainable_Signals_Whitepaper.pdf; *Sustainable Signals: Individual Investor Interest Driven by Impact, Conviction and Choice* (Morgan Stanley, 2019), 4, https://www.morganstanley.com/pub/content/dam/msdotcom/infographics /sustainable-investing/Sustainable_Signals_Individual_Investor_White_Paper _Final.pdf; The Economist Intelligence Unit, *The New Face of Wealth and Legacy: How Women Are Redefining Wealth, Giving and Legacy Planning* (RBC Wealth Management, 2018), https://www.rbcwealthmanagement.com/us/en/research-insights /the-new-face-of-wealth-and-legacy-how-women-are-redefining-wealth-giving -and-legacy-planning/detail.

19. *Gender Lens Investing: Bending the Arc of Finance for Women and Girls* (Veris Wealth Partners, 2018), 3, https://www.veriswp.com/research/gli-bending-arc-of -finance-women.

20. Kostka, "More Women Became VC Partners Than Ever Before In 2019."

21. "Fund Right Homepage," Fund Right, https://fundright.nl, accessed November 29, 2019.

22. "Governor Signs Jackson's #MeToo Bills to Combat Sexual Harassment in the Workplace," Hannah-Beth Jackson: Representing Senate District 19, October 1, 2018, https://sd19.senate.ca.gov/news/2018-10-01-governor-signs-jacksons -metoo-bills-combat-sexual-harassment-workplace.

23. National Women's Business Council, "Billions of Federal Contracting Dollars Go to Women-Owned Businesses—but It's Still Not Enough," National Women's Business Council, October 18, 2017, https://www.nwbc.gov/2017/10/18 /billions-of-federal-contracting-dollars.

24. "Federal Government Achieves Small Business Contracting Goal for Sixth Consecutive Year with Record-Breaking $120 Billion to Small Businesses," Small Business Administration Newsroom, June 25, 2019, https://www.sba.gov/about -sba/sba-newsroom/press-releases-media-advisories/federal-government-achieves -small-business-contracting-goal-sixth-consecutive-year-record-breaking.

25. Milton J. Valencia, "Boston Awarded $664m in Contracts. Less Than 1% Went to Women- and Minority-Owned Businesses," *Boston Globe*, May 2, 2019, https://www.bostonglobe.com/metro/2019/05/02/the-city-awarded-million -contracts-last-year-only-percent-went-minority-owned-businesses/K4Tto4 GndWBF1MHdvipcNP/story.html.

26. *Office of Economic Opportunity Fiscal Year 2019 Annual Report* (City of Phila-delphia: November 4, 2019), 4, https://www.phila.gov/media/20191031160732 /OEO-FY-2019-Annual-Report-1.pdf.

27. "Small Business: Minority- and Women-Owned Business Enterprises," Dallas Economic Development, https://www.dallasecodev.org/382/Minority-and -Women-Owned-Business-Enter, accessed November 30, 2019.

28. "De Blasio Administration Reaches Milestone Goal of 9,000 City-Certified M/WBEs," City of New York, July 8, 2019, https://www1.nyc.gov/office-of-the -mayor/news/333-19/de-blasio-administration-reaches-milestone-goal-9-000-city -certified-m-wbes.

29. Emily Washcovick, "Yelp Makes It Easy to Find and Support Women-Owned Businesses," *Yelp Official Blog*, February 27, 2020, https://blog.yelp.com /2020/02/yelp-makes-it-easy-to-find-and-support-women-owned-businesses.

30. Harvard Business School, "Public Programs Encourage Entrepreneurship," YouTube Video, 3:19, October 25, 2016, https://www.youtube.com/watch?v =hoA7W5wlGkY.

31. Gareth Olds, "Food Stamp Entrepreneurs," Harvard Business School Working Paper No. 16–143, May 2016, https://www.hbs.edu/faculty/Publication %20Files/16-143_2cf7ba14-5bfa-4c34-85d9-oedcoddc7ce6.pdf; Gareth Olds, "En-trepreneurship and Public Health Insurance," Harvard Business School Working Paper No. 16–144, May 2016, https://www.hbs.edu/faculty/Publication%20 Files/16-144_d9ce8326-eeaa-4650-a8af-6ff03c3f7e77.pdf.

32. Harvard Business School, "Public Programs Encourage Entrepreneurship."

33. Lydialyle Gibson, "Food Stamp Entrepreneurs," *Harvard Magazine*, July–August 2016, https://harvardmagazine.com/2016/07/food-stamp-entrepreneurs.

34. Walter Frick, "Research: Want More Entrepreneurs? Make College Cheaper," *Harvard Business Review*, July 7, 2016, https://hbr.org/2016/07/research -want-more-entrepreneurs-make-college-cheaper.

35. Walter Frick, "Welfare Makes America More Entrepreneurial," *Atlantic*, March 26, 2015, https://www.theatlantic.com/politics/archive/2015/03/welfare -makes-america-more-entrepreneurial/388598.

36. Elizabeth Warren (@ewarren), "The racial wealth gap tilts the playing field against entrepreneurs of color, holding back our economy . . . ," Twitter, June 14, 2019, 9:30 a.m., https://twitter.com/ewarren/status/1139525444628299777.

37. Elizabeth Warren, "Leveling the Playing Field for Entrepreneurs," *Medium*, June 14, 2019, https://medium.com/@teamwarren/leveling-the-playing -field-for-entrepreneurs-2a585aa2b6d7; "Reducing the Opportunity Gap: Investing in HBCUs and Black Entrepreneurship," KamalaHarris.org, https://kamalaharris .org/opportunity-gap/#I7GvBdaeyeyXJmVB.99, accessed October 9, 2019; "The Douglass Plan: A Comprehensive Investment in the Empowerment of Black America," PeteforAmerica.com, https://peteforamerica.com/policies/douglass-plan /#EqualEmploymentandBusinessOpportunity, accessed October 9, 2019.

38. *Trends in College Pricing 2018* (College Board, 2018), 12, https://research .collegeboard.org/pdf/trends-college-pricing-2018-full-report.pdf.

39. *Deeper in Debt: Women and Student Loans* (American Association of University Women, May 2019), https://www.aauw.org/aauw_check/pdf_download/show _pdf.php?file=deeper-in-debt-onepager.

40. Karthik Krishnan and Pinshuo Wang, "The Cost of Financing Education: Can Student Debt Hinder Entrepreneurship?," *Management Science* (2018): 7, 23, https://pubsonline.informs.org/doi/10.1287/mnsc.2017.2995.

41. *Millennial Women Entrepreneurs: Opportunities and Challenges* (National Women's Business Council, November 28, 2018), 2, https://www.nwbc.gov /2018/11/28/profile-of-millennial-women-the-future-of-entrepreneurship-in -america.

42. "Balancing Paid Work, Unpaid Work and Leisure," OECD, May 3, 2018, https://www.oecd.org/gender/balancing-paid-work-unpaid-work-and-leisure.htm.

43. *The Alison Rose Review of Female Entrepreneurship*, 9, 56–60.

44. Netherlands Enterprise Agency, "Maternity Allowance for Self-Employed Professionals," Business.gov.nl, https://business.gov.nl/regulation/prenatal-and -childbirth-allowance-self-employed-professionals, accessed November 28, 2019.

45. *The Alison Rose Review of Female Entrepreneurship*, 60.

46. Kimberly Zeuli, Kathleen O'Shea, and Austin Nihuis, *Building Strong Clusters for Strong Urban Economies: Insights for City Leaders from Four Case Studies in the U.S.* (JPMorgan Chase & Co. and Initiative for a Competitive Inner City, June 2017), 6–7, http://icic.org/wp-content/uploads/2017/06/JPMC-Cluster-Report _Building-Strong-Clusters_FINAL_v2.pdf.

47. "Cortex: About," Cortex Innovation Community, https://www.cortexstl .com/about/mission, accessed November 30, 2019.

48. *Creating Inclusive High-Tech Incubators and Accelerators: Strategies to Increase Participation Rates of Women and Minority Entrepreneurs* (JPMorgan Chase & Co. and Initiative for a Competitive Inner City, 2016), 1–7, 11–12, http://icic.org/wp -content/uploads/2016/05/ICIC_JPMC_Incubators_post.pdf.

49. "MassChallenge: FAQ for Start-ups," MassChallenge, https://masschallenge .org/about-faq, accessed November 30, 2019.

50. Callum Borchers, "For the First Time, Majority of MassChallenge Start-Up Teams Include a Woman," WBUR, July 12, 2018, https://www.wbur.org /bostonomix/2018/07/12/women-masschallenge-start-up-finalists.

51. "Babson WIN Lab Venture Accelerator," Babson, https://www.babson.edu /academics/centers-and-institutes/center-for-womens-entrepreneurial-leadership /cwel-programs/win-lab-accelerator, accessed November 30, 2019.

52. *Amazon HQ2 RFP* (Seattle: Amazon, 2017), https://images-na.ssl-images
-amazon.com/images/G/01/Anything/test/images/usa/RFP_3._V516043504_.pdf;
Nick Wingfield, "Amazon Chooses 20 Finalists for Second Headquarters," *New
York Times*, January 18, 2018, https://www.nytimes.com/2018/01/18/technology
/amazon-finalists-headquarters.html.

53. Ben Casselman, "A $2 Billion Question: Did New York and Virginia Over-
pay for Amazon?," *New York Times*, November 13, 2018, https://www.nytimes.com
/2018/11/13/business/economy/amazon-hq2-va-long-island-city-incentives.html.

54. Kurt Badenhausen, "The Top 10 Rising Cities for Start-Ups," *Forbes*, October 1, 2018, https://www.forbes.com/sites/kurtbadenhausen/2018/10/01/the-top
-10-rising-cities-for-startups/#52823ec26b37.

55. Caro Berry, "Being Non-Binary in a Binary Business World," PrettyinPunk.co,
November 16, 2017, https://prettyinpunk.co/blogs/pretty-in-punk/being-non
-binary-in-a-binary-business-world.

56. "Gen Z More Familiar with Gender-Neutral Pronouns," Pew Research
Center, January 14, 2019, https://www.pewsocialtrends.org/2019/01/17/generation
-z-looks-a-lot-like-millennials-on-key-social-and-political-issues/psdt_1-17-19
_generations-02.

57. Emily Chang, *Brotopia: Breaking Up the Boys' Club of Silicon Valley* (New
York: Portfolio/Penguin, 2018), 11.

58. "Women's College Coalition: Our History," Women's College Coalition,
https://www.womenscolleges.org/history, accessed November 30, 2019.

59. Scott Jaschik, "A Trump Bump in Yields at Women's Colleges," *Inside
Higher Ed*, August 13, 2018, https://www.insidehighered.com/admissions/article
/2018/08/13/womens-colleges-see-boost-yield-wake-2016-election.

60. Kimberly Wright Cassidy, Jacquelyn Litt, and Rebecca Roloff, "Women's
Colleges Play Unique Role in Quest for Equality," *Conversation*, September 11,
2018, https://theconversation.com/womens-colleges-play-unique-role-in-quest
-for-equality-95913.

61. Susan Lennon and Jim Day, *What Matters in College After College: A Comparative Alumnae Research Study* (Women's College Coalition, March 7, 2012), 37,
https://www.womenscolleges.org/sites/default/files/report/files/main/2012hardwick
daycomparativealumnaesurveymarch2012_0.pdf.

62. *The State of Black Women Founders: ProjectDiane 2018*, 5.

63. Ellen Bara Stolzenberg et al., *The American Freshman: National Norms
Fall 2017* (Los Angeles: Higher Education Research Institute, UCLA, 2019), 76,
https://heri.ucla.edu/publications-tfs.

64. Cara Buckley, "Why the Oscars, Emmys and Tonys Are Not Ready for
They and Them," *New York Times*, October 17, 2019, https://www.nytimes.com
/2019/10/16/movies/oscars-gendered-categories.html.

65. Ashley Lee, "Oscar Nominations Shut Out Female Directors—Again," *Los
Angeles Times*, January 22, 2019, https://www.latimes.com/entertainment/la-et-mn
-oscars-nominations-female-directors-20190122-story.html.

66. *Bank of America Business Advantage: 2019 Women Business Owner Spotlight*
(Bank of America, 2019), https://about.bankofamerica.com/assets/pdf/2019
-Women-Business-Owner-Spotlight.pdf.

67. *Bank of America Business Advantage: 2018 Women Business Owner Spotlight*
(Bank of America, 2018), https://newsroom.bankofamerica.com/system/files/2018
_Women_Business_Owner_Spotlight_0.pdf.

68. Saadia Zahidi, "Acceleration Gender Parity in Globalization 4.0," World Economic Forum, June 18, 2019, https://www.weforum.org/agenda/2019/06/accelerating-gender-gap-parity-equality-globalization-4.

69. *Public Papers of the Presidents of the United States: Jimmy Carter, 1977, Book II—June 25 to December 31, 1977* (Washington, DC: US Government Printing Office, 1978), 1429; "Klobuchar, Scott Introduce Legislation to Enhance Entrepreneurship for the 21st Century," Amy Klobuchar: United States Senator, September 24, 2019, https://www.klobuchar.senate.gov/public/index.cfm/2019/9/klobuchar-scott-introduce-legislation-to-enhance-entrepreneurship-for-the-21st-century.

70. Betty Friedan, *The Feminine Mystique* (New York: W. W. Norton, 2013), 452.

ABOUT THE AUTHOR

SUSANNE ALTHOFF is a veteran journalist and an assistant professor at Emerson College in Boston, where she teaches the business of publishing, publishing entrepreneurship, and women's media. She's served as an adviser to student-led start-ups. Previously, Althoff was the editor in chief of the *Boston Globe Magazine* and worked as a magazine editor for twenty-two years. Her writing has appeared in *WIRED*, the *Boston Globe*, and other publications. She has a master's degree from the Columbia University Graduate School of Journalism. She lives outside Boston with her husband and son.